The Art of the Self in D. H. Lawrence

THE ART OF THE SELF
IN D. H. LAWRENCE

Marguerite Beede Howe

Ohio University Press
Athens, Ohio

Published 1977
Ohio University Press
Athens, Ohio 45701
Printed in the United States of America
Library of Congress Catalog Card Number: 75-39864
ISBN 8214-0234-X

To Marion Savage

We have no one law that governs us. For me there is only one law: I am I. And that isn't a law, it's just a remark. One is one, but one is not all alone. There are other stars buzzing in the centre of their own isolation. And there is no straight path between them.

D. H. Lawrence
Fantasia of the Unconscious

CONTENTS

Introduction   1

1. *Sons and Lovers:* The Struggle to Exist   4

2. *The Rainbow:* Coming of Age   28

3. Chaos: Who Survives in *Women in Love?*   52

4. Solipsism: *Aaron's Rod and Kangaroo*   79

5. Death and *The Plumed Serpent*   105

6. The Lesson in *Lady Chatterley's Lover*   133

Notes   141

Selected Bibliography   153

Index   158

ACKNOWLEDGEMENTS

I would like to thank Professor George Stade for his generous advice and encouragement. Thanks to Earlene Stundis, who typed and re-typed without complaint. And I deeply appreciate the great editorial wisdom of Mr. Edwin Seaver.

ABBREVIATIONS

CL   H. T. Moore, ed. *The Collected Letters of D. H. Law-
           rence.* 2 vols. New York: Viking, 1962.

CSS   *The Complete Short Stories of D. H. Lawrence.* 3 vols.
           New York: Viking, 1961.

Nehls   Edward Nehls, *D. H. Lawrence: A Composite Biog-
           raphy.* 3 vols. Madison: University of Wisconsin
           Press, 1958.

Phoenix E. D. McDonald, ed. *Phoenix: The Posthumous Papers
           of D. H. Lawrence.* London: Heinemann, 1936.

Phoenix II Warren Roberts, and H. T. Moore, eds. *Phoenix II:
           Unpublished and Other Prose Works by D. H. Law-
           rence.* New York: Viking, 1968.

SCAL   D. H. Lawrence, *Studies in Classic American Litera-
           ture.* New York: Viking, 1961.

SLC   D. H. Lawrence. *Sex, Literature and Censorship.* H. T.
           Moore, ed. New York: Viking, 1959.

All quotations from Lawrence not otherwise specified are
from the Viking Edition.

INTRODUCTION

D. H. Lawrence's main concern is identity, and the fragmented self. It is not "blood" religion, nor modern sexuality, nor the vicissitudes of the industrial age. Each one of his novels, no matter what its avowed subject, is fundamentally an attempt to create through the medium of fiction an image of the self adequate to the demands reality will make on it. Lawrence's study of the self is extensive and systematic enough to be properly considered an ego psychology. In this, as in so much else, he anticipates the present day. His notions of personality prefigure, and sometimes surpass, in their complexity, those of contemporary academic psychologists, many of whose constructs have become household words in an egocentric age. In a culture where the self has become the subject of anxious scrutiny, it seems particularly relevant to study Lawrence's ideas about being.

His notions of personality serve to organize his art. Each of the novels presupposes a concept of self which governs not only the characterization, but the theme and structure of the work as well. Thus, in Lawrence's first novel, *The White Peacock*, personality is seen as consisting of animal instincts and spiritual impulses. This antithesis of mind and body dictates the book's characterization and symbolism, as well as its plot, which is a dramatization of the conflict between these instincts and impulses.

Lawrence redefines and elaborates his ideas about personality continuously in the novels. In *The White Peacock*, for instance, where the subject is the mind-body split, there are suggestions—but no more than suggestions—that the split originates in the sexual conflicts of the oedipal personality. *Sons and Lovers* then deals explicitly with the origin of the mind-body dichotomy in

1

this situation. The oedipal personality is the subject of the book, yet in the course of the narrative a new concept of self begins to appear: an ego structure which is, metaphorically, a living core surrounded by a hard dead shell—a seed. This analogy, in turn, becomes the central metaphor for personality in *The Rainbow*, and it, again in turn, is superseded by another, which becomes central in *Women in Love*. The succession continues throughout the novels (with slight exception); each novel contains in embryo the psychology—and ultimately the structure—of the one that succeeds it.

The chapters that follow examine the various ideas of personality as they appear in *Sons and Lovers, The Rainbow, Women in Love, Aaron's Rod, Kangaroo,* and *The Plumed Serpent*. These books register the significant shifts in Lawrence's ego psychology. (*The Lost Girl* and *Lady Chatterley's Lover* are instances of recidivism rather than advance; their psychology and their themes are mostly derived from Lawrence's own earlier work.) Taken as a whole, the novels describe the progress of the self from childhood (*Sons and Lovers*), through youth (*The Rainbow*), marriage (*Women in Love*), maturity (*Aaron's Rod* and *Kangaroo*), and death (*The Plumed Serpent*). Each phase has, for Lawrence, its own struggles, which inspire its particular image of self; and we follow the chain of these images through his work. Each represents an attempt to reach an equilibrium with reality; we watch each effort succeed for a time, then flounder, and in the end, finally, fail.

It has been my intention to avoid, whenever possible, the luxuriant swamp of Lawrence's own psychopathology. He was almost certainly a schizoid personality. He assumes throughout the novels that the self is weak in relation to reality, and requires defenses of every sort: insulation, infinite growth, equilibrium, isolation, duplication, rearrangement, rerelation, infinite life, infinite power, and so on. Whatever the solution, the problem is fundamentally that the ego is perceived as vulnerable, even to death, in the face of an alien reality.

Lawrence is frequently criticised as an artist driven by his pathology to create. But it is irrelevant whether or not he was a madman spurred on to literary achievement by (besides his delusions of grandeur and incipient homosexuality) the need for ego defense, a need strong from the first, apparently, and grown stronger in every novel. In relation to the self "sanity" is more often than not a question of degree rather than any essential difference. The novels encompass the extremes of unthinkable

2

danger and blissful certainty, areas which "sane" people never experience. But the books only exaggerate (and in so doing, emphasize and clarify) the difficulties inherent in the modern human condition. They show the struggles that any individual who has a modicum of sentience must, with greater or lesser intensity, experience, as he proceeds through life, in his relation to the reality that surrounds him.

The critical method used in this study is allegorical. It treats character primarily as idea, and the material world as symbol. This deprives Lawrence's novels of their considerable sense of immediate life, which will strike many readers—quite correctly—as unforgivable. Neither does this approach offer a valid aesthetic index for judging the novels as works of art. Just the opposite, in fact: the novels generally agreed to be Lawrence's weakest (*Aaron's Rod, The Plumed Serpent* and *Kangaroo*) are the clearest presentations of his ego psychology. But it is the paradoxical nature of allegory to be both coldly schematic and at the same time the most precise possible rendering of inner states. The dramatic is limited by being verbal, external and sensory. A large part of our psychic life is unconscious, and the language of the unconscious is the symbol.

Lawrence distrusted analytical awareness. The constant and powerful undertow of images in his fiction represents an attempt to bypass it. He appeals directly to the reader's unconscious through symbols and patterns which follow their own logic. That he is successful, anyone who has been hypnotized by a logically unintelligible passage of incantatory Lawrence can testify. Whether he succeeds in defining the self by these means, is something else.

1

SONS AND LOVERS:
THE STRUGGLE TO EXIST

At the outset it is necessary to say a word about Lawrence's psychological systems, as distinct from the ideas of psychology expressed in the novels. Their chronological relationship indicates that most often Lawrence explores and discovers his ideas of the self in the process of writing his fiction. As a rule he formulates these discoveries by recasting them into the discursive theories of non-fiction prose written in approximately the same period. Most of Lawrence's non-fiction prose contains some theorizing—however symbolical—on the nature of the self, which can enrich our understanding of the concurrent novel.[1] His psychological systems also tend, sometimes with unfortunate results, to be reflected back into his subsequent fiction.

Lawrence's psychological systems are far from consistent, when considered either throughout his life or at any particular moment. However, they all show similar attitudes and prejudices, and they invariably show the rigidly dualistic thinking that stamps, unmistakably as a trademark, every one of his ideas about human personality. From first to last Lawrence believes that the self is created by warring opposites, both without and within the ego. To him, the fragmented personality—incomplete, crippled, perverted—is the result of imbalance in the existential opposition.

He also assumes that everything which exists is in some sense either male or female. This notion represents an almost inevitable extension of dualism as extreme as his is. "But except in infinity," he writes in the "Study of Thomas Hardy," "everything of life is male or female, distinct." "But the consciousness, that is of both. Every impulse that stirs into life, every single impulse, is

4

either male or female, distinct, except the being of the complete flower, of the complete consciousness, which is two in one, fused. These are infinite and eternal. The consciousness, what we call the truth, is eternal, beyond change or motion, beyond time or limit. But that which is not conscious, which is Time and Life, that is our field." *(Phoenix, 43)* And, as far as Lawrence is concerned, except in an ideal state, which is attainable only in theory or fantasy, the only condition of existence possible between male and female is warfare. No event and no character in his work escapes this symbolic male-female dualism.

Another characteristic of his thought is that often it proceeds by analogy. His fictional universe reveals a system of correspondences. Thus a cosmic fact or event has always social and individual parallels. In his metaphysics, for example, the female principle is necessary because it provides the creative opposition to the male principle, a tension that is necessary for existence. In his fictional society, women are essential because they act as Other to the men. In his personality theory, the feminine element is needed to balance the masculine within the individual ego.[2]

Lawrence's dualism and his use of analogy are nowhere better illustrated than in *The White Peacock*, his first novel. It is based on the three great dualities in Western thought: ontological, societal, and individual. These are form and matter, Eros and civilization, mind and body. As an example of the first dualism Lettie Beardsall, the book's heroine, is form to George Saxton's matter. She calls him "blind," "half-born," "gross with good living and heavy sleeping." "As for me," she says, "the flower is born in me but it wants bringing forth." George's relation to Lettie should be one of mutual realization, but it is not. Instead they destroy each other. After she rebuffs him he gets physically sick, and deteriorates into a drunk who sinks into a sodden torpor without spirit or hope. The failure between them partly explains the deadly atmosphere that hangs over *The White Peacock*. If we assume that physical reality comes into being through the conjunction of form and matter, then because Lettie and Gorge fight rather than marry, the universe disintegrates.

The second dualism in *The White Peacock*, and the one that Lawrence stresses most, is between civilization and instincts. It is dramatized in an antagonism between over-civilized women and uncivilized men. One of these men is the gamekeeper Annable, first of the Lawrentian dark men of the earth, who lives with his litter of children in the woods (his house is called "Kennels"), rants bitterly about the deadly effects of civilization, and advocates the least civilized behavior possible: animality. "Be a good animal," Annable says, "whether it's man or woman." (202) Annable was once nearly destroyed by a mistress, Lady Crystabel, who rejected him "in the pride of [his] body." Another animalistic man, George Saxton, is destroyed—actually destroys himself—because Lettie effectively unsexes him. The book opens with him pulling the wings off bees, symbolizing his destruction of his own animal nature with drink.

Certain women, in contrast, represent civilization, or "spirituality," or "idealism." This kind of woman instinctively and without malice tries to annihilate animal nature. The book is full of maimed animals, human and other, who are victims of women. Emily Saxton kills a wild dog; George's well-intentioned mother tries to incubate some chicks, but burns them alive in the stove. It is implied that women's antagonism to animality is antagonism to sex. "A woman is so ready to disclaim the body of a man's love," the narrator observes, "she yields him her own soft body with so much gentle patience and regret, she clings to his neck, to his head and cheeks, fondling them for the soul's meaning that is there, and shrinking from his passionate limbs and his body." (423) In such a universe a virile man must be a misogynist in self-defense. Annable watches a peacock dirty the head of an angel on a tombstone and remarks, "That's the soul of a woman—or it's the devil." (227) To these unhappy men, confronting the grave of their own masculinity, there is very little difference.

The Trespasser, Lawrence's second novel, also deals with the conflict between spiritual women and animalistic—actually sexual—men. The hero's *doppelgänger*, Hampson, tells him,

> The best sort of women—the most interesting—are the worst for us, ... By instinct they aim at suppressing the gross and animal in us. Then they are super-sensitive—refined a bit beyond humanity. We, who are as little gross as need be, become their instruments. Life is grounded in them, like electricity in the earth; and we take from them their unrealized life, turn it into light or warmth or power for them. The ordinary woman is, alone, a great potential force, an accumulator, if you like, charged from the source of life. In us her force becomes evident.
>
> She can't live without us, but she destroys us. These deep, interesting women don't want *us;* they want the flowers of the spirit they can gather of us. We, as natural men, are more or less degrading to them and to their love of us; therefore they destroy the natural man in us—that is, us altogether.(69-70)

And in fact, this is the way the hero, Siegmund, is destroyed.

In both these early novels, the conflict between sexual men and civilized women also reflects the third great dualism, the

Christian dualism of the spirit and the flesh. In a sense *The White Peacock*, especially, is a *psychomachia,* an allegory of the spirit's battle with the corporeal. Lettie and George stand for a single being whose mind and body are out of balance. Lawrence stresses that George belongs to an ancient race, the Saxons; hence he embodies the primitive and instinctive in human nature. That Lettie destroys him symbolizes the subjection of the body by the more powerful spirit.

Individual characters in the novel also suffer inner conflicts because mind and body are out of balance. Lettie, for example, is sexually repressed. She feels a vague, Arnoldian mourning for some loss she cannot define. She rejects George, who attracts her sexually, for Leslie Tempest (the first mechanical man in the Lawrence canon), who does not. When she is out walking with George, some flowers happen to remind her of "something out of an old religion, that we have lost. They make me feel afraid.... They belong to some knowledge we have lost, that I have lost and I need. I feel afraid.... I believe I have lost something." (198) What she has lost, and what she fears, is the primitive, instinctive part of her personality—her sexuality—that she has repudiated in rejecting George.

There are women in *The White Peacock* who are not repressed, overrarified creatures of spirit. One is Annable's wife; another is George's wife Meg, who is "fleshly," and a fertile mother. Although George is matter in relation to Lettie's spirit, he is spirit to Meg's matter. Metaphorically, as spirit, he is trammelled by Meg's physicality; literally, as a man, he is enslaved by her maternity. "In the marital duel," he says, "Meg is winning. The woman generally does; she has the children on her side."(140) Beginning with *The White Peacock* Lawrence's characters are polarized thus, stereotyped according to the antitheses of matter and form, instinct and civilization, body and spirit. Throughout Lawrence's works characters retain overtones of this polarization. In *The Rainbow*, for instance, Will Brangwen acts as matter to Anna's spirit. The tension between Ursula and Skrebensky is partly due to the fact that she is a symbol of transcendence, and he of immanence. In "The Man Who Died," one of the last stories Lawrence wrote, the characters are totally polarized as flesh and spirit. Mary Madelaine, the spiritual bride, is contrasted to the earthy peasant wife. Christ is spirit before his crucifixion, and seeks the divinity of the flesh after it.

From a psychological point of view the crucial antithesis in *The White Peacock* is between mind and body. The other polarities are only analogies for it. As the novel unfolds skirmish by

7

skirmish, it implies that this conflict is simply inherent in human nature. Yet *The White Peacock* does suggest obliquely the etiology of the self's disease. This is the oedipal mother. The book's original title was *Nethermere*, which breaks down etymologically into "nether' (under, below) and "mere" (French "mother," and Old English "pond, swamp").[3] The hero, Cyril, at the end of book leaves both the swampy woods of Nethermere and his domineering mother. George Saxton, on the other hand, is unable to escape the women around him, and symbolically suffocates in a drunken miasma.

Every woman in the book acts as a domineering mother. The only physicality these women permit is maternal, and that is smothering and obscene as Cyril describes it. In one scene the women bathe their sons, while the adult males stand in the doorway, jealously excluded. "I always remember the inarticulate delight with which she took the child in her hands," Cyril says, "when at last his little shirt was removed, and felt his soft white limbs and his body."(422) Cyril is obsessed by infantile sexuality: "In my heart of hearts I longed for someone to nestle against, someone who would come between me and the coldness and wetness of surroundings."(336) In the supposedly "homoerotic" bathing scene with George Saxton, Cyril also seems envious of the infantile:

> [George] saw I had forgotten to continue my rubbing, and laughing he took hold of me and began to rub me briskly, as if I were a child, or rather, a woman he loved and did not fear. I left myself quite limply in his hands, and, to get a better grip of me, he put his arm round me and pressed me against him, and the sweetness of the touch of our naked bodies one against the other was superb. It satisfied in some measure the vague, indecipherable yearning of my soul. (340)

The encounter has more overtones of infant care than homosexual love. Yet not until Lawrence's third book, *Sons and Lovers*, does the author make an explicit connection between the domineering mother and the destructive mind-body split, with the theory of mother-incest.

That an oedipus complex is the theme of *Sons and Lovers* there is no doubt. Lawrence describes his intentions in the much-quoted letter to Edward Garnett.

> A woman of character and refinement goes into the lower class, and has no satisfaction in her own life. She has a passion for her husband, so the children are born of passion and have heaps of vitality. But as soon as her sons grow up she selects them as lov-

ers—first the eldest, then the second. These sons are *urged* into
life by their reciprocal love of their mother—urged on and on. But
when they came to manhood, they can't love, because their mother
is the strongest power in their lives, and holds them . . . As soon as
the young men come into contact with women, there's a split.
William gives his sex to a fribble, and his mother holds his soul.
But the split kills him, because he doesn't know where he is. The
next son gets a woman who fights for his soul—fights his mother.
The son loves the mother—all the sons hate and are jealous of the
father. The battle goes on between the mother and the girl, with
the son as the object. The mother gradually proves the stronger,
because of the tie of blood. The son decides to leave his soul in
his mother's hands, and, like his elder brother, go for passion. He
gets passion. Then the split begins to tell again. But, almost un-
consciously, the mother realizes what is the matter and begins to
die. The son casts off his mistress, attends to his dying mother. He
is left in the end naked of everything with the drift towards death.
(CL, 160)

Lawrence, like Freud, believes the sexual schizophrenia pro-
duced by the oedipus complex is the most prevalent form of
degradation in modern erotic life. He calls it "the tragedy of
thousands of young men in England." Lawrence disclaimed any
debt to Freud in *Sons and Lovers,* and later attempted to refute
him, but the novel conforms to Freud's theory of the oedipus
complex on all important points. An incestuous attachment to the
mother causes what Freud calls "psychical impotence." The
erotic life of such people remains dissociated; "where such men
love they have no desire and where they desire they cannot
love."[4] In other words, because of mother-incest there is a mind-
body split.

In *Sons and Lovers* Lawrence makes the same division of
women into "dark and fair, sinful and innocent, sensual and
pure" that he accuses Cooper and Hardy of making in their novels.(SCAL, 86) This lily-rose stereotype is a familiar Victorian
compound of evangelical prudery and oedipal anxiety. William
Morel is typical; he gives himself to a "fribble," as many Victorian sons did. Paul sees Miriam and Clara as the lily and the
rose; one is a "nun," the other an "Amazon," a "Brunhild." Dark
and fair women are stereotyped projections of man's bodily and
spiritual sides; Clara and Miriam, battling over Paul, symbolize
his divided self.

In his essay on Hawthorne Lawrence cites his own parents as
examples of this antagonism between idealism and physicality.
They, like Dimmesdale and Chillingworth, represent the "basic
hostility in all of us between the physical and the mental, the

blood and the spirit. The mind is 'ashamed' of the blood. And the blood is destroyed by the mind, actually."(SCAL, 86) A man contains the "black, vengeful soul of the crippled, masterful male, still dark in his authority; and the ghastliness of the fallen saint! The two halves of manhood mutually destroying one another." (99)

Lawrence's ideas about mother-incest resemble Freud's even in their limitations, which are the limitations of a metaphorical system that is a concrete analogy used as a model for human behavior. Freud's is essentially a system of hydraulic pressure that makes us see emotional life as the eruption of psychic geysers through the weakest point in the bedrock of defenses. Lawrence's system is predicated on electrical polarization of positive and negative charges. *Fantasia of the Unconscious* and *Psychoanalysis and Unconscious*, which Lawrence wrote as a rebuttal to Freud, describe mother-incest in symbols taken from Kundalini yoga and occult physiognomy. The upshot of his theory is that "idealism" recognizes as the highest earthly love the love of mother and child, and this is asexual, "a persistent starving of the lower centres," particularly the "centre of sensual, manly independence." (150) The worst result of this "dynamic *spiritual* incest"—Lawrence will not call it an oedipus complex—is the derangement of the son's sex, a terrible puritanism and denial of his own body. (Of which Lawrence himself was an example. "I remember," he writes, "when I was a very young man I was enraged with a woman, if I was reminded of her sexual actuality. I only wanted to be aware of her personality, her mind and spirit. The other had to be fiercely shut out.")(*Phoenix II*, 568)[5]

The extent to which the mind-body split affects *Sons and Lovers*—and all of Lawrence—is obvious. What is perhaps not so obvious is that mother-incest in the novel has other than sexual ramifications. Specifically, the domineering mother threatens more than her child's sexuality; she threatens his ego.

The oedipal mother in *Sons and Lovers* is presented in a split image, consisting of Mrs. Morel, Miriam and Clara.[6] Clara is, of course, the sexual fragment of the personality. Mrs. Morel is presented as sexually neutral to Paul, and even her passion for her husband, which must have been considerable, is underplayed. She is not described as a sexual being. The worst traits of the oedipal mother are displaced from Mrs. Morel onto Miriam. For example, Miriam denies Paul's sex. The oedipal mother-son relationship is inevitably one of repressed sexual desire and outward frustration, as is Miriam and Paul's. Miriam is called "willful." Lawrence's rhetoric flatters Mrs. Morel and paints Miriam as a monster, but to judge from their actions, Miriam is an unhappy girl who likes to pick flowers, and Mrs. Morel is a hard, domineering woman who destroys her husband when he doesn't conform to her ideas of gentility, and her elder son when he does. Miriam is called "possessive." The anxiety a domineering mother causes in her son is considerable, yet none is ever mentioned in Paul; instead it is Miriam who makes him feel anxious and trapped, Miriam whom he inexplicably hates. His horror of the girl's "possessiveness" and "willfulness" (which are never demonstrated in any act of hers) are absent from his feelings about his mother, for whom he feels love untainted with fear or anger.

Mrs. Morel is perhaps the most vampirish woman in Lawrence, yet he never damns her, or any mother, outright, by showing her to be a monster to her son. Instead he uses surrogates to express this unacceptable repugnance.[7] So the figure of the domineering mother, in various guises, extends in a long line of female vampires through Lawrence. Escape from the mother appears as a theme in nearly every Lawrence novel. In *The White Peacock*, Cyril Beardsall, being tied to his mother, is consequently of uncertain gender (he's nicknamed "Sybil"). A go-between for his estranged parents, he sees his father die a drunk because his mother rejected him. For most of the book Cyril vascillates between his mother and his manly independence, and ultimately escapes Nethermere.

In *The Trespasser*, Siegmund escapes his motherly wife with a child-lover, Helena; only to discover that Helena metamorphoses into a Great Mother too. In this role she literally saps his strength. After a sexual encounter,

> He felt stunned, half-conscious. Yet as he lay helplessly looking up at her some other consciousness inside him murmured: "Hawwa—Eve—Mother!" She stood compassionate over him. Without touching him she seemed to be yearning over him like a mother. Her compassion, her benignity, seemed so different from his little Helena. This woman, tall and pale, drooping with the strength of her compassion, seemed stable, immortal, not a fragile human being, but a personification of the great motherhood of women.
> "I am her child, too," he dreamed, as a child murmurs unconscious in sleep. He had never felt her eyes so much as now, in the darkness, when he looked only into deep shadow. She had never before so entered and gathered his plaintive masculine soul to the bosom of her nurture.
> "Come," she said gently, when she knew he was restored. "Shall we go?"
> He rose, with difficulty gathering his strength.(60-61)

Lawrence emphasizes that Siegmund on the walk back is deathly weak. Ultimately the women drive him to suicide.

Paul Morel actually poisons his dying mother. But Gertrude Morel's ghost is not easily laid to rest. She appears in the person of Mrs. Crich in *Women in Love;* there "the dead hold the living." (177) Mrs. Crich releases her son Gerald from her, as he stands with Gudrun, in a ghostly parting scene. "Don't come any further with me," she said in her barely audible voice. "I don't want you any further." (320) Hermione, as a "spiritual bride," is a continuation of Miriam, and by extension, of Gertrude Morel. She calls Rupert "little boy," and would keep him a sexless child. Gerald is in effect killed by Gudrun (Gertrude?), whom he repeatedly forces into the perverted role of his mother. These mother-figures are death-dealers.

In *The Lost Girl* a myth of the overthrow of the matriarchy—or the mother—is performed by a mime troupe. As Madame Rochard wrote their act, she kills Ciccio, the "son," disguised as a bear. But one night during a performance the beast-hero revolts, and stands up saying *"Vivo sempre,* Madame!" (183) Eventually her power over him is crushed, and he can elope with the heroine.

Aaron Sisson flees a houseful of squabbling females in *Aaron's Rod,* with only a flute to symbolize his endangered masculinity. "It seemed a burden just then, a millstone around his neck." (40) Aaron fears that women possess the power, in our matriarchal civilization, to envelop men with their "infernal will." He escapes to Italy and a fantasy world of male values not unlike Hemingway's.

Kangaroo, in the book by the same name, is a stifling surrogate mother who tries to coerce the hero, Richard Somers, into loving him, but dies when Somers rejects him instead. Another advocate of "love" is Carlota in *The Plumed Serpent,* who is also killed by the hero. A descendent of Miriam, Carlota represents the frigid female who denies her man's sex and vampirizes him with Christian spirituality. (Lawrence often accuses a woman's frigidity of making a man impotent. In fiction it is possible to invert the law of cause and effect when the occasion demands.) Carlota is the "sneak-thief of the world's virility," and Kate Leslie laughs dispassionately as a fertility goddess to hear Cipriano curse Carlota, the killing frigid principle of "spirit."

> You stale virgin, you spinster, you born widow, you weeping mother, you impeccable wife, you just woman. You stole the very sunshine out of the sky and the sap out of the earth. Because back

again, what did you pour? Only the water of dead dilution into the mixing bowl of life, you thief. Oh die!—die! die! Die and be a thousand times dead! Do nothing but utterly die. (381)

Lawrence's dislike of the spiritual vampire does not diminish over the years; if anything, it increases.

Such hostility to the mother-figure is generally rationalized in Freudian—or at least sexual—terms: she is hateful because she denies a man's (her son's) sex. Lawrence suggests that Paul's outbursts of anger are due to his sexual difficulties (as would Freud if Paul Morel came to him as a patient). Paul may love his mother above all others, but she has cost him his masculinity and is therefore hated. The death-obsession of the Morel sons can be interpreted as a sign of their murdered masculinity, or as anger turned upon themselves. When Paul hopes to hurt himself riding his bicycle, or suffers through his many illnesses, he wants revenge on his women. His "drift toward death" may be suicide as an acceptable substitute for homicide—his mother's. Yet these explanations all accept the assumption that the book itself consciously makes, which is that loss of masculinity is loss of life itself. Conversely, Paul, to save his masculinity, must destroy his mother.

Paul tries to reconcile his mind and his body in his relations with Miriam and Clara, who are symbols of the two parts of himself. Miriam fails because she has no sex, according to Paul, and Clara because she has sex only. But the failure is Paul's, he realizes, and since his mother creates the fatal schism in him, it is impossible for him to integrate mind and body while she lives. For this reason she must die. We may ask why love is always a question of life and death in Lawrence, why a bad marriage can be literally fatal, and the wrong woman a killer. ("My boy, remember," Mrs. Morel tells William when he gets engaged, "you're taking your life in your hands.") Frigid women are murderers as well. "Idealism," "Christian love" and especially Protestantism[8] are anti-life forces embodied in women. Miriam's spirituality, like that of her descendents Hermione and Carlota, is potentially fatal. Both sex and lack of sex with Miriam makes Paul brood on death, supposedly because the lovers are brimful of Protestant prudery. But if we disentangle what Lawrence is doing from what he says he is doing, it becomes clear that in *Sons and Lovers*, in spite of the appearance of psychological realism, we are dealing with a myth, and a rather rigid one at that. This is the myth of the mother as murderer.

The murder is metaphorical; it is a crime committed against the self. *Sons and Lovers*—and much of Lawrence—deals in sexual terms with an aspect of the human psyche that is anterior to sex. That aspect is the sense of self. *Sons and Lovers* describes the growth of a sense of identity in terms of sexuality; the sexual events in the novel are metaphors. Thus love is a question of do-or-die in Lawrence because for Paul to fail to win his masculinity in spite of his mother would be to lose his identity altogether; that is, he would be nonexistent, and, in effect, dead.

Mother-incest is still the crucial relationship in the novel; but this incest can, and does in Paul's case, involve more than a person's sexuality. Erich Neumann in *The Origins and History of Consciousness* makes a distinction between two kinds of incest, which is relevant here.[9] Oedipal incest, which Freud deals with, means coming into manhood by replacing the father. It is an act of self-definition. What Neumann calls "uroboric incest" (*uroboros* is the snake of eternity devouring its own tail) is an act of self-effacement. It is the desire to return to the "original unity" of the womb, where self is relinquished in order to merge with the mother. In uroboric incest ego-consciousness is dissolved, as if one were *in utero* or in the earliest infant state where one does not differentiate self from environment.

Regression to infantile experience is typical of neurosis and mysticism, and of both as they appear in *Sons and Lovers*. Freud sees regression to the earliest consciousness of infancy as the source of the "oceanic feeling" of the religious mystic.[10] Neumann compares uroboric incest with romantic nature mysticism where self dissolves into nature, and with the "death-romanticism of the Germanic races."[11] The capacity for this experience, Freud notes, generally belongs to people without a strong sense of *ego*. In this category Paul Morel must be included.

Uroboric incest is a return to the monosexuality of infancy.[12] In *Sons and Lovers*, as well as subsequent books, the sexual ecstasies of the hero often resemble infant eroticism. At one point, for instance, Paul and Clara sit at the theatre:

> The drama continued. He saw it all in the distance, going on somewhere; he did not know where, but it seemed far away inside him. He was Clara's white heavy arms, her throat, her moving bosom. That seemed to be himself. Then away somewhere the play went on, and he was identified with that also. There was no himself. The grey and black eyes of Clara, her bosom coming down on him, her arm that he held gripped between his hands were all that existed. Then he felt himself small and helpless, her towering in her force above him. (331)

The play is a metaphor for the unreality of their "adult" love, which is an acting out of Paul's infant need. His erotic impulse is to merge himself with the body of his lover, especially with her maternal bosom, and to make himself nothing.

The core of Paul's nature mysticism, and of the related sexual mysticism that he discovers through Clara with the "cry of the peewit, the wheel of the stars," is the uroboric outflux of the self. The experience of merging is atavism. Diana Trilling sees the "precognitive flow" which was "love" to Lawrence as the animal affection that exists between mother and infant.[13] "Understanding," she maintains, is the force which interrupts this relationship when the social connection replaces the earlier physical one. "In all his adult life ... Lawrence looked to reproduce the noncognitive connection of this earliest love experience, his infant experience. It is what he meant by the blood consciousness."

His metaphors for blood connection are decidedly infantile, not to say prenatal. *Psychoanalysis and the Unconscious* describes the breaking of ties with the mother, and the desire for oneness again, "a strange sinking back into the old unison, the old organic continuum" and "the lovely polarized vitalism." (22) To Lawrence blood union is a state of grace from which we have fallen into the alienation of individuality. The history of the race parallels the history of the individual in this respect. "Class hate and class-consciousness are only a sign that the old togetherness, the old blood-warmth has collapsed, and every man is aware of himself in apartness." (*Phoenix II,* 513) The attempt to return to Eden can be public or private. In the early and late novels salvation is individual; in the middle books—*Aaron's Rod, Kangaroo* and *The Plumed Serpent*—the emphasis is social.

When he wrote *Sons and Lovers* Lawrence had not yet formulated his theory of blood consciousness. Lacking as yet his own terminology, he describes uroboric experiences in conventional mystical language, some of which resembles Whitman's. Paul's religious ecstacy is a "strange, gentle reaching-out to death." "To be rid of our individuality," he says to Miriam, "which is our will, which is our effort—to live effortless, a kind of curious sleep—that is very beautiful, I think; that is our after-life—our immortality." (288) And "the highest of all" is "to melt out into the darkness and sway there, identified with the Great Being." (287) Paul's ecstasy is consummately pleasurable. Yet a weak ego also has the capacity, and in fact the tendency, to experience the obverse: excruciating feelings of nonexistence. In Christian terminology, the mystic wins illumination in Divine union, but he also must endure the dark night of the soul.[14]

Paul Morel's experience of non-existence has two forms, as Lawrence describes it. The first is that Paul confronts, and is himself, a void. The other is that he is being merged into a greater being, but against his will. After his mother's death Paul suffers the agonies of the void around and within him:

> He could not bear it. On every side the immense dark silence seemed pressing him, so tiny a spark, into extinction, and yet, almost nothing, he could not be extinct. Night, in which everything was lost, went reaching out, beyond stars and sun. Stars and sun, a few bright grains, went spinning round for terror, and holding each other in embrace, there in a darkness that outpassed them all, and left them tiny and daunted. So much, and himself, infinitesimal, at the core a nothingness, and yet not nothing.
> "Mother!" he whispered—"Mother!"
> She was the only thing that held him up, himself, amid all this. And she was gone, intermingled herself. (420)

This experience is the obverse of Paul's loss of self in sexual ecstasy with Clara, which is also described as the wheel of stars in space.

For most of the novel Paul's ego is defined by his women. Away from them on vacation, he is "like another man. None of himself remained—no Clara, no Miriam, no mother that fretted him." (369) Consequently, when Paul loses his women in the final chapters, he is nearly nonexistent. The paradox of Paul's situation is that the loss of his mother nearly annihilates him, yet he must get rid of her precisely because she threatens his being.

The negative characteristics of the domineering mother—the reasons Paul must escape from her—are displaced from Mrs. Morel onto Miriam. Paul's cruelty to the girl is confused with his feelings toward his mother: "and why did he hate Miriam, and feel so cruel towards her, at the thought of his mother? If Miriam caused his mother suffering, then he hated her. Why did she make him feel as if he were uncertain of himself, insecure, an indefinite thing, as if he had not sufficient sheathing to prevent the night and space from breaking into him? How he hated her! And then, what a rush of tenderness and humility." (193) Paul hates Miriam because she makes him feel non-existent, like "an indefinite thing." From his point of view, she is trying to annihilate him.

To Paul the girl is a vampire; she wants to absorb everything. "To her, flowers appealed with such strength she felt she must make them part of herself." (173) "Paul hated her for it," because his vitality is symbolized in those flowers. The "soul union" he thinks Miriam craves would be for her to engulf him. The lovers'

16

communion at the white rose-bush makes Paul feel "anxious and imprisoned" not because Miriam denies his sex (as Lawrence intimates), but because she threatens his being. Mrs. Morel says Miriam is "one of those who will want to suck a man's soul out till he has none of his own left ... and he is such a gaby as to let himself be absorbed." (160) And later the mother thinks Miriam "wants to absorb him ... wants to draw him out and absorb him until there is nothing left of him, even for himself ... she will suck him up." (193) Miriam has the significant habit of sucking on her finger, especially in conversations with Paul.

To the weak ego the mother-image is equivocal. It is Mrs. Morel; it is also Miriam. That is, it supports a sense of self but on the other hand it threatens to destroy self. The contradictions in Paul's affair with Miriam reflect this. They are summarized at the lovers' final meeting, when Paul complains both that Miriam is too possessive, and that she has failed to take possession of him. "You love me so much," he says, "you want to put me in your pocket. And I should die there smothered." (417) But Miriam fails, according to Paul, also because she cannot assert herself: "she could not take him and relieve him of the responsibility of himself .... He wanted her to hold him and say, with joy and authority: 'Stop all this restlessness and beating against death. You are mine for a mate.'" (418) Graham Hough accuses Lawrence of "impurity of motive" in this scene; according to him it is an instance of tortured, "enigmatic" confusion. "The situation hardly explains itself, or rather, two inconsistent explanations are offered."[15] But Paul's behavior is not a "neurotic refusal of responsibility," nor an artistic or psychological inaccuracy. It is a perfect description of his ambivalence, and his dilemma about the role women should play in his life.

That one has a weak ego is attributable to one's earliest relationship with his mother. It was first noted by Freud that in normal development, the infant first depends on his mother's presence for his sense that he is real. As the baby matures, he internalizes his need for her presence: he develops a sense of autonomy and doesn't need his mother there to feel he exists. However, Paul would be a case of abnormal development. He suffers from what existential psychologist R.D. Laing calls "ontological insecurity,"[16] that is, chronic uncertainty about whether or not one actually exists.

The sense of self in the ontologically insecure person has somehow failed to become independent of his mother. He therefore longs for contact, because that alone gives him a sense that

17

he is real; yet since his ego is weak, such contact carries the threat of engulfing him at the same time. In this sense it is trying to "kill" him, and he vascillates between seeking the contact that will save him, and seeking to avoid that same contact because it will destroy him.

Left alone, this individual feels empty, as though he were a vacuum. Laing calls this a sense of "implosion." It is a felt impingement of reality, "the world as liable at any moment to crash in and obliterate a vacuum." On the other hand, contact is sensed as engulfment; it is "to be swallowed up, drowned, eaten up, smothered."[17] Since love involves this contact, where the ego is "buried," or "dragged into quicksand," or "smothered," all love is seen as a version of hatred. Caught between these two contradictory impulses, such a personality is defined somewhere between the desire to merge and the act of resisting it.

This tendency to see existence as relationship, and all relationship as some form of engulfment, is the single most important fact in Lawrence's world view. It radically affects his ideas about religion, society and history, as well as psychology. It is the major premise of the psychological system that he elaborates in *Fantasia of the Unconscious* and *Psychoanalysis and the Unconscious*. Here Lawrence uses images of positive and negative electrical polarization to describe the relationship between mother and infant wherein the self is created. These currents of attraction and repulsion resemble the opposing impulses of the weak ego. The attraction of the "sympathetic system" draws the child to the mother in a unity of "creative flux." Its counterpart is "the negation of connection," the rejection of the mother, the "revolt from connection, the revolt from union. There is a violent antimaternal motion, anti-everything." (23) As the child matures this revolt alternates with the tendency to merge again with the mother, "to re-establish the old oneness" in "a strange sinking back to the old unison, the old organic continuum—a recovery of the prenatal state." (21) Ideally the self and mother achieve a balance of impulses where each supports but does not invade the being of the other. This is "the at-last-clarified singleness of each being, a singleness equilibrized, polarized in one by the counterposing singleness of the other." (22)

If nothing goes wrong with this process of development its result is "the central fulfillment for a man," which is "that he possess his own soul in strength within him deep and alone. The deep, rich aloneness, reached and perfected through love. And the passing beyond any further *quest* of love." (156) In other words, the individual ego ideally is self-sufficient. "The essence of morality," Lawrence writes, "is the basic desire to preserve the perfect correspondence between the self and the object, to have no trespass and no breach of integrity, nor yet any refaulture in the vitalistic interchange." (28)

However, according to him, self-sufficiency is rarely the case. He attributes the ego-dependence of modern man to prevalence of the oedipus complex. "Coming to fulfillment of single alone-ness is made impossible for us by the ideal monomania of more love" on the part of the mother. Unsatisfied by her husband, "the unhappy woman beats about for her insatiable satisfaction, seek-ing who she may devour. And usually, she turns to her child." (157) The child, trapped in the old patterns of attraction and rejection, cannot be independent.

In the novels we find a great many characters with weak egos, who are both threatened by women and yet nonexistent without them. Cyril Beardsall's vision of nullity at the end of *The White Peacock* is a revelation worthy of Pascal. "I felt the great wild pity," he says, "and a sense of terror, and a sense of horror, and a sense of awful littleness and loneliness among a great empty space. I felt beyond myself as if I were a mere fleck drifting un-consciously through the dark." (36-37) Paul Morel has a similar sense of his own non-existence after his mother's death, when "always alone, his soul oscillated, first on the side of death, then on the side of life, doggedly. The real agony was that he had no-where to go, nothing to do, nothing to say, and *was* nothing him-self." (412) When the hero of *Aaron's Rod* escapes his women, he too endures anxiety in solitude:

> "Does he seek another woman?" said Lilly. "Do you, Aaron?"
> "I don't *want* to," said Aaron. "But—I can't stand by myself in the middle of the world, and in the middle of people, and know that I am quite by myself, and nowhere to go, and nothing to hold on to. I can for a day or two—But then, it becomes unbearable as well. You get frightened. You feel you might go funny—as you would if you stood on this balcony wall with all the space beneath you."

Another character says to Aaron, "You like your own company? Do you? Sometimes I think I'm nothing when I'm alone. Some-times I think I surely must be nothing—nothingness." (63)

Women in Love deals with the dilemma of the weak ego by contrasting a failed affair to a successful one. Gerald Crich repre-sents the weak ego. When he is alone he does not feel real: "once or twice lately, when he was alone in the evening and had

19

nothing to do, he had suddenly stood up in terror, not knowing what he was." (224) He feels "such a strange pressure upon him, as if the very middle of him were a vacuum, and the outside were an awful tension." (225) And he is frightened by the void outside himself as well as inside: "for another night he was to be suspended in chain of physical life, over the bottomless pit of nothingness. And he could not bear it . . . . He did not believe in his own strength any more. He could not fall into this infinite void and rise again. If he fell, he would be gone forever. He must withdraw, he must seek reinforcements. He did not believe in his own single self any further than this." (330) Because he is "faced with the ultimate experience of his own nothingness" Gerald seeks Gudrun.

He turns to Gudrun to restore him, but what he wants to be restored to is the primal unity of the prenatal state. He wants to be "suffused out" in sex. Gudrun remains fully conscious, but

> the lovely creative warmth flooded through him like a sleep of fecundity within the womb. Ah, if only she would grant him the flow of this living effluence, he would be restored, he would be complete again. He was afraid she would deny him before it was finished. Like a child at the breast he cleaved intensely to her, and she could not put him away. And his seared, ruined membrane relaxed, softened, that which was seared and stiff and blasted yielded again, became soft and flexible, palpitating with new life. He was infinitely grateful, as to God, or as an infant at its mother's breast. He was glad and grateful like a delirium, as he felt his own wholeness come over him again, as he felt the full, unutterable sleep coming over him, the sleep of complete exhaustion and restoration. (338)

But Gerald is, in Lawrence's eyes, a pervert because he seeks this passive merging instead of self-integrity.

Many Lawrence characters are guilty of such infantile passivity. Like Gerald, Clifford Chatterly attempts to regain this condition with his wife, and then his nurse. In *The Rainbow* Will Brangwen is damned because he stays childish and "unformed," because he "lapses back for his fulfillment" to Anna, his wife. (204) Lawrence complains in his essay "The Crown" that "we want to reduce ourselves back, back to the corruptive state of childishness." (*Phoenix II*, 395) "For a grown person," he continues, "to be slimily, pornographically reaching out for child-gratification is disgusting . . . . It is the desire to be reduced back, reduced back in our accomplished ego: always within the unshattered rind of our completeness and our complacency, to go backwards, in sentimentalized disintegration, to the states of childhood."[18] For this reason Gerald and Gudrun are flowers of "universal dissolution."

Such lapsing back as Gerald's is condemned because it makes the ego vulnerable to engulfment. Gudrun, cast in the role of Gerald's mother by Gerald himself, devours him. She threatens his being:

> Like a victim that is torn open and given to the heavens, so he had been torn apart and given to Gudrun. How should he close again? This wound, this strange, infinitely-sensitive opening of his soul, where he was exposed, like an open flower, to all the universe, and in which he was given to his complement, the other, the unknown, this wound, this disclosure, this unfolding of his own covering, leaving him incomplete, limited, unfinished, like an open flower under the sky, this was his cruellest joy. (437)

Yet Gerald cannot stand independent of Gudrun; "his brain turned to nought at the idea. It was a state of nothingness." (436) Consequently Gerald straddles the horns of his fatal dilemma; unable to survive with her or without her, he seeks in her to save himself yet finds only his own destruction.

Because he cannot free himself from Gudrun, Gerald perishes in the Alps. The mode of his death symbolizes the opposing tendencies of his life. The mountains represent the void, and when Gerald dies he dissolves into snowy inhuman nothingness. They also represent the womb that engulfs: Gerald relinquishes his life in a womb-like hollow basin of snow. "I've had enough," he says, "I want to go to sleep." (464) His corpse is found in the fetal position, "curled up as if for sleep," and Birkin thinks, surveying the spot where Gerald fell, that his friend might have hauled himself to safety up out of the "shallow pot" where he died. That is, Gerald could have escaped from the overwhelming womb.[19]

Gerald and Gudrun demonstrate how imperfect egos are destroyed. On the other hand, Ursula and Birkin offer—or at least, attempt to offer—an ideal. They create one another by attaining a state of ideal balance between egos. The "stellar equilibrium" that Birkin wants is a dramatization of the perfect equilibrium between mother and infant that Lawrence posits as ideal in *Fantasia of the Unconscious*. Each supports but does not invade the other. Birkin says that in love, as he would have it,

> the man is pure man, the woman pure woman, they are perfectly polarized. But there is no longer any of the horrible merging, mingling self-abnegation of love. There is only the pure duality of polarization, each one free from any contamination of the other. In

each, the individual is primal, sex is subordinate, but perfectly polarized. Each has a single, separate being, with its own laws. The man has his pure freedom, the woman hers. Each acknowledges the perfection of the polarized sex-circuit. Each admits the different nature of the other. (193)

Gerald's "love" constellates around fear of merging and the void, Birkin's around individuation. Yet Birkin's theory when applied in the novel is less than equitable between man and woman and, in this respect, it is like the dependent relation between Gerald and Gudrun. But Birkin's idea of love involves several strategies whereby he avoids Gerald's fate.

Gerald returns to the womb; Birkin is born from it. Ursula gives birth to his individuality in the chapter titled "Excurse," where he is described as "an infant," "a thing that is born," and "as if born out of the womb." (303) When she gives him a flower it symbolizes the individuality he gains through her. She compares him to a flower "because he seem[s] so separate." (304) However Ursula, like Gudrun, is seen as having the power to engulf her lover. In the chapter "Moony" she is a "polyp" who wants "to drink him down," who demands his "complete self-abandon." (257) She can also annihilate him by cutting him off from herself in her self-contained "radiance," her "maddening self-sufficiency." Birkin needs Ursula to fulfill him as Gerald needs Gudrun: "There is a golden light in you," he says, "which I wish you would give me." (241) Thus Ursula, like the moon, has a double aspect to Birkin; she sustains him, but she can destroy him also.

Birkin overcomes Ursula's potential danger by depriving her of her will and individuality. At first she resists him because she feels, correctly, that "he wanted her to yield, as it were her very identity." (178) Eventually she does. Her will is eradicated by what Birkin terms "true sex," and she becomes his "belonging," (360) and his "child." When he throws stones at the reflected moon he tries to annihilate Ursula: "Ursula was dazed, her mind was all gone. She felt she had fallen to the ground and was spilled out, like water on the earth." (240) But she does give the thing he wants, "the surrender of her spirit." (242) After their marriage Ursula's self evaporates. She exists with "no identity," (381) "in the midst of profound darkness." (379) She is made out to be an infant, and Birkin her mother: on the trip abroad he sits "enfolding Ursula round about," and "then her spirit came home to him nestling unconscious in him." Ursula now lives in another, interior world. "Why not a bath of pure oblivion," she wonders, "a new birth, without recollections or blemish of a past life .... What had she to do with parents and antecedents? She knew herself new and unbegotten ... she was herself, pure and silvery, she belonged only to the oneness with Birkin, a oneness that struck deeper notes, sounding into the heart of the universe, the heart of reality, where she had never existed before." (400) In effect Birkin prevents Ursula from overwhelming him by inverting the proposition: he engulfs her.[20]

He also deifies her, and such apotheosis becomes a means of manipulation. To identify Ursula with the moon is a way of "maintaining the self in mystic balance and integrity," in Birkin's words, and insuring "mutual union in separateness." The problem in Lawrence's fiction is one of balance: how to insure that woman will provide the essential otherness for the ego, yet not engulf it. To make her a goddess is to make her both permanent and impersonal. Divested of her social identity Ursula is an impersonal female sapience; without volition she is immobilized, powerless to impinge on Birkin.

The same strategy to protect man from woman occurs in *Sons and Lovers*. Paul Morel and his women become mythic figures, even to Paul himself. The novel is a seasonal myth in the great tradition of Frazer's *Golden Bough* (which Lawrence had read). It follows the cycles of yearly combat of the vegetation god, only the protagonists are reversed: Paul is the May queen, the central "female" figure to whom lovers are sacrificed annually. These lovers are the dying and reviving gods. Miriam is every year tested and tortured in the spring. "We're always like this toward Easter-time," Paul tells her. (221) The next year, "with the spring came the old madness and battle between them." (278) Miriam combats first Mrs. Morel, then Clara. The mother is a fading goddess; she ages most, in Frazer-like fashion, when beside the "luxurient" Clara. (321) Mrs. Morel is joined to earth's diurnal course at her funeral, where she becomes a part of the natural cycle. Clara herself is taken in the fields to insure the growth of the crops—or at least, of Paul, whose emancipation from his mother in a sexual "fire-baptism" is described as a "ripening." (317) "It almost seems," he tells Clara, "to fertilize your soul and make it so that you can go on and mature."

The seasonal myth makes Paul's growth away from his mother seem part of an ineluctable organic process, as though it is only natural that she be usurped by younger women, and inevitable that he grow away from her. It also reduces the power of the women—or attempts to—by depriving them of some measure of their humanness. Paul especially romanticizes Clara, the most alarmingly sexual, as a goddess, "a wistful sphinx," a vehicle for "something bigger than herself," (331) a Brunhild, a Juno. Married to Hades Dawes, this Demeter has a Ceres-like mother in Mrs. Radford, who possesses a mysterious aura. (333) The accoutrements of myth emphasize the fact that Paul persistently reduces Clara to an elemental being. He refuses to acknowledge her as a personality. "Sometimes," he tells his mother, "when I see her as just *the woman,* I love her. But when she talks and criticizes, I don't often listen to her." (350) By abstracting Clara to the level of myth, Paul traffics with a principle instead of relating to a human being. Her sensuality is an idea to him, since he sees her as an impersonal abstraction; she has no human presence. During their vacation at the seashore Paul looks at Clara through the wrong end of a telescope (belittling her literally as well as figuratively). He says to himself, "Why does she absorb me? . . . But what is *she?*" "It's not her I care for," he concludes, having reassured himself that she is only a vessel of the "elemental." (359)

In *The Lost Girl* Alvina Houghton is reduced to an elemental consciousness in order to provide the sole source of reality for her husband and his uncle. She has her apotheosis in the Italian mountains as Demeter, identified with the "eternal pig," she becomes "dumb and elemental." The mountains and valleys strive to obliterate Alvina, "not only her, but the very natives themselves. Ciccio and Pancrazio clung to her, essentially, as if she saved them also from extinction. It needed all her courage. Truly, she had to support the souls of the two men." (35) At the end of the book Alvina comes to know "the ancient gods that knew the right for human sacrifice" because she—or at least her social self—is that sacrifice.

Like Ursula, Alvina is required to relinquish her social personality. The lost girl is transformed not so much by her husband, however, as by the Italian Alps. "The place began annihilating the soul of the Englishwoman, . . . it stole away the soul of Alvina." Later,

> she woke with a start . . . . The moon was in the room. She did not
> know where she was. And she was frightened. And she was cold. A
> real terror took hold of her. Ciccio in his bed was quite still. Everything seemed electric with horror. She felt she would die instantly, everything was terrible around her. She could not move.
> She felt that everything around her was horrific, extinguishing her,
> putting her out. In another instant she would be transfixed. (349)

The irony of *The Lost Girl* is that Alvina suffers the anguish of dissolving personality in order to extinguish her social self; and that in doing so, she becomes a goddess who insures that her men not suffer the same existential anguish.

Lawrence's most unabashed instance of subjection by apotheosis is Kate Leslie's transformation in *The Plumed Serpent.* Kate's "individual self" is relinquished in a series of ritualistic experiences and internal crises. In exchange for her identity she is installed as the goddess Malintzi in the pantheon of the new Mexican religion of the blood that is being "revived" by Don Ramon and his disciple Cipriano. As a goddess she provides essential support for the men.

Whereas in the earlier novels the theme of loss of self is presented mainly dramatically and symbolically, in *The Plumed Serpent* it is brought to such a high degree of analytical self-consciousness that the book sometimes seems less like a novel than a tract. Kate thinks, for instance, that "it is all very well for a woman to cultivate her ego, her individuality. It is all very well for her to despise love, or to love love as a cat loves a mouse, that it plays with as long as possible, before devouring it to vivify her own individuality and voluptuously fill the belly of her own ego." (48) Here "woman" is the devouring mother who preys on the ego of her lover-child, and as such she must be symbolically subjugated in the person of Kate.

That sexuality is a metaphor for the sense of identity is abundantly clear in the novel. "Woman has suffered far more from the suppression of her ego than from sex suppression," Lawrence writes. (481) Kate, in relinquishing her sexual autonomy, that is, her orgasm, to Cipriano, yields her very self to him. Like Ursula, Kate is engulfed by her husband; she feels "he wanted his bloodstream to envelop hers," (349) and Kate "felt she wanted to be covered with deep and living darkness, the deeps where Cipriano could lay her." (386) Cipriano, like Birkin, imitates the devouring mother.[21]

The religion of Quetzalcoatl also coerces Kate by engulfing her. The divine state Ramon and Cipriano want to restore is called "blood-unison," (456) "the old mode of consciousness, the old, dark will, the unconcern for death, the subtle, dark consciousness, non-cerebral but vertebrate." (455) It is an atavistic lapse back to a state of uroboric consciousness, treated as a religious conception. *"In the blood, you and I are undifferentiated,"* (457) Kate realizes. *"We are one blood.* It was the assertion that swept away all individualism, and left her immersed, drowned in the grand sea of living blood." At first she complains to Cipriano that "You treat me as if I had no life of my own. But I have got it. And I must live it. I can't just be swallowed up." (406) But eventually she capitulates: "The blood is one blood—it meant a strange, marginless death of her individual self." (457) Kate as a goddess is "consummate in living lifelessness, the sheer solid mystery of passivity." (342) In other words, woman ideally is reduced to minimal existence.

In this condition, Kate, like her deified predecessors in Lawrence, does not threaten the man whose being she gives indispensable support. Cipriano needs her "dumb" and "perfect in her proneness," (341) in order to be the god Huitzilopochtli. "I am the Huitzilopochtli, Malintzi," he says. "But I cannot be it without you." (428) That is, he needs her in order to exist. "She was not real until she was reciprocal.... The same was true of him, and without her to give him the power, he too would not achieve his own manhood and meaning.... failing her, he would never make his ultimate achievement, he would never be whole." (424-425) Thus Kate fulfills him.

The Plumed Serpent also deals with the other side of the ego's dilemma, which is the fear of being nothing. When Kate joins the religion of Quetzalcoatl, in which she must merge her being in "blood-unison," she is driven to do so partly by fear that without it she will be left in the opposite condition: alone in a vacuum. "She knew she could not live quite alone. The vacuity crushed her. She needed a man there, to stop the gap, and to keep her balanced." (276) Her house at Lake Chapala is the objective correlative of her self, alternately invaded and abandoned. There Kate experiences the horrible nothingness of solitude, "the anguish of night terror." (149) "'Now,' she thought to herself, 'I am at the mercy of this thing, and I have lost myself.' And it was a terrible feeling, to be lost, scattered, as it were, from herself in a horror of fear." The land of Mexico tries to annihilate her with "silence, an aboriginal, empty silence, as of life *withheld*." (105) Kate feels that there is "doom written on the very sky, doom and horror." (110) Yet at the end of the book the cosmos is a living one, for Kate brings life to Mexico by the sacrifice of herself.

Kate also fears that the Mexican peasants will destroy her by pulling her "down into the homogeneity of death, plucking at the created soul of man." "They would pull her down," she senses, "pull her down to the dark depths of nothingness." (82) They would do so because they themselves are incomplete: "uncreated," "unbuilt," "unable to win their own souls out of

26

chaos." (153) And she senses "the heavy, bloody-eyed resentment of men who have never been able to win themselves a nucleus, an individual integrity out of the chaos of passions and potencies and death." (147) Kate is married to Mexico; that is, she gives herself to a union which is "the only step to a new world of man" where "a new germ, a new conception of human life ... will arise from the fusion of the old blood-and-vertebrate consciousness [of the Mexicans] with the white man's present mental-spiritual consciousness. The sinking of both beings into new being." (455) Actually it is the sinking of Kate's being into Mexico's new being.

In short, Kate fulfills both roles in relation to the self, for she is being both victim and victimizer. She is the "modern woman"— anathema to Lawrence—who "voluptuously fills the belly of her own ego" with her lover's being. As such she is deified, and by that means brought low. However she is also the individual who tries and fails to stand alone against nothingness, who is faced with the alternatives of nonexistence in isolation, or being devoured by the "blood" of her husband and merged into the "warm oblivion" of the living cosmos.

The theme of loss of self, where ego's merging is opposed to ego's annihilation in nothingness, appears in each of Lawrence's novels. Each puts a different construction on it, however, as if Lawrence were recasting what he sees as the one irreducible *given* of existence into terms which are variously religious, sociological, mystical, mythic, or simply psychological. *Sons and Lovers*, with its premise of the oedipal origin of the mind-body split and its underlying assumption of ontological uncertainty, is Lawrence's last novel to deal with the theme in the style of psychological realism. In his next book, *The Rainbow*, he shifts to the mythic mode, and refines his notions of personality further by means of an ontological myth.

2

THE RAINBOW:
COMING OF AGE

In *The Rainbow,* which was rewritten seven times, Lawrence invents a narrative method that is one of the great innovations of the modern novel. He seems to recognize as much himself when he says about the work in progress: "It is all crude as yet, most cumbersome and floundering—but I think it's great—so new, so really a substratum deeper than I think anybody has ever gone, in a novel. But there, you see, it's my latest. It's all analytical—quite unlike *Sons and Lovers,* not a bit visualized." (CL, 193)

Sons and Lovers is "visualized" in the sense that the characters, like those in most novels, are presented as visible, concrete entities. We understand Paul, for instance, mainly through the activity of his social self and his conscious mind. However in *The Rainbow* Lawrence wants to present not the social self so much as the essential being. Like Van Gogh, whom he admired, Lawrence has a vision of reality which is not a quality of surface but an emanation from a living center. And like Van Gogh, he developed an idiosyncratic technique to express this essence. Thus *The Rainbow* is "analytical" in that Lawrence is concerned with essence rather than substance, with things felt and understood rather than things seen.[1]

Lawrence's new idea of personality that is the basis of *The Rainbow* is that we have a social self and an essential one. The split originates in the opposition of ordinary consciousness and the heightened, mystical states of melting out that are scattered through Lawrence's first three novels. There the experience of dissolving out into infinity is described in conventional mystical terminology reminiscent of Wordsworth, Whitman or St. John. In *Sons and Lovers,* for example, it occurs when Mrs. Morel, pregnant with Paul, stands among the lilies in her garden. Later Paul, making love to Clara in a field, also feels a sense of cosmic unity. The two selves hinted at in *Sons and Lovers*—the "passional" and the everyday—become split apart in *The Rainbow*. Here the passional, or mystical experience is not the infrequent occurrence it was in *Sons and Lovers;* it becomes the general rule rather than the exception. In fact this desirable state becomes the basis of the morality and the religion of *The Rainbow*.

Lawrence's new conception of personality involves what he calls "blood" consciousness and "mental" consciousness. The terminology is unique, but the idea is as traditional as his earlier mind-body split. In brief, he sets up an opposition between a reasoning self and an instinctual one. The first is public and social; the other is internal and—for want of a better word—religious. The social self experiences through the rational mind (what Lawrence calls nervous or cerebral or mental consciousness), but this artificially stimulated self is not genuinely alive; its activity is a simulacrum of life. According to the metaphor Lawrence uses in *The Rainbow* the social self is a dead husk, or shell; only the inner core self, the blood consciousness, is truly alive.

The term "blood consciousness" is merely Lawrence's neologism for the experience of uroboric incest which was discussed earlier. In this state the social ego seems to evaporate; but mental consciousness precludes this primal awareness, and so to Lawrence the blood and the mind are mutually exclusive, and ultimately antagonistic.[2] *The Rainbow* deals with the transition between one state of awareness and the other. Again and again characters pass from blood to mind, mind to blood, as Lawrence attempts to clarify the process of changing consciousness. To do this he relies on metaphors, mainly of two kinds.

A number of descriptive images are taken from the activity of physical matter: change is described as hardening, melting, fusing or crystallizing.[3] The main images are of birth and death: when one consciousness dies, the other is born. This trope occurs particularly in reference to coitus. Characters die or swoon during sex and often emerge as newborn. A sexual encounter like the first one between Tom and Lydia Brangwen, for example, involves first his "obliteration," "sleep," "oblivion"; and then his return, "gradually, but newly created, as after a gestation, a new birth, in the womb of darkness." "Their new life came to pass, it was beyond all conceiving good, it was so good, that it was almost like a passing away, a trespass." (41) The germ of this idea occurs as early as Lawrence's second novel, *The Trespassers*, where the lovers likewise trespass—literally, "pass over"—into a new state through coitus.

Lawrence's premise is that the sense of touch is the means of communication between the blood consciousness of two individuals. Therefore in sex, which is the closest possible touch, the ultimate blood relationship is possible. "There is the blood consciousness, with the sexual connection holding the same relation as the eye, in seeing, holds to the mental consciousness." (CL, 393) The blood relation is important as a means to realize one's vital self, for it creates this vital self by giving birth to it.

> When I *see,* there is a connection between my mental consciousness and an outside body, forming a percept; but at the same time there is a transmission through the darkness which is never absent from the light, into my blood consciousness; but in seeing the blood-percept is not strong. On the other hand, when I take a woman, then the blood-percept is supreme, my blood-knowing is overwhelming. There is a transmission, I don't know of what, between her blood and mine in the act of connection. So that afterwards, even if she goes away, the blood connection persists between us, when the mental consciousness is suspended, and I am *formed* then by my blood consciousness, not by my mind or nerves at all.

It is mainly as a metaphor for this all-important theme, the creation of self, that Lawrence uses sex in *The Rainbow*. It is ironic that the puritanical Lawrence's metaphor should be so universally misconstrued: "And I," he complained, when *The Rainbow* was suppressed, "who loathe sexuality so deeply, am considered a lurid sexuality specialist." (CL, 954)

Blood consciousness provides the basis of the religion in *The Rainbow,* a religion for which the book is intended to serve as a bible. The divinity is the Blood, an impersonal life force that is experienced directly in blood awareness. The Blood resembles Bergson's *élan vital* (Lawrence had read *Creative Evolution*)[4] in being the creative impulse behind the process of cosmic evolution that is seen as reality. His characters have a modicum of mundane psychological trappings, but they do not behave like ordinary characters in novels. They do not develop by shedding illusions or gaining awareness; that belongs to the social self, and in *The Rainbow* the emphasis is elsewhere. Instead individual characters are vehicles for the superhuman force of life that is the Blood. They participate in it, much as, in scholastic theology, individual souls each contain a fragment of God. Lawrence's characters are intended to reveal the divine process, the great unfolding, through their actions. They are sometimes difficult to tell apart, not being individualized in the way we have come to expect from characters in fiction, for the reason that the Blood is suprapersonal and is not individualized in its manifestations.

The protagonist of *The Rainbow* is not a character; it is the Blood. The realistic presentation of *Sons and Lovers* is abandoned for the allegorical, and the allegory is the manifestation of the Blood in human events. "I don't so much care what the woman *feels*," Lawrence writes, "in the ordinary sense of the word. That presumes an *ego* to feel with. I only care about what the woman *is*—what she *is*—inhumanly, physiologically, materially—according to the use of the word: but for me, what she *is* as a phenomenon (or representing some greater, inhuman will), instead of what she feels according to the human conception." (CL, 281) He replaces the conventional idea of character development by a sort of choreography, where characters are subordinate to the pattern they describe.[5] "Don't look," he continues, "for the development of the novel to follow the lives of certain characters: the characters fall into the form of some other rhythmic form, as when one draws a fiddle-bow across a fine tray delicately sanded, the sand takes lines unknown." In *The Rainbow* these "lines unknown" are dictated by the life power in the cosmos; its unfolding is expressed mainly through the birth metaphor which dominates the book.

The Blood is an organic force. Like Bergson's *élan vital* it is intended as an anodyne to the mechanistic world view of a cosmos made sterile by utter determinism. Paradoxically, Lawrence, by blowing life up to larger-than-life size, has a tendency to make a dead, mechanical process out of it. A similar tendency is seen in his psychology, in which he often attempts to describe the indescribable—unconsciousness—with analogies taken from physics. Human behavior is reduced to the certainty of scientific law: "What is interesting in the laugh of the woman is the same as the bonding of molecules of steel or their action in heat. It is the inhuman will, call it physiology, or like Marinetti, physiology of *matter*, that fascinates me." Marinetti was one of the Futurists whom Lawrence had recently read. He rejected them: "That is where the futurists are stupid. Instead of looking for the new human phenomenon, they will look only for the phenomenon of the science of physics to be found in human beings." However, he seems to have absorbed some of their vocabulary as well as their methods. The two metaphors—or laws—of human behavior Lawrence constantly invokes are "polarity" and "allotropy," both of which smack of the very mechanicalism the notion of the Blood is supposed to repudiate.

Lawrence first refers to his theory of polarity in 1914, in "The Crown" essay. *Fantasia of the Unconscious* and *Psychoanalysis and the Unconscious* summarize his thought on the subject. He finds the basis of psychic activity in the currents of "attraction" and "repulsion" flowing between the four "centres"—two upper and two lower—of the human body. These currents are compared to positive and negative electrical charges. Thus a relationship with another person, according to Lawrence, is formed first on an unconscious level by means of polarization between the bodies' centres. Relationship occurs remote from conscious understanding, and inevitable as a magnet picking up iron filings, or as atoms of hydrogen and oxygen bonding into a water molecule. The idea that one makes a rational decision to marry, for instance, is absurd in Lawrence, since polarization alone determines "love," and love, once fixed, is immutable. Thus in his novels men and women who barely know each other, whose conscious minds may be antipathetic, find themselves permanently wed through this mysticized sex appeal, this polarization.

"Daughters of the Vicar" (1914) is Lawrence's first fiction based on his new ego psychology. The main events of the story take place between unconscious minds and are described almost exclusively in metaphors of polarity. Louisa is first polarized to Alfred when she sees his body.

> His skin was beautifully white and unblemished, of an opaque, solid whiteness. Gradually Louisa saw it: This also was what he was. It fascinated her. Her feelings of separateness passed away: she ceased to draw back from contact with him and his mother. There was this living centre. Her heart ran hot. She had reached some goal in this clear, beautiful male body. She loved him in a white, impersonal heat. (171)

But Alfred is weak; polarized to his mother who seems "positive," he cannot break this strongest bond. After her death he endures chaos. "Without knowing it, he had been centralized, polarized in his mother." (176) But her death also releases him for bonding with Louisa:

> Then, gradually, as he held her gripped, and his brain reeled round, and he felt himself falling, falling from himself, and whilst she, yielded up, swooned to a kind of death of herself, to wake up again as if from a long sleep. He was himself.

* * *

> And at last she drew back her face and looked up at him, her eyes wet, and shining with light. His heart, which saw, was silent with fear. He was with her. She saw his face all sombre and inscrutable, and he seemed eternal to her. And all the echo of pain came back into the rarity of bliss, and all her tears came up.
> "I love you," she said, her lips drawn to sobbing. He put down his head against her, unable to hear her, unable to bear the sudden coming of the peace and passion that almost broke his heart. (181)

The second metaphor from physics that Lawrence applies to human personality is allotropy. He explains his new conception of character in a letter which should be published in every edition of *The Rainbow* and *Women in Love:* "You mustn't look in my novel for the old stable *ego* of character. There is another *ego*, according to whose action the individual is unrecognisable, and passes through, as it were, allotropic states which it needs a deeper sense than any we've been used to exercise, to discover are states of the same single radically unchanged element." (CL, 282) Allotropy is the property chemical elements have of existing in several forms. The two Lawrence uses most are carbon and water. Water, for example, occurs in the novels first as a liquid, then is transformed into a vapor (the rainbow), and ultimately into a crystal (snow). Thus images of allotropy link *The Rainbow* and *Women in Love* into one large structure. The tale begins at Marsh Farm, where life is fluid and, in a sense, submarine; it concludes a thousand pages later in the snow of the Alps, where characters like Loerke—brittle, frigid and separate—exemplify modern life.

Allotropy becomes the main metaphor in Lawrence's next ego theory, and determines the structure of *Women in Love*. As, in *Sons and Lovers,* the oedipal mind-body split was supplanted by the organic metaphor of the core-and-shell ego, so, in *The Rainbow*, allotropy supplants the core-and-shell. Like its precursors, the allotropic theory of ego structure—or "ego process" may be more accurate—begins to emerge in the middle of the previous novel. In *The Rainbow* certain characters are unmistakable instances of negative allotropy, an unvital inorganic hardening. Will Brangwen is "too special, self contained . . . too much abstracted, like a separate thing." (110) "He lay awake for many hours, hard and clear and unthinking, his soul crystallizing more inalterably." (122) Anger always "hardens" him, in his "hard, evil moments." (149) When Anna is angry with him she is "hard and cold as a jewel" . . . . "So he kissed her, whilst his heart was ice." (185) Baron Skrebensky is "so detached, so purely objective," "something separate and interesting; his hard, intrinsic being, . . . so dis-

tinct in its surety, . . . his cool, hard separate fire." (195-196) Anna's father, by comparison, is described as fluid: "'He was'—the
mother made a quick, running movement with her hands—'his figure was alive and changing—it was never fixed. He was not in
the least steady—like a running stream.'" (174) Allotropic images
occur also in relation to Anton Skrebensky and Uncle Tom
Brangwen, which associate them with crystals, jewels, stones,
and metals. These scattered instances of hardened isolation become the main theme of alienation in *Women in Love,* and in that
novel allotropy governs the action of all but a few characters.

Allotropy is not always negative, but in *The Rainbow* it contrasts as a state of disconnected deadness with the central image
of birth that symbolizes living connection. The marsh and the
rainbow stand at the fluid, volatile end of the allotropic spectrum,
which is akin to vitalism. At the other end, Will Brangwen's
metal working is a sign of his "abstraction, a sort of instrumental
detachment from human things." The stone cathedral at Lincoln,
with the stone men carved on it, is an inorganic foil to Anna
Brangwen, the living woman. Uncle Tom Brangwen, who is "as
if soft and affable, yet quite removed from everybody," gives Ursula a "little necklace of rough stones, amethyst and opal and
brilliants and garnet." (240) When she is out walking with
Skrebensky, Ursula gives this necklace to the baby on the barge
the "Annabel." (312) Skrebensky disapproves. The necklace signifies Ursula's option of being an alienated person like
Skrebensky or her Uncle Tom; that is, allotropically hardened
and cut off from the Blood. By giving it to the barge people Ursula casts her lot with vitalism. The bargeman "gave her a pleas-
ant warm feeling. He made her feel the richness of her own life.
Skrebensky, somehow, had created a deadness around her, a
sterility, as if the world were ashes." (314)

In *Women in Love* the conflict between vital and mechanical
becomes central, but in *The Rainbow* mechanical images of polarity and allotropy are overwhelmed by the central metaphor of
living birth. The birth process gains its overriding power through
the cumulative effect of literally thousands of repetitions. Birth
describes the unfolding of the Blood, and assumes the magnitude
of a religious event. This divine fecundity is fluid. The novel
pulsates with the flow of life, like a foetal heartbeat. To act in it
is to "merge," "lapse" or "absorb." The governing spatial relation is enclosure; innumberable boundaries contrast to bound-
lessness. Almost everything in the book, including the landscape,
is feminine; and almost everything feminine is pregnant.[6]

In *The Rainbow* the life process is essentially a living core bursting through a dead shell. The plot consists of three generations, in the etymological sense: three eruptions out of a confining past into a new life. The impulse behind the process is the Blood. Lawrence's choice of the birth metaphor to describe it is not unlike Bergson's image for the *élan vital,* according to which the creative impulse shoots forward like a rocket from which the dying embers fall away. The rocket is new life; the embers are matter and the dead past, against which inertia life is always struggling.[7] Lawrence's newborn is like Bergson's rocket in that both symbolize a breaking away from the dead forms of the past. But the peculiarity of Lawrence's metaphor is that it takes on a reality of its own. Birth ceases to be an analogy used, like the rocket, for the purposes of illustration. Lawrence, unlike Bergson, considers his life force religious, and raises his image for it to an object of worship. He deifies the birth process into the Blood, and as such the process does not describe reality, but becomes itself the higher, divine reality which "real" events only reflect.

The Rainbow resembles the Bible in that both intimate the divine in the mundane. Furthermore, both require exegesis. Lawrence uses the Old Testament as a model for *The Rainbow,* just as he bases *Women in Love* on the New. Besides its copious biblical ornamentation—allusions and rhetorical phrases used chiefly for their emotional and religious association—*The Rainbow* is constructed to invite the kind of allegorical interpretation long given the Old Testament. The novel is intended to be interpreted as a revelation of divine will, and yields at least four levels of meaning.[8] Literally, it is a family chronicle that follows three generations. It is also a historical narrative that traces the change from agrarian life to cottage industry to industrial society.[9] On the mythological level many characters are representative of gods, demigods or biblical characters, sometimes self-consciously so.[10] On the metaphysical or mystical level (which is the equivalent of Dante's "anagogic"), the Blood is the divine antitype that persons and events in the novel symbolize.

In *The Rainbow* history is the process of mankind's deterioration. Succeeding generations descend from a higher, happier, integrated state to a condition of increasing disharmony and disorder—albeit of higher consciousness also. Lawrence's allegory combines the Christian myth of the fall from grace with the classical motif of the four ages of mankind. *The Rainbow* begins in a Golden Age. The earliest Brangwens are godlike, barely differentiated from each other or from the cosmos they inhabit in unreflecting harmony. In this Eden, the women are dissatisfied; Tom Brangwen's mother aspires to education for her son, and so he goes to school. That is, he gets knowledge, and in so doing, falls from grace. His generation marks the beginning of disharmony. The age is patriarchal; he himself is Noah. Anna's generation represents a further lapse. It is matriarchal; she is the virgin mother, but even more she is a pagan fertility goddess, the great mother. Ursula, in the third generation, is utterly fallen into the confusion of the present age of iron—literally the machine age. It is a time of false gods; the pagan religion of her mother is defunct, and the present era secular. The book concludes without a resolution, as Ursula, one of the "daughters of men," waits for one of the "sons of God" to realize the divinity that is latent in her.

On the mystical level *The Rainbow* deals with an experience that transcends ordinary awareness, and a realm that transcends time and matter. Lawrence describes the metaphysical theme of the novel in his essay "The Crown" (1915). Reality is a dialectical coming into being, a sort of cosmic coitus that occurs beyond time and matter. "What are we," he says, "but light and shadow lying together in opposition." (*Phoenix II*, 370) The dark "receives and interpenetrates the light" in a crisis of orgasm, then recedes, "save for one enfolded ripple, the tiny, silent, scarce-visible enfolded pool of seeds." (376) He describes the birth of matter and time in "the eternal light of germination and begetting, the eternal light, shedding our darkness like the fruit that rots on the ground." "First of all the flesh develops in splendor and glory out of the prolific darkness, begotten by light it develops to a great triumph, till it dances naked in the glory of itself." (360) Mind and consciousness are born in this womb also. "The flesh is made perfect within the womb, the spirit at last is made perfect also, within the womb. They are equally perfect, equally supreme, the one adhering to the infinite darkness of the beginning, the other adhering to the infinite light of the end." (370) This is the most elevated significance of the pleurysignificant rainbow; it is a symbol of eternal reality, born of the interpenetration of light and matter.

Since Lawrence compares existence in eternity to an act of conception he considers history, which is the descent from infinity into time and matter, to be a birth. Each new social order gestates within the old, and eventually emerges from it. "For the womb is full of darkness, and also flooded with the strange white light of eternity. And we, the peoples of the world, we are enclosed within the womb of our era, we are there begotten and conceived, but not brought forth." (367) This theme of birth gone wrong—abortion and stillbirth—dominates the end of *The Rainbow*. Thus Ursula's abortion signifies the end of plentitude, the end of the reality that is seen as infinite creation. It also symbolizes the end of the matriarchy, the end of the notion of woman as primarily a child-bearer, and the shift from child-parent love to spouse-centered love. In *Women in Love* reality is seen as cosmic deterioration rather than creation; marriage supplants maternity; and the religion is death- rather than birth-worship.

Lawrence's metaphysics and metahistory tend to obscure the fact that *The Rainbow* is fundamentally a study in ego psychology. In this it is very much like Dante's *Divine Comedy*, for it is not as philosophy or theology that the latter endures, but as psychological allegory. In the *Comedy*, Christian doctrine provides a theoretical framework on which Dante demonstrates the salvation of the soul in the progress from a condition of sin to a state of grace. In the same way the religion in *The Rainbow* serves as a background against which Lawrence presents an allegory of the evolution of human consciousness. He deals with the spirit's progress toward the modern equivalent of the state of grace, which is the state of wholeness.

The Rainbow deals with the racial evolution of modern consciousness. Lawrence assumes that mankind passes from a life that is in harmony with nature, and remote from large, impersonal societies, to a life in society cut off from nature. He shows man in past agrarian communities as unreflective and in harmony with the universe he does not try to understand. Tom Brangwen's experiences have a quality of "mystery" and "the unknown" which he does not try to analyze. In the second generation, the Brangwens have evolved into village society. The individual is more articulated. Set off from his surroundings, he is no longer at one with nature. He is self-conscious and critical, as, for instance, Will Brangwen is, but he is still partly bound by his environment. In Will's case his home and church constitute his society; to both of these he is so dependently attached he cannot escape. Will's generation is transitional between the agrarian, preoccupied with the soil and fertility, and the modern industrial, preoccupied with money, metal and time.

The villager, with his cottage industry, is in turn superseded by the industrial man, whose consciousness sets him apart from his environment so completely that he is alienated. At the conclusion of *The Rainbow*, the modern self is represented by Ursula. She is cut adrift from her family's past, from Cossethay, and from the greater society she feels she has no part in. Ursula culminates the evolution of consciousness from archaic harmony to modern alienation. "As Ursula passed from girlhood to womanhood, gradually the cloud of self-responsibility gathered upon her. She became aware of herself, that she was a separate entity in the midst of an unseparated obscurity, that she must go somewhere, she must become something." (281) *The Rainbow* as a "historical" novel is a prelude to *Women in Love*, for it brings us to the brink of modern times with Ursula's existential dilemma. In the sequel Lawrence is concerned mainly with the vicissitudes of such alienation and man's attempts to overcome it.

In Lawrence's ego psychology, ontogeny recapitulates phylogeny. As the race develops, so the individual passes through stages, symbolized in *The Rainbow* by the generations of Brangwens. Thus besides the history of the race the novel describes a single consciousness as it grows from inchoate, foetal awareness to fully articulated adult consciousness in agrarian society. Not even named, the earliest Brangwens are undifferentiated from each other and their environment. Their existence is dominated by the great pulse of natural being, a rhythm that suffuses the cosmos like a maternal heartbeat of a Great Mother, the Earth. They live in "the drowse of blood intimacy," "feeling the pulse and body of the soil." (2) The Blood in the cosmos pulses through them: "they lived full and surcharged, their senses full fed, their faces always turned to the heat of the sun." (3) Thus these Brangwens also symbolize the individual ego *in utero*, for they exist in blood-unity with a living matrix.

In the next generation Tom and Lydia represent the infant ego and the mother. Their relationship is symbiotic and instinctual, with the directness of primitive biological response. Their awareness is mainly physical and emotional. Lawrence stresses that they do "not take much notice of each other, consciously." (55) They are not articulate or analytical. In spite of their biological—or blood—connection, Tom, like a very young child, eventually is prey to vague fears that he will lose Lydia-mother. Even the expression of his anxiety is child-like: "Did he own her? Was she here forever? Or might she go away?" (55) And later, "He was safe with her now, till morning. She was curiously self-sufficient and didn't say much." (55) Another point of similarity between Tom as infant and Lydia as mother is that she seems self-sufficient, that is, a whole, mature ego; and Tom, the unformed ego, depends on her presence. Often she lapses "into a sort of sombre exclusion, a curious communion with mysterious powers, a sort of dark mystic state which drove him...nearly mad." (57) He depends on her for his sense of his own reality. Lydia can "obliterate" him by withdrawing, and Tom feels the panic and rage of an infant deprived of his mother's attention when she does. Lastly, Lydia is like a mother because she has a great range of experiences, in this case her past with her first husband, that Tom feels are inaccessible to him. They make him feel excluded and powerless to compete.

The succeeding Brangwens, Anna and Will, represent the mother and the ego of the child. However, at this point in the development Lawrence introduces the pathological. Like Erik Erikson, Lawrence assumes in his psychology that the ego's growth proceeds in stages, and that the transition to each new stage is a crisis. During this crisis the old forms of behavior are cast aside, the old self is burst; there follows regression and confusion, and then assumption of a new self. Erikson's image for such a transition is a birth; according to his scheme men can be seven times "reborn" in the course of their lives. Some men are "once-born," meaning that they fit themselves to the prevalent ideology of their age and experience no identity crisis.[11] Erikson, like Lawrence, considers that these crises are not only not pathological but essential for the evolution of racial consciousness. The individual in crisis can find a new identity which determines a new direction for the whole of mankind.

Pathology enters in with what Erikson calls "identity diffusion," which is a severe disorientation that occurs in the identity crisis.[12] Describing a hypothetical case he notes that "most of all this kind of person must shy away from intimacy. Any physical closeness, with either sex, arouses at the same time both an impulse to merge with the other person, and a fear of losing autonomy and individuation."[13] The desire to merge, in order to be whole, coupled with the "fear of losing autonomy and individuation," are opposing impulses Erikson postulates on the basis of his clinical experience. The terminology is different from Laing's, but these are in effect the fears of engulfment in merging and implosion in solitude, cited by Laing, which were discussed earlier. In fact Erikson's "identity diffusion" attributes to adolescence what Laing's "ontological insecurity" describes in infancy: the double impulse of the weak ego to merge with and to reject another person. This other person is ultimately the mother or a figure identified with the mother.

Erikson (as well as Laing, and Lawrence in *The Rainbow*) attaches paramount importance to the mother in relation to the ego because she is almost solely responsible for the child's sense of his own wholeness, or lack thereof. Lawrence's emphasis on the mother-child relation in *The Rainbow* suggests parallels with Erikson's assertion that during the identity crisis, especially in the therapeutic situation, a patient regresses to an infantile kind of relationship. He "wants to fuse with the therapist in order to derive from him everything the parents were or were not; yet he is afraid to be devoured by an identification with the therapist."[14] In *Psychoanalysis and the Unconscious* Lawrence describes the same double impulse of the ego, toward and away from the mother, as "attraction" and "repulsion":

> The unconscious subjectivity is, in its positive manifestation, a great imbibing, and its negative, a definite blind rejection.... [It] includes alike the sweet and untellable communication of love between the mother and child, [and] the irrational reaction into separation of the two. (28)

To Lawrence these are the fundamental movements of the psyche.

Like *Psychoanalysis* and *Fantasia of the Unconscious*, *The Rainbow* deals with the development of the ego, but it is a weak ego, ambivalent in its relations to others because it fears both too much closeness and none at all. The purpose of all three works is to achieve some kind of balance, at least in theory or fantasy, between ego and mother, self and Other. In *The Rainbow*, with each generation of Brangwens, Lawrence rehearses different possibilities of relationships available to the weak ego. Tom and Lydia at various times represent a fantasy of the ideal: a perfect balance of mother and child. Lydia mostly is no danger to Tom's ego. She provides the essential Other, in the words of Simone de Beauvoir, in reference to which Tom defines himself. He always sees her as "other than himself." (76) Yet there is no threat of merging because of their unlikeness. She is foreign, and Tom feels they are "such strangers, they must forever be such strangers." (44) He feels a "terror of foreignness," but this irreducible difference keeps him intact. It is no coincidence that Lydia is "fra th' Pole," (25) that is, a Polishwoman; she is Tom's polarized opposite.

The second reason that Tom and Lydia have a perfect balance in their relationship is that the sex distinctions are so clearly marked in their era that male and female are almost like different species. Later, in the generation of Will and Anna, sex-roles grow uncertain, and the ego is threatened with merging and dissolution. However the marriage between Tom and Lydia exemplifies the phenomenon of "separate spheres." Tom's ego is secure in its wholeness, and the institution of marriage is secure in its eternality. For Tom and the generations before him, a woman is an angel in the house. "The woman was the symbol for that further life which comprised religion and morality. The men placed in her hands their own conscience, they said to her, 'Be my conscience keeper, be the angel in the doorway guarding my incoming and outgoing.'" (13) And, Lawrence continues, "they depended on her for their stability."

In the age of Tom and Lydia a great chasm separates the sexes. The unlikeness of male and female is presented as highly erotic:

> [Tom and Lydia] had had their hour, and should it chime again they were ready for it, ready to renew the game at the point where it left off, on the edge of outer darkness, when the secrets within the woman are the man's adventure, and they both give themselves to the adventure. (58)

But here, as perhaps generally, insisting on the "mystery" of woman gives rise to predatory sexuality. The relationship of Tom and Lydia only proves once again the impossibility of sexual roles being "separate but equal." Lydia is near-deified as moral exemplar and transcendent being; just as the medieval lyric turned the erotic into the religious, so Tom (or Lawrence) sees woman as intermediary and approach to God.[15] Nevertheless, man is unquestionably her master, and maintains her for the purpose of providing his ideal and his complement.

Yet Lawrence does not present the nineteenth century as a golden age of male supremacy, from which men have fallen into parity. Rather he undermines these—at least—Victorian values. Tom's attitude toward Lydia is typical of the nineteenth century in its ambivalence: she is a symbol of (his) carnality, therefore his inferior, yet she is also a symbol of (his) spirituality, and therefore infinitely superior. He feels superior, although uneasy, before her sexual aspects, which are "dark" and "deathly." Yet he is prostrate before the "mystery" of Lydia the transcendent being, Lydia the Unknown.

> "My dear!" she said. He knew she spoke a foreign language. The fear was like bliss in his heart. He looked down. Her face was shining, her eyes full of light, she was awful. He suffered from the compulsion to her. She was the awful unknown. He bent down to her, suffering, unable to let go, unable to let himself go, yet drawn, driven. She was now the transfigured, she was won-

derful, beyond him. He wanted to go. But he could not as yet kiss her. He was himself turned apart. Easiest he could kiss her feet. But he was too ashamed for the actual deed, which was like an affront. She waited for him to meet her, not to bow before her and serve her. She wanted his active participation, not his submission. She put her fingers on him. And it was torture to him, that he must give himself to her actively, to participate in her, that he must meet and embrace and know her, who was other than himself. There was that in him which shrank from yielding to her, resisted the relaxing towards her, opposed the mingling with her, even when he most desired it. He was afraid, he wanted to save himself. (90)

Yet Lawrence exposes Tom's self-abasing woman-worship as narcissism. His love is reverential selfishness. His relationship to Lydia is so distant, except physically, and so clouded with fantasy that he does not perceive her as another human being. He sees her as a manifestation of the divine, as "the unknown," "mysterious," "inspired," "transfigured," "not human." He comforts himself when she is in childbed that "Woman [is] immortal, whatever happened, whoever turned towards death." (69) For most of the novel Lydia is presented from the point of view of Tom's consciousness, and it is not until their first quarrel that Tom's image of Lydia, a false conception, cracks, revealing to Tom, and to us, that she is not at all as he has seen her. " 'Why do you deny me?' " she cries at him. "Suddenly in a flash, he saw that she might be lonely, isolated, unsure. She had seemed to him utterly certain, satisfied, absolute, excluding him. Could she need anything?" (89) The relationship between Tom and Lydia, like that between mother and infant, is perfect, but limited. It is a state before the fall into self-consciousness, before I and you, before the division occurs between the child's ego and the mother. It survives in memory as an ideal. In retrospect it seems to be an untroubled, unreflecting time when the ego is whole. Yet this perfect egoism, as Lawrence shows, has its negative as well as positive aspects.

With the second generation of Brangwens, Will and Anna, the disturbance of previously polarized sex roles begins. In the patriarchal order of the elder Brangwens there is no uncertainty about male and female roles, and no confusion of self with Other. Old Baron Skrebensky, even more than Tom Brangwen, is secure in both his masculinity and the integrity of his ego. He has "the quality of the male in him. . . . so detached, so purely objective. A woman was thoroughly outside him. There was no confusion." (195) But with Will and Anna the patriarchy gives way to the "little matriarchy." Anna Victrix feels she is "the earth, mother of everything." (205) In her fecundity she dominates her husband: "like a child on its mother, he depend[s] on her for his living." (186) Like a child, Will lacks—to use Erikson's phrase— autonomy and individuation. In fact, he seeks the opposite.

Will is self-conscious to a degree that Tom Brangwen never is; yet if one is to be whole, Lawrence implies, such awareness must be joined with independence, and this Will does not possess. His name is ironical, for he has not enough volition. He is powerless to act without Anna; he cannot "go forward without her." (201) Will, Lawrence stresses, has failed to be "born." He is described repeatedly as "unformed," "uncreated," and not brought forth. In "The Crown," which was written directly after *The Rainbow* in 1915, Lawrence describes such a self, which has self-con- sciousness but cannot "beat back the old body that surrounds it":

> Then the darkness, having overcome the light, reaching the dead null wall of the womb, reacts into self-consciousness, and recoils upon itself. At the same time the light has surpassed its limit, be- come conscious, and starts in reflex to recoil upon itself. Thus the false I comes into being: the I which thinks itself supreme and in- finite, and which is, in fact, a sick foetus shut up in the walls of an unrelaxed womb." (*Phoenix II*, 390)

Will's failure is one of passivity; he actually shuns the exercise of will which is essential for self-definition, according to Law- rence. The will is an energy of resistance that keeps the ego from being absorbed, from merging into non-existence.

The aim of Will's life is to be absorbed in an ecstasy of passiv- ity. Lawrence says he is "like a man who has failed, who lapses back for his fulfillment." (204) Will wants, quite simply, to return to the womb. This is the issue in the marital battle with Anna. In the end he capitulates: "he relaxed his will, and let everything go.... she had conquered, really." (203) His ego dissolves: "A vagueness had come over everything, like a drowning. And it was an infinite relief to drown, a relief, a great, great relief." (186)

Will's life becomes a quest for the ultimate interior. He turns away from the world, towards his home and his wife. He seeks to obliterate his self in ecstasies of sensual love to find "this su- preme, immoral Absolute Beauty, in the body of a woman." (234) Will, like Tannhäuser lingering in the cavern of the Venusberg, is shamed by his weakness, but nevertheless unable to leave the dwelling place of his wife. The cave, house and woman are patent womb symbols. Likewise the transcendent experience Will seeks in religion is uroboric merging. The source of his ecstasies is the buildings themselves; with their rounded Roman arches, they are to him great wombs. Lincoln Cathedral is the "perfect womb." (198) So on a smaller scale is the little church at Cossethay a stone and wood symbol of Will's desire. It permits him to lose himself: many times "in its shadowy atmosphere he sank back into being. He liked to sink himself into its hush as a stone sinks into water." (204) That Will's self-annihilation is most nearly perfect in a religious setting suggests there is little difference between quietism and retrogression, between the mystical temperament and the weak ego.

In some of the prose writings concurrent with *The Rainbow* Lawrence discusses the evolution of racial consciousness, especially of man's religious sense. His theories are based on the same double impulse, towards merging and away from it, that is central in the ego psychology of *The Rainbow*. In *Twilight in Italy*, which was written in between drafts of the novel, Lawrence distinguishes "pagan" from "Christian" mysticism. The "pagan transport" is to absorb all into the ego. The Christian consummation is the opposite—to dissolve the ego into the Otherness. The Christian God, says Lawrence, is "Not-me," and the Christian infinite is reached through renunciation of self and dissolution into Not-me. According to Lawrence's racial history, the Christian ecstasy has superseded the pagan one:

> The old transport, the old fulfillment of the Ego, the Davidian ecstasy, the assuming of all power and glory unto the self, the becoming infinite through the absorption of all into the Ego, this gradually became unsatisfactory. . . .
> The world, our world of Europe, had now really turned, swung round to a new goal, a new ideal the Infinite reached through the omission of Self. God is all that which is Not-me. I am consummated when my Self, the resistant solid, is reduced and diffused into all that which is Not-me: my neighbor, my enemy, the great Otherness. Then I am perfect. (92-93)

Anna Brangwen is a pagan who absorbs all things in a "Davidian" ecstasy, and who, when pregnant, dances naked like David before the Lord. On the other hand, Will is a Christian; in his transport he is absorbed.

In *Twilight in Italy* Lawrence says that the "two opposing ways to consummation" are both equally valid and equally necessary, yet from his choice of ersatz historical fact it is obvious that he favors the pagan. The Christian he identifies with "negative Puritanism" which "destroyed, symbolically, forever, the supremacy of the Me who am the image of God, the Me of the flesh, of the senses. Me, the tiger burning bright, me the king, the lord, the aristocrat, me who am divine because I am the body of God." (49) Pagan mysticism exalts the self: it is "a tiger," "supreme, imperial, warlike." "Then simulate the action of the tiger," Lawrence writes. "A tiger devours because it is consummated in devouring, it achieves its absolute self in devouring." (51) The essence of the metaphor is that the self is active rather than passive. It is a commonplace of existential psychology that individuality is the product of activity; through acts, through will, one differentiates oneself from the matrix of Otherness.[16] In *Twilight in Italy* Lawrence elaborates this assumption further by equating individuality, activity, and masculinity. "The supreme male" is "the ideal Self, the King and Father." (90) "The whole Greek life," he writes, "was based on the idea of the supremacy of the self, and the self was always male." (89) Conversely, denial of the flesh and annihilation of the self in Christian worship are passive—childlike or feminine. The Not-me into which such an ego dissolves is also implicitly feminine; that is, it is a matrix in the etymological sense, a womb.

The paradox of the womb as an image in Lawrence's oeuvre is that while it gives birth to the self, it also threatens to annihilate it. To Lawrence the very existence of self depends on the constant conflict between self and Not-me, where each tries to absorb the other. Such conflict, according to Lawrence, is inherent in all modern relationships: "The unconsummated soul, unsatisfied, uncreated in part, will seek to make itself whole by bringing the whole world under its order, will seek to make itself absolute and timeless by devouring its opposite." The "unconsummated soul" suggests the oedipal mother, turning her energies onto her child, who becomes, in turn, "unconsummated" himself. According to Lawrence's metaphorical logic, the tiger "devours" to make himself whole; the individual must absorb the matrix, or else it will absorb him. The struggle between male and female, to overwhelm before one is overwhelmed, is central in the love relationship of Will and Anna, Skrebensky and Ursula, in *Women in Love*, and in much of later Lawrence.

However, in *The Rainbow* as well as *Twilight in Italy* the distinction Lawrence makes between what is masculine and what feminine, is doubtful at best. When in *Twilight in Italy* he defines "the man's soul," he in effect figuratively defines the self. Male spirit, he says, has both its spiritual and its fleshly sides. On the spiritual side is the "real man's soul, the soul that goes forth and builds up a new world out of the void." It is the "male divinity, which is the spirit that fulfils in the world the new germ of an idea." (78) On the other hand, man's flesh has the phallus as a symbol of its creative divinity. The phallic principle, Lawrence says, involves the desire to expose oneself to death, and also "the phallic principle is to absorb and dominate all life." (78) Yet if absorbing is taken as it generally is, and as it generally is by Lawrence, to be a metaphorical attribute of the female, the matrix, then the "supreme male, the ideal Self" (since he defines himself by absorbing) is only an imitation of the female.

According to Lawrence the present age is a matriarchy. The women, he says, destroy the male self:

> Some strange will holds the women taut. They seem like weapons, dangerous. There is nothing charming or winning about them; at the best a full, prolific maternity, at the worst a yellow poisonous bitterness of the flesh that is like a narcotic. But they are too strong for the men. The male spirit, which would subdue the immediate flesh to some conscious or social purpose, is overthrown. The woman in her maternity is the law-giver, the supreme authority. The authority of the man, in work, in public affairs, is something trivial by comparison. (*Twilight in Italy*, 75)

It is an era of the belittled male, and, by extension, of the endangered ego. This imbalance in favor of women has come about because men lack that essential "soul that goes forth and builds up a new world out of the void." That is, they lack "purposive activity," a recurrent phrase of Lawrence's in this period, and one applied frequently to Will Brangwen. Will and Anna's marriage is matriarchal because he has no social identity. He has no saving relation to society, no "respect for his conscious or public life" to counterbalance his physical relationship to his wife. He prefers to lapse into Anna, to live "simply by her physical love for him," and in this he fails her. Not "publicly proud" of him, she learns to be "indifferent" to public life, "but his abandoning of claims, his living isolated upon his own interest, [makes] him seem unreal, unimportant." (205)

Eventually Will joins the community as a crafts teacher. His intimate life has "set another man in him free," and "developed a real purposive self." (235) Will's newly-assumed social identity brings vitality to himself, and indirectly to his family. "The house by the yew trees was in connection with the great human endeavor at last. It gained new vigor thereby." (236) In spite of this, he is never fully realized as a person. His impulse, typically enough, is to merge himself with mankind, rather than differentiate himself: "he want[s] to be unanimous with the whole of purposive mankind." (235) With the third generation, Ursula, Lawrence shows that, from the point of view of either racial consciousness or individual's development, it is no longer possible or desirable to be at one with society in this way. A modern individual must be an outsider.

If Will Brangwen is unborn, his daughter's lover, Skrebensky, is an abortion. Rather than being born through his relationship with Ursula, his vital self is destroyed by it. In Skrebensky the core-and-shell concept of personality that dominates *The Rainbow* has its final and clearest incarnation. Even Anton himself believes he has an inner, vital self, and an outer, dead social one. In his affair with Ursula he inhabits "the fecundity of universal night." "The puppet shapes of people, their wooden mechanical voices, he was remote from them." (450) The traditional means of integrating the erotic dyad, which is essentially antisocial, into society is the wedding. Skrebensky hesitates to marry Ursula because he intuits, correctly, that marriage would transform their erotic relationship into a predominantly social one. "One's social wife was almost a material symbol," he thinks, and they would "become part of that complication of dead reality—then what was his under-life to do with her?" (453) As lovers Ursula and Skrebensky are outsiders; at no point is their affair contingent with society.[17]

Skrebensky as a character is full of contradictions, and when he is destroyed, it is for contradictory reasons: because he is too vulnerable and because he is invulnerable. His destruction occurs in acts that are like rituals of exorcism, that rehearse the contradictory disasters which can befall the weak ego. Skrebensky is invulnerable because he is the civilized man. He and Ursula have their first quarrel essentially over the relative merits of Eros and civilization. In the person of Ursula, Lawrence holds that modern civilization is fatal to the life impulse, and must be escaped. When she and Anton meet the animalistic bargeman of the "Annabel," the Eros figure, Ursula says it is necessary to be outside society, as he is. She commits herself to this by giving up her necklace. But her lover "could not see, it was not born in him to see, that the highest good of the community is no longer the highest good of even the average individual." (327) He believes in doing his "duty by the nation." (309) To her this social identity is no identity at all: "It seems to me," she says, "as if you weren't anybody—as if there weren't anybody there, where you are. Are you anybody, really? You seem like nothing to me." (309) Yet paradoxically it is Ursula who makes Skrebensky "nothing."

She destroys his "under-life" in the mortal combat of their affair. Theirs is not the blind dependence of Tom and Lydia, nor the benign dominance of Anna Brangwen; from the start Ursula and Skrebensky are "enemies come together in a truce." While they walk in "unison" it is never in "union." There is no blood connection between them, and no birth. The parturition images which overflow all intercourse between the earlier couples are conspicuously absent from Ursula and Skrebensky's lovemaking.

Ursula is a vampire who sucks out Skrebensky's vital soul during sex. After one encounter, his "core" is gone. He is progressively "reduced" by her, fearful of death and Ursula, which are linked in his mind. He loses vitality as she gains it, dwindles in stature as she grows more like a goddess, elemental even to herself. In their final sexual encounter at the seashore Ursula completes the obliteration of Skrebensky's inner self. With her "fierce, beaked harpy's kiss' she attacks him "pressing in her beaked mouth till she ha[s] the heart of him." (479) Perverted into the male role she rides over him, presses "down to a source and a core" until he succumbs and gives way "as if dead." If her lover is a hollow man, Ursula is at least partly responsible.

She is referred to as "Aphrodite" at the seashore, and in *Twilight in Italy* Lawrence describes "Aphrodite of the foam" as a destructive goddess who "reduces" men as Skrebensky is reduced.

> Aphrodite, the queen of the senses, she born of the sea foam, is the luminousness of the gleaming senses, the phosphorescence of the sea, the senses become a conscious aim unto themselves; she is the gleaming darkness, she is the luminous night, she is goddess of destruction, her white, cold fire consumes and does not create. [In this Aphrodite worship] the flesh, the sense, are now self-conscious. They know their aim. Their aim is supreme sensation. They seek the maximum of sensation. They seek the reduction of the flesh, the flesh reacting upon itself, to a crisis, an ecstasy, a phosphorescent transfiguration in ecstasy. (43)

That Ursula's lovemaking gives birth to sensation but not to a new self for her or Skrebensky is the "bitterness of ecstacy."

When he has Ursula destroy Skrebensky, Lawrence is exorcising both the deadened social self that is cut off from a living relationship, and the dependent self that seeks only to exist at the living center, so to speak. Skrebensky suffers the nightmare fate of the ontologically insecure: his being is sapped by the very person who sustains it. He depends on Ursula for his sense of reality, and he fears to lose her because then "life was extinct, only

ash moved and stirred or stood rigid, there was a horrible, clatter-
ing activity, a rattle like the falling of dry slag, cold and sterile."
(456) As a shell, Skrebensky is also dead. Ironically Ursula ad-
mires him at first for this self-sufficiency. "He permitted no ques-
tions about himself. He was irrevocable in his isolation.... So
Ursula thought him wonderful, he was so finely constituted, and
so distinct, self-contained, self-supporting." (290) However such
isolation cuts him off from any possibility of vital contact: he is
"perfectly, even fatally established." (289) Lawrence stresses that
Ursula and Anton have no blood connection by using allotropic
images; the lovers are described as metals, stones, physical properties. Ursula's soul "crystallizes" in triumph when she corrodes
the "soft iron" of Skrebensky. At the wedding at the Marsh
where they tryst, the guests are stones, magnets, jewels. The
world has changed; Ursula's predecessors met in a living cosmos,
but images of silver and steel dominate the landscape where she
and Skrebensky meet.

Finally, Skrebensky, inasmuch as he embodies stifling social
forms, symbolizes the dead past which trammels the life force,
Ursula. He is cast in the metaphorical role of matter, to her spirit.
When they dance at her uncle's wedding, he trammels her as
substance does essence: "But he must weave himself around her,
enclose her in a net of shadows, of darkness, so she would be
like a bright creature gleaming in a net of shadows, caught. Then
he would enjoy her. How he would enjoy her when she was
caught." (319) The antagonism between Ursula and Skrebensky
is thus the result of his cloying physicality which encumbers her
aspiration. Ursula, like the earlier Brangwen women, aspires to
the "beyond." Her relation with Skrebensky is only physical; he
worships and fears her body, she is obsessed by and jealous of his.

The turning point in their relationship comes at the cathedral
of Rouen. Her father's experience in cathedrals led him back to
physicality, for the rounded Norman and Roman arches raise the
eye and spirit only to return them to earth. In contrast, Rouen
cathedral is Gothic; its arches lead only upward, out of the realm
of matter. Its lesson for Ursula is that she must not remain sunk
in the past or sensuality with Skrebensky. He "aroused no fruit-
ful fecundity in her. He seemed added up, finished. She knew
him all round, not on any side did he lead to the unknown. Poignant, almost passionate appreciation she felt for him, but none of
the dreadful wonder, none of the rich fear, the connection with
the unknown, or the reverence of love." (473) For this reason she
"must insist on having the moon" for her own. Ursula's abortion

signifies the end of the matriarchy and the end of the worship of immanence. She waits for a new creation, where "the man should come from the Infinite and she should hail him." (493)

Ursula breaking free from Skrebensky signifies the individual emancipating himself from his parents, his past, his society. If Tom Brangwen is the infant, and Will the child, Ursula is the adolescent. No longer "enclosed" she is "in her final isolation," (489) yet she has achieved integrity. "She was in some way like the stone at the bottom of the river, inviolable and unalterable, no matter what storm raged in her body. Her soul lay still and permanent, full of pain, but itself forever." (490) The river in tumult prefigures the chaotic cosmos of *Women in Love,* where Ursula's inviolability, so hard won, will sustain her.

In *Women in Love* the conflict is not between self and matrix so much as between self and disintegrative chaos. *The Rainbow* is unique among Lawrence's novels in its theme of self-differentiation. It is a literary rite of transition to adult status. Like a rite of passage in primitive society, the novel celebrates the shift from mother-dependence to independence. The essence of the rite is imitation of the female ability to give birth, which undoes man's birth from woman and marks his rebirth as an adult in the society of men.[18] *The Rainbow,* too, is a rite of symbolic emancipation from the mother.

Margaret Mead notes in her studies on New Guinea that initiatory cults assume that men can become men only by their ritualizing birth and taking over—as a collective group—the functions that women perform naturally. Motherhood is superiority, according to Mead, and the men "steal" it from her.[19] By imitating women, Lawrence's men give birth to themselves.

The most striking example of a man who imitates woman is Will Brangwen in his pursuit of the Nottingham shopgirl. With "this girl, whom he wanted to absorb," Will parodies his wife. With the girl he "was purely a world to himself, he had nothing to do with any general consciousness. Just his own senses were supreme." (227) For once, he is "perfectly self-contained." (225) After this Will returns to his wife as much a man as he will ever become. Later Skrebensky battles Ursula by trying "with all his energy, to enclose her, to have her." (320) He even has a "womb," (326) a symbol of his power to create (and destroy) a self. But he fails to engulf Ursula, and consequently fails to gain himself.[20]

The tendency for men to imitate women in Lawrence is always strong, and it is always related to self-integrity. In *The Rainbow* the birth metaphor belongs to a primitive layer of thought that coincides with actual primitive custom. It may seem untoward to accuse Lawrence of practicing primitive magic in his writing. Yet according to his symbols, imitation is self-creation, and art is like sympathetic magic in that the act of creating is precisely the act of imitating.

3

CHAOS:

WHO SURVIVES IN *WOMEN IN LOVE?*

The Rainbow and *Women in Love* are complements; one praises birth and the other exalts death. *The Rainbow* presents a living cosmos where existence unfolds as continuous creation, synthesis and evolution. In contrast, *Women in Love* reveals a moribund universe dominated by dissolution, by devolution and disintegration into lower forms of disorder. The orderly progression of the seasons and the cycles of birth and growth that provide a harmonious ground bass in *The Rainbow* are replaced by universal chaos. Against this background characters pursue lives whose issue is no longer development but deterioration, no longer the act of becoming but un-becoming—or at best maintaining equilibrium against the tide of universal dissolution.

As *The Rainbow* uses birth as a metaphor for creation, *Women in Love* takes death as the image of dissolution. But "death" as Lawrence uses it is not what we usually understand it to be, the final cessation of life; instead it is a continuous process, a going asunder in stages of lesser organization in inverted imitation of the way growth moves toward greater complexity. "There's a long way to go, after the point of intrinsic death, before we disappear," Birkin tells Gerald.

> "There is," said Gerald. "But what sort of way?" He seemed to press the other man for knowledge which he himself knew far better than Birkin did.
> "Right down the slopes of degeneration—mystic, universal degeneration. There are many stages of pure degradation to go through: agelong. We live long after our death, and progressively, in progressive devolution." (196)

Women in Love also inverts the organic imagery that in *The Rainbow* signifies the life process, so that the sprouting of swamp flowers symbolizes the growth of decay, a contradiction in terms. *Women in Love* is symmetrical to the point of paradox: almost every object has a counterpart, nearly every character his complement, and every process, completing itself, engenders its opposite. However the balanced arrangement of *Women in Love* only emphasizes the fact that the novel's underlying assumption is profound disorder.

Chaos is the central fact of *Women in Love.* "I am doing another novel that really occupies me," Lawrence writes. "The world crackles and bursts, but that is another matter, external, in chaos. One has a certain order inviolable in one's soul."[1] During the first World War Lawrence was stricken with an alarmed sense of universal disintegration, and this sense of dissolution pervades the novel. "We are now in a period of crisis," he writes in the "Foreword" to *Women in Love.* "Every man who is acutely alive is acutely wrestling with his own soul. The people that can bring forth the new passion, the new idea, this people will endure. Those others, that fix themselves in the old idea, will perish with the new life strangled unborn within them. Men must speak out to one another," he concludes, and to this end Lawrence adopts the tone of a prophet and the literary accoutrements of the visionary.

Visionary worldviews valued by the Western mind tend to be very much alike. Yeats and Plotinus, Swedenborg, and Blake envision approximately the same kind of cosmos. Lawrence is no exception; his visionary cosmology as it is described in his essays and novels is quite traditional. He has the tendency of the visionary to see an overabundance of analogies where most men see none and to accept cause and effect where ordinary reason denies it. To him there are similarities between cosmic process, human history and the state of the soul. Lawrence the visionary is also reductive; he attempts to explain all events in terms of the same few universal laws. He is also typical in that his visionary expression takes the form of extended metaphors, and these are generally based on antithesis. The cosmos is divided into north and south, into upper and lower realms. Existence is a conflict between light and dark, fire and ice, earth and air, male and female. Lawrence's visionary cosmos, like most, bears little resemblance to empirical reality. In spite of the appearance that he deals with public things, the prophet—at least the literary prophet—is directed towards an inner reality and not a social one. For this reason the "social implications" of *Women in Love* are misleading; society in the novel, like the cosmos depicted in it, reflects primarily a subjective state.

Many Lawrence commentators take his pronouncements on society at face value, with the result that even the most charitable is forced to concede he is "impractical."[2] But Diana Trilling is more accurate in perceiving that when Lawrence sees dissolution and corruption in society he simply sees his own madness. She asserts that the War coincided with the onset of Lawrence's insanity and became for him the cause of chaos.[3] Lawrence mentions both insanity and the visionary mode in letters of 1915:

> I cannot help being very much interested in God and the devil—particularly the devil—and immortality. I cannot help writing about them in the "philosophy." But all the time I am struggling in the dark—very deep in the dark—and cut off from everybody and everything. Sometimes I seem to stumble into the light, for a day, or even two days—then in I plunge again, God knows where and into what utter darkness of chaos.... sometimes I am afraid of the terrible things that are real, in the darkness, and of the entire unreality of these things I see.... The whole universe of darkness and dark passions—the subterranean universe—not inferno, because that is "after"—the subterranean black universe of things which have not yet had being—has conquered me for now, and I can't escape. (Cl 329)

In another letter he writes, "I feel quite sad, as if I talked a vulgar little language of my own which nobody understood," and "my world is real, it is a true world.... it is a world you can inhabit with me, if I can't inhabit yours with you." (CL, 324)

His prose writings of this period show unequivocally that his metaphysics like his social pronouncements are a form of existential discourse. In "The Crown" he writes of

> Angels that cleave asunder, terrible and invincible. With cold irresistible hands they pull us apart, they send us into like, darkness into darkness. They thrust the seas backward from embrace, backward from the locked strife. They set the cold, phosphorescent flame of light flowing back to the light, and cold heavy darkness flowing back to the darkness. They are the absolute angels of corruption, they are the snake, the newt, the water-lily, as reflected from below." (*Phoenix II*, 389)

Then, he adds, "I cease to be, my darkness lapses into utter stone darkness, my light into a light that is keen and cold as frost."

The visionary cosmos of *Women in Love* is also a form of existential discourse. Like *The Rainbow*, the novel is an allegory about being. But *The Rainbow* deals with the development of the self, from birth through childhood to maturity. *Women in Love* deals with the ways in which this self, once achieved, is maintained—or fails to be—against the forces that would destroy it.

According to the paradigm discussed in relation to *Sons and Lovers* and *The Rainbow*, being, as Lawrence sees it, depends on relation, and relation consists of vascillation between merging and annihilation in nothingness. *The Rainbow* describes how this dual motion is necessary to the creation of the self. *Women in Love* sets out to show the opposite: how these antitheses destroy the self.[4] Chaos in *Women in Love* reflects the disintegration of a being, but it is disintegration predicated on the two extremes of merging and isolation, and therefore coherent. In fact Lawrence in *Women in Love* organizes chaos, analyzing it into a spectrum of disorder. At one end is "the burning death-abstraction" of the "African process," a "mindless progressive knowledge through the senses, knowledge arrested and ending in the senses, mystic knowledge in disintegration and dissolution." (245-46) At the other end of the spectrum is the process of the "Arctic north," the "vast abstraction of ice and snow" that is "a mystery of ice-destructive knowledge, snow-abstract annihilation." (246) "African" dissolution corresponds to merging; "Arctic" annihilation to isolation. This antithetical pattern governs the novel. The image Lawrence uses to express it is allotropy.

Allotropy we saw is the property of an element (or compound, as Lawrence uses it) to exist in several forms. Besides water, which appears as fluid, vapor and crystal, other allotropic images he uses are mud, earth and stone, and coal dust, coal and diamond. When this metaphor for personality appears in *The Rainbow* it describes anger, detachment and the quality of anti-life. Anton Skrebensky, Uncle Tom Brangwen, and sometimes Will Brangwen are associated with jewels, stones and metals. Against the fluid vitality of the Brangwen family and the overwhelming tide of life in the cosmos these characters are set in contrast. *Women in Love* makes the same contrast of organic to inorganic, but the proportions are reversed: Birkin and Ursula stand out as exceptions of vitality against a background that is predominantly inorganic. They exist in an isolated pocket of living nature. Their relationship is compared to a live seed that contains the promise of order, but it is a seed that is falling through chaos, where the dominant image is allotropic transformation: water to ice, earth to jewels.

As in *The Rainbow* the ubiquitous birth process determines most events and behavior, so in *Women in Love* allotropy is nearly universal. It is almost invariably presented as a progression to hardness, a solidification. The book begins in a world that is fluid and amorphous. Events occur around water. Even English society is a watery element, epitomized by the "Pompadour," a "small, slow central whirlpool of disintegration and dissolution." (372) The ambience of the café reflects a cosmic process that is also fluid: "a reducing back to the origin, a return along the Flux of Corruption, to the original rudimentary conditions of being," in Birkin's words. (375) *Women in Love* moves from fluid to solid, from volatile to fixed form. The novel concludes in the frozen North. Gerald's water is crystallized into the snow that kills him; the mud that sustained the *fleurs du mal* is hardened into the stone that Loerke sculpts. The process of the fluid cosmos is replaced by the static finality of the Alps, the cessation beyond which one cannot pass. In this universe "the cradle of snow ran on to the eternal closing-in, where the walls of snow and rock rose impenetrable.... This was the centre, the knot, the navel of the world, where the earth belonged to the skies, pure, unapproachable, impassable." (391)

In *Women in Love* character is also conceived as being allotropic. Because the image is essentially materialistic, personality tends to behave like substance. When characters are angry, for instance, they "harden" against each other. Ursula repudiates Birkin thus: "for several days she went about possessed by this exquisite force of hatred against him.... He was the enemy, fine as a diamond, and as hard and jewel-like, the quintessence of all that was inimical.... Her relation was ultimate and utterly beyond words, the hate was so pure and gem-like." And "she saw him as a clear stroke of uttermost contradiction, a strange gem-like being whose existence defined her own non-existence." (190) Eventually Ursula rejects hate for love, nonexistence for living relation, and Birkin's jewelled rings for flowers.

The implication is that hardening cuts one off from vital relation, as if "hardness" were a state where no reciprocity—or, to continue the metaphor, no mixture of elements—were possible. In Lawrence such characters often have also an insect-like completeness, as if the individual in his "character armour," as Reich calls it, were impervious to relationship.[5] One of Hermione's guests is beetle-like in her "neat, brittle finality of form. She was like some elegant beetle with thin ankles.... How repulsive her completeness and her finality was!" (231) The most insect-like and the most jewel-like character in the novel is of course Loerke. He is a "topaz," (448) a sculptor in stone and metal whose granite frieze (an allotropic pun) first attracts Gudrun's attention in conversation. In Gudrun's eyes, Loerke is "the rock bottom of all life" (another allotropic pun) because he has no illusions. "In the last issue he cared about nothing, he made not the slightest attempt to be at one with anything. He existed a pure, unconnected will, stoical and momentaneous." (417) He possesses "insect-like comprehension" because he "in his inner-most soul, was detached from everything, for him there was neither heaven nor earth nor hell. He admitted no allegiance, he gave no adherence anywhere. He was single and, by abstraction from the rest, absolute in himself." (443)[6] Loerke's hardened independence makes him something of a tragic (or at least, satanic) hero in *Women in Love,* for Lawrence's premise is that relationship is salvation and life.

For this reason Gerald dies when Gudrun becomes a "pure thoughtless crystal," (410) since he is cut off from life-giving relationship. His alienation is illustrated when they are in the snow of the Alps together.

> When she reached the top of the slope, in the wind, she looked round, and saw peak beyond peak of rock and snow, bluish, transcendent in heaven. And it seemed to her like a garden, with the peaks of pure flowers, and her heart gathering them. She had no separate consciousness for Gerald.
> She held on to him as they went sheering down over the keen slope. She felt as if her senses were being whetted on some fine grindstone that was keen as flame....

Gudrun swoons in "utter oblivion":

> When she came to, she stood up and looked round, astonished. Her face was white, her eyes brilliant and large.
> "What is it?" he repeated. "Did it upset you?"
> She looked at him with her brilliant eyes that seemed to have undergone some transfiguration, and she laughed, with a terrible merriment.
> "No," she cried, with triumphant joy. "It was the complete moment of my life."
> And she looked at him with her dazzling, overweening laughter like one possessed. A fine blade seemed to enter his heart, but he did not care, or take any notice. (410)

The plunge down the hill is a barely-disguised reference to their sexual intercourse, where Gudrun, who was at first involuntarily excluded, now withdraws her consciousness from Gerald, and in doing so annihilates him.

Thus images of allotropic hardening correspond to one, deadly, end of the allotropic spectrum. Conversely, fluidity and volatility are the other extreme, which corresponds to the state of being where the ego lapses out. Both extremes are encompassed in Gerald's love affair with Gudrun, which shows how the imperfect ego is destroyed. From the beginning it is made clear that Gerald is not whole. "Gerald," says Mrs. Crich to Birkin, "he's the most wanting of them all. You'd never think it, to look at him now, would you?" (19) There is "a certain isolation, a fear about him, as of something wanting." (229) Gerald's existence is a microcosm of chaos:

> ... life was a hollow shell all round him, roaring and clattering like the sound of the sea, a noise in which he participated externally, and inside this hollow shell was all the darkness and fearful space of death, he knew he would have to find reinforcements, otherwise he would collapse inwards upon the great dark void which circled at the centre of his soul. His will held his outer life, his outer mind, his outer being unbroken and unchanged. But the pressure was too great. He would have to find something to make good the equilibrium. For day by day he felt more and more like a bubble filled with darkness, round which whirled the iridescence of his consciousness, and upon which the pressure of the outer world, the outer life, roared vastly. (314-15)

His need sends him to Gudrun, but she only dramatizes his ontological weakness.

With Gudrun Gerald experiences the one extreme of merging. After their first sexual encounter he feels "perfect as if he were bathed in the womb again.... dissolving and sinking to rest in the bath of her living strength." (337) To emphasize Gerald's tendency to self-dissolution, Lawrence associates him with water. Out in the boat with Gudrun, Gerald's "mind was almost submerged, he was almost transfused, lapsed out for the first time in his life, into the things about him." (170) This imagistic association culminates when, in the chapter "Water Party," he dives down again and again into the lake: significantly, he is in search of a woman.

Gerald can survive neither with Gudrun nor without her. In the Alps, his dilemma becomes clear to him:

> "Where shall I go?" he asked himself.
> "Can't you be self-sufficient?" he replied to himself, putting himself upon his pride.
> "Self-sufficient!" he repeated.
> It seemed to him that Gudrun was sufficient unto herself, closed round and completed, like a thing in a case. In the calm, static reason of his soul, he recognised this, and admitted it was her right, to be closed round upon herself, self-complete, without desire. He realised it, he admitted it, it only needed one last effort on his own part, to win for himself the same completeness. He knew

that it only needed one convulsion of his will for him to be able to
turn upon himself also, to close upon himself as a stone fixes upon
itself, and is impervious, self-completed, a thing isolated.

This knowledge threw him into a terrible chaos. Because, however much he might mentally *will* to be immune and self-
complete, the desire for this state was lacking, and he could not
create it. He could see that, to exist at all, he must be perfectly free
of Gudrun, leave her if she wanted to be left, demand nothing of
her, have no claim upon her.

But then, to have no claim upon her, he must stand by himself,
in sheer nothingness. And his brain turned to nought at the idea. It
was a state of nothingness. (436)

Without a relationship Gerald is isolated as a "stone," "isolated
as if there were a vacuum round his heart, or a sheet of pure
ice." (452) When he merges in contact Gerald is associated with
water and mud; in dead isolation he is frozen and hardened into
an "icy pebble" (467) with "the horrible hardness somehow evident." (468) His paradoxical fate is to be too vulnerable and yet
inaccessible.

Thus Gerald's life (and his death, which symbolizes nonexistence by both merging and annihilation in nothingness) embodies a logical contradiction that is nevertheless, in terms of the
ego, a fact. The contradiction is reflected in the allotropic images
that describe him. From the beginning of the novel he is both
fluid and "crystal," (170) "immune and perfect, without bond or
connection anywhere." (40) At the end he is crystalline and yet
suffers in his affair with Gudrun "the unwillingness to harden
himself against her." (439) However, generally Gerald's development moves from one end of the allotropic (and ontological)
spectrum to the other, from fluid merging to hardened isolation.
In his early sexual encounter with Gudrun he is like fluid; he
pours himself into her, (337) he is a "sea of darkness." (339)
Later he becomes like a machine in his hardness, "his hands like
living metal," his "passion like bronze." (391) "His heart went
up like a flame of ice, he closed over her like steel." (392) His
association with coal becomes association with diamonds: "his
brain seemed hard and invincible now like a jewel." (435) Ultimately there can be no resolution for Gerald except that, fatally
discrete and yet diffuse, he dies.

Gerald's affair shows how the weak ego is destroyed. On the
other hand, Birkin's marriage insures that the ego is made perfect. Gerald and Gudrun are creatures of flux; because their relationship is unstable, their very existences are uncertain. The affair is "an eternal see-saw, one destroyed that the other might

exist, one ratified because the other was nulled." (436) Birkin's alternative is "ultimate marriage," essentially a relationship that will transcend chaos.

At the beginning of *Women in Love* Birkin is the embodiment of mutability. His social position is undefined; he is "indefinite, not to be assigned." (71) He is constantly moving from place to place: "his life seemed uncertain, without any definite rhythm, any organic meaning." (18) He is emotionally unstable, "readily-changing," (18) "wavering, indistinct, lambent," (155) with "the odd mobility and changefulness which contains the quintessence of faith." (225) Birkin's self is protean. "He is a changer," says the Contessa, "he is not a man, he is a chameleon, a creature of change." (85) But Birkin wants stability.

The "ultimate marriage" he describes to Gerald provides a "centre and core" to one's life. "I want the finality of love," he tells Gerald. (50) The "stellar equilibrium" he has such difficulty persuading Ursula to accept is a static union of perfect balance: "If you admit a unison," he tells her, "you forfeit all the possibilities of chaos." (143) He answers her remark that "love is freedom" with the reprimand, "Sentimental cant.... You want the state of chaos, that's all. It is ultimate nihilism, this freedom-in-love business." (144) Even Mino the cat, who is Birkin's alter ego, wants "superfine stability" when he cuffs his mate. (141) As Birkin explains it,

> "The old ideals are as dead as nails—nothing there. It seems to me there remains only this perfect union with a woman—a sort of ultimate marriage—and there isn't anything else."
> "And you mean if there isn't the woman there's nothing?" said Gerald.
> "Pretty well that, seeing there's no God."
> "Then we're hard put to it," said Gerald. (51)

But it is not a substitute religion compounded of mysticism and sexuality that Birkin wants. The crucial issue in the novel is not surety of religious belief but certainty about one's being. Gerald's remark that if there isn't the woman there's nothing, is to be taken quite literally, for both he and Birkin (like Lawrence himself) require women in order to exist.

> The supreme effort each man makes, for himself, is the effort to clasp as a hub the woman who shall be the axle, compelling him to true motion, without aberration.... And the vital desire of every woman is that she shall be clasped as axle to the hub of man, that his motion shall portray her motionlessness, convey her static

being into movement, complete and radiating out into infinity, starting from her stable eternity, and reaching eternity again, after having covered the whole of time. (*Phoenix*, 444)

No man can endure the sense of space, of chaos, on four sides of himself. It drives him mad. He must be able to put his back to the wall. And this wall is his woman. . . . From her he has a sense of stability. She supplies him with the feeling of Immutability, Permanence, Eternality. He is himself a raging activity, change potent within change. He does not even conceive of himself, save when he is sure of the woman permanent beneath him, beside him. (446)

The difficulty is to establish a relationship where one does not suffer Gerald's fate, and "stellar equilibrium" does precisely that. This "mutual unison in separateness" (257) is fantasy of self-sufficiency. It is a means of self-preservation, where the two egos support and define, but do not invade and destroy, each other. It is a "mystic dualism in otherness," (237) "an equilibrium, a pure balance of two single beings—as the stars balance each other." (139) There is no "meeting and mingling" because the self does not lapse out; there is only conjunction: "one must commit oneself to a conjunction with the other—for ever," Birkin says. "But it is not selfless—it is a maintaining of the self in mystic balance and integrity." (144) "Stellar equilibrium" is an ideal of safety and stasis where there is neither conflict nor threat to being. "I want us to be together without bothering about ourselves," Birkin says to Ursula, "to be really together because we *are* together, as if it were a phenomenon, not a thing we have to maintain by our own effort." (242) They should be "glad and sure and indifferent," (243)—that is, their egos should be self-sufficient. The "ultimate marriage" is a fantasy wherein the self transcends chaos, and "chaos" is simply the vicissitudes of merging and annihilation, the danger and struggle of relationship.

Not only do Birkin and Ursula transcend the morass of English society, imagistically they abandon the realm of physical existence altogether, transcending time and matter into eternity.

She looked at him. He seemed still so separate. New eyes were opened in her soul. She saw a strange creature from another world in him. It was as if she were enchanted, and everything were metamorphosed. She recalled again the old magic of the Book of Genesis, where the sons of God saw the daughters of men, that they were fair. And he was one of these, one of these strange creatures from the beyond, looking down at her, and seeing she was fair. (304)

Ursula seems likewise transcendent to Birkin: "He looked at her with his strange, non-human singleness," and "she lifted her face to him, all shining and open. It was as if he might enter straight into the source of her radiance." (309) They are compared to perfectly balanced stars above the flooding and confusion of earth, and they are associated with flame, spirit, heavenly bodies, light and air. Their relationship is a pure, paradisical flower, a mystic rose.

On the other hand, Gerald and Gudrun are immersed in chaos, symbolically trapped in time and matter. He is an industrialist, his life is an endless manipulation of materials for material ends. Gudrun, a sculptress, is likewise a shaper of matter. (Ursula, on the other hand, prefers flowers since they hold the spirit of life.) Gudrun and Gerald have characters that are allotropic: they are like water or "pure thoughtless crystal," (410) "hard, metallic," (407) "like steel," like jewels, or machine-like. Their own "transcendence" is to be abstracted beyond matter to the state of physical properties.

> The first days passed in an ecstasy of physical motion, sleighing, ski-ing, skating, moving in an intensity of speed and white light that surpassed life itself, and carried the souls of the human beings beyond into an inhuman abstraction of velocity and weight and eternal, frozen snow. (411)

Their velocity and momentum are mechanical travesties of the organic living spirit in Birkin and Ursula.

Gerald and Gudrun are also trapped in time. During her first tryst with Gerald, Gudrun listens for the church clock. (339) Her flat has a "long case clock" with a "ruddy, round slant-eyed joyous-painted face, that wagged over with the most ridiculous ogle when the clock ticked, and back again with the same absurd glad-eye at the next tick. . . . She stood for minutes, watching it, till a sort of maddened disgust overcame her, and she laughed at herself hollowly." (369) Gudrun's identification with time is complete when, in the Alps during a night of insomnia, she feels herself transformed into a clock. "She was watching the fingers twitch across the eternal, mechanical, monotonous clock-face of time. She never really lived, she only watched. Indeed, she was like a little, twelve-hour clock vis-à-vis with the enormous clock of eternity. . . . Didn't her face really look like a clock-dial—rather roundish and often pale, and impassive." (457) Both she and Gerald, Lawrence stresses, are finite. Gudrun, struck by Gerald's beauty, realizes that "it was all no good, and that she would never go beyond him, he was the final approximation of life to her." (173) His beauty makes her want "to die, to die . . . . This was too much for her, a final vision." Likewise Gerald seems limited to Birkin:

He [Birkin] seemed now to see, not the physical, animal man, which usuallv he saw in Gerald, and which usually he liked so much but the man himself, complete, and as if fated, doomed, limited. This strange sense of fatality in Gerald, as if he were limited to one form of existence, one knowledge, one activity, a sort of fatal halfness, which to himself seemed wholeness, always overcame Birkin after their moments of passionate approach, and filled him with a sort of contempt, or boredom. It was the insistence on limitation which so bored Birkin in Gerald. Gerald could never fly away from himself, in real indifferent gaiety. He had a clog, a sort of monomania. (199)

To Gudrun Gerald is "a piece of radium," a "fatal, living metal," (387) and to Birkin Gerald in death has a "last terrible look of cold, mute Matter." (472)

Gudrun is material, rather than, like Ursula, spiritual, and being immanent she is associated with finite limitation, as is Gerald. She is always hemmed in, seeking release beyond further horizons. Gerald is the "*ne plus ultra* of the world of man as it existed for her. In knowing him she knew the world, and had done with it." (443) The only further experience possible is not with men but with "little, ultimate *creatures* like Loerke. The world was finished now, for her. There was only the inner, individual darkness, sensation within the ego, the obscene religious mystery of ultimate reduction, the mystical frictional activities of diabolic reducing down, disintegrating the vital organic body of life." Images of finite limitation in *Women in Love* are invariably deathly. For one thing, Gerald and Gudrun's symbolic immanence, their immersion in the stream of chaos, is "fatal" because it signifies their mortality. For another, they are associated with death because of their finite intactness. The "sensation within the ego" of "ultimate reduction" is a kind of sexuality that is solipsistic; there is no interchange and replenishment. It is a fatal reducing down of the self to utter singularity.[7]

On the other hand, Birkin and Ursula, according to the metaphorical logic of the book, become transcendent like gods, and are saved. However their transcendent marriage fails to satisfy them (and us) for a number of reasons. First is that "stellar equilibrium" cannot be equitable as far as Ursula is concerned and still insure the safety of Birkin's self. She must relinquish her "female ego," her "assertive *will*," her "frightened apprehensive self-insistence." (243) Yet once this is accomplished their relationship fails to fulfill its *raison d'être*, which is to create and sustain Birkin's ego. According to Lawrence's thinking, an Other is necessary in order to be. The tension between self and Other is what defines the ego; thus conflict is an existential necessity.

The need for conflict is an important theme in many of Lawrence's writings, both psychological and metaphysical: "All truth—and real living is the only truth—has in it elements of battle and repudiation." (CL, 932) And, "once you have conquered a thing, you have lost it. Its real relation to you collapses." (*Phoenix*, 29)[8] This observation applies to the marriage of Birkin and Ursula. When her identity is nullified, when she becomes too pliant and is reduced to the point where Birkin absorbs her, she fails to provide a satisfactory Other. Birkin turns to Gerald because Gerald offers resistance.

Ursula is relegated to the position of essential background:

> "Did you need Gerald?" she asked Birkin one evening.
> "Yes," he said.
> "Aren't I enough for you?" she asked.
> "No," he said. "You are enough for me as far as a woman is concerned. You are all women to me. But I wanted a man friend, as eternal as you and I are eternal." (472)

Birkin weeps over the dead body of Gerald: "He should have loved me . . . I offered him." (471) The *blutbrüderschaft* he wants is a counterpart to his "ultimate marriage," "Something abiding," he calls it, "something that can't change." (268) But this equilibrium is never attained between him and Gerald, and fortunately so, for it would necessitate nullifying Gerald as Ursula is nullified, and again leave Birkin with the need to find another person to—in Lawrence's word—"ratify" him.

"Stellar equilibrium" is static. When this "unison" denies movement in time and space, which is the "possibilities of chaos," it denies also the "possibilities" of relationship—that is, the tendency toward merging, or, conversely, annihilation in nothingness. However, these two tendencies are essential to define the self. Without activity, which can consist only of this dual motion toward and away from another being, there is no existence. The contradiction between stasis and process is reflected in Lawrence's two definitions of love in the essay "Love" (1918).

> We are like a rose, which is a miracle of pure centrality, pure absolved equilibrium. Balanced in perfection in the midst of time and space, the rose is perfect . . . in the realm of perfection . . . neither temporal nor spatial but absolved by the equality of perfection, pure immanence of absolution. (*Phoenix*, 153)

On the other hand,

> Love is the hastening gravitation of spirit towards spirit, body towards body, in the joy of creation. But if all be united in one bond of love, then there is no more love. And therefore, for those who

are in love with love, to travel is better than to arrive. For in arriving one passes beyond love, or rather, one encompasses love in a new transcendence.... Love is not a goal; it is only a travelling. (151)

The desire for stasis cannot be reconciled with the necessity for process. Stellar equilibrium is a fantasy possible only in the reality of the unconscious. Birkin and Ursula, once their battle is over and their equilibrium achieved, become less important in *Women in Love*, and their relationship seems to continue outside the scope of the novel. Attention shifts to the combat of Gerald and Gudrun, and of Birkin and Gerald. Lawrence intimates that the "ultimate marriage" is mystical and therefore ineffable, but it is ineffable only because the notion of perfect equilibrium denies that any thing exists to be described. Birkin and Ursula's "final love which is stark and impersonal and beyond responsibility," (137) which is "not a thing they have to maintain by their own effort," is not only an impersonal denial of human characteristics in them, it is a state of perfect passivity tantamount to nonexistence. No "development" is possible between them, even in terms of the metaphors Lawrence himself establishes for personality.

However there are several contradictions in *Women in Love* as to the relative merits of stasis and process. What is condoned in one character is condemned in another. For instance, Birkin wants a relationship with Ursula that is "final and irrevocable." (136) "It is irrevocable," he insists, "and it is never pure till it is irrevocable. And when it is irrevocable, it is one way, like the path of a star." (144) "Stellar equilibrium," transcending chaos, brings him this permanence: "this was the first time that an utter and absolute peace had entered his heart, now, in this final transit out of life." (379) Likewise, with Ursula, "the paradisal glow in her heart, and the unutterable peace of darkness in his, this was the all in all.... The peace and bliss in their hearts was enduring." Yet this state of finality is what Gerald also seeks in his relationship.

Both he and Gudrun move toward a state of ultimate cessation. Near its end their affair is a "perfect, static unity" (410) that is a parody of "stellar equilibrium." The Alpine valley becomes an objectification of their stasis: a "great cul-de-sac of snow and mountain peaks," (391) which is "the pivot of all existence, there was no further reality." (432) As Birkin wants Ursula's irrevocable commitment to him on an "inhuman" plane of existence, so Gerald wants to possess Gudrun finally and perfectly. The difference is that in Gerald's case cessation is associated with death. "The affair is over, is it?" he says to himself. "I believe it is over. But it isn't finished. Remember it isn't finished. We must put some sort of a finish on it. There must be a conclusion, there must be a finality." (452) Birkin kills Ursula figuratively; he "kills" the willful part of her personality. Gerald wants to kill Gudrun, quite literally, also in order to possess her. "What a perfect voluptuous consummation it would be to strangle her," he thinks, because then "he would have her finally and for ever; there would be such a perfect, voluptuous finality." (452) Birkin's equilibrium insures life, and Gerald's finality is deadly; yet in terms of the ego they are the same goal.

The notion of changeability is also equivocal in the novel. The difference between Gudrun and Ursula, for instance, is essentially rhetorical. Ursula's changeableness indicates her vitality: "she was so quick, so lambent, like discernible fire, and so vindictive, and so rich in her dangerous flamy sensitiveness." (142) No images of light and fire are applied to Gudrun's mutability. She is a watery changer, a water-lily undulating in the swamp of disintegration, a seagull above the flood of chaos, an angel of corruption. Yet her mobility is different from Ursula's only in that it is associated with images of disintegration instead of life.

As with changeability, so with self-sufficiency: what is self-centrality in Ursula is fatal intactness in Gudrun. Ursula doesn't need others to ratify her existence. "Their presence [Birkin and her father] was not vital to her. She was withheld, she did not take them in. It was a subtle insult that never failed to exasperate her father." And "she was in some self-satisfied world of her own. He and his hopes were accidentals, violations to her. It drove her father to a pitch of mad exasperation." (253) To Gudrun she says, "I do feel like a swan among geese—I can't help it. They make one feel so. And I don't care what *they* think of me. Je m'en fiche." Gudrun's response is to look up "at Ursula with a queer, uncertain envy and dislike. 'Of course, the only thing to do is despise them all—just all,' she said." (45) Ursula is associated with images of static plentitude like the moon. "She had her queer, radiant, breathless manner, as if confused by the actual world, unreal to it, having a complete bright world of her self alone." (252) It seems to Birkin as if she is "suffused from within by a powerful sweet fire.... like a strange queen, almost supernatural in her glowing smiling richness." (122) However any such self-sufficiency in Gudrun is presented not as plentitude, but as murderous intactness.

As Ursula seems complete to Birkin, so to Gerald Gudrun seems "so finished, and of such perfect gesture, moreover." (114) But Gudrun's wholeness is exclusive. "One must preserve oneself," she thinks, when Gerald leaves her family's house. Her character development, in terms of allotropic images, is progressive hardening, until she reaches a "jewel-like" intactness and a frozen integrity that cuts Gerald off from the quick of life and the possibility of self-definition.

Women in Love has a symmetrical structure and a symmetrical value system. Flux is death and it is life; the same is true of stasis. Each character embodies both stasis and flux, but in one couple they are associated with life, and in the other, with death.

Gudrun is in fact very much like Birkin, but again, as with Ursula, there is a discrepancy in the way similar states are described. "One must be free," she says, "above all one must be free. One may forfeit everything else, but one must be free." (366) She, like Birkin, refuses to be trammelled. She also leaves English society to embark on a nomadic existence. "Wohin?" Loerke asks her. "That was the question—wohin? Whither? Wohin? What a lovely word! She never wanted it answered. Let it chime for ever." (461) Gudrun's wanderlust is presented as irresponsibility and decadence. She has a scheme to visit a Russian couple (a sculptor and a jewel-maker, significantly) because "the emotional, rather rootless life of the Russians appealed to her." (203) "Her nature, in spite of her apparent placidity and calm, was profoundly restless." She is "one of life's outcasts, one of the drifters that have no root." (368)

On the other hand, Birkin avoids a settled existence with the imagistic justification that he is spirit transcending matter, "You must leave your surroundings sketchy, unfinished," he tells Ursula, "so that you are never contained, never confined, never dominated from the outside." (349) He shuns "materialism" and anything that is "complete ... a horrible tyranny of the fixed milieu." (348) His self-imposed exile has overtones of Lord Byron's; "I want to be disinherited," he says. "We will wander about the face of the earth, ... and we'll look at the world beyond just a bit." (354) Essentially his wanderlust does not differ from Gudrun's; the only dissimilarities are rhetorical—one is associated with aerial transcendence and the other with watery death.

Gudrun appraises Birkin's marriage ideal of equilibrium levelly. "Birkin has a great yearning to be safe," she says, "to tie himself to the mast." (282) Unlike him she does not try to rise above the flood of life; she immerses herself in the destructive element, embracing impermanence as a condition of existence. Gudrun's stance is more heroic than Birkin's, as indeed is Loerke's. But we are persuaded by Lawrence's rhetoric and the imagery of life and death that "stellar equilibrium" is transcendent, and "perfect static unity" is immanent; that Birkin and Ursula's mutability is "lambent," divine "changeableness," whereas Gerald and Gudrun's is "deathly" and "phosphorescent" disintegration.

There is one most outstanding instance of Lawrence's unequal treatment of two virtually identical phenomena. What Gerald wants from sex and what Birkin wants are the same thing. Gerald's sex with Gudrun, as we saw, is a return to the womb. His self dissolves: "he felt himself dissolving and sinking to rest in the bath of her living strength." (337) It recreates him: "he felt his limbs growing fuller and flexible with life, his body gained an unknown strength." And because he lapses out into infantile passivity Lawrence condemns him as one who reduces himself back to the "corruptive state of childishness."

But Birkin's ideal in sex is the same infantile merging, where self is relinquished: "I deliver *myself* over to the unknown in coming to you," he says to Ursula. "I am without reserves or defenses, stripped entirely, into the unknown. Only there needs be the pledge between us, that we will cast off everything, cast off ourselves even, and cease to be, so that which is perfectly ourselves can take place in us." (138) When his ideal is realised, it is—like Gerald's sex with Gudrun—a parody of the mother-infant relation.

> In the new, superfine bliss, a peace superseding knowledge, there was no I and you, there was only the third, unrealised wonder, the wonder of existing not as oneself, but in a consummation of my being and of her being in a new paradisal unit regained from the duality. How can I say "I love you" when I have ceased to be, and you have ceased to be: we are both caught up and transcended into a new oneness where everything is silent, because there is nothing to answer, all is perfect and one. Speech travels between the separate parts. But in the perfect One there is perfect silence of bliss. (362)

He wants to return to a state of primal unity before the ego differentiates itself from the Other. This is the "paradisal unit regained from the duality." In effect this is precisely what Gerald's desire to suffuse himself out in sex signifies except that with him such merging is not paradisiacal but—to apply Lawrence's words —slimily pornographic.

Gerald's loss of his self is fatal, as in his associations with process and stasis. Birkin's, on the other hand, are not. Whereas his changeability is a sign of vitality, like Ursula's, Gudrun's mobility is corrupt. Her self-sufficiency is deathly intactness. Ursula's is plentitude. In short, the angels of light and the angels of darkness in *Women in Love* both proceed from the same set of premises about the nature of existence, but they proceed in opposite directions. The difference between the saved and the damned is, objectively, not great; it is mostly a question of the rhetorical distortion of their behavior, which is considerable. There is, however, one crucial difference between the race of light and the damned who are flowers of corruption.

The only and essential difference between the two is contingent on the kind (or the degree) of their sexuality. Whereas Gerald is an adult, sexual male, his counterpart Birkin is not. Birkin's love ideal denies male-female (i.e., genital) sexuality, and instead imitates, in part, infant-mother love. He merges into Ursula, and she into him. Through love he is reborn from her, "childlike." He kisses her face and brow, "slowly, gently, with a sort of delicate happiness which surprised him extremely, and to which she could not respond. They were soft, blind kisses, perfect in their stillness." (179) But Birkin's infantile erotic bliss is rudely disrupted by Ursula's—to him, insensitive—insistence on lovemaking.

> Then suddenly, to show him she was no shallow prude, she stopped and held him tight, hard against her, and covered his face with hard, fierce kisses of passion. In spite of his otherness, the old blood beat up in him.
> "Not this, not this," he whimpered to himself, as the first perfect mood of softness and sleep-loveliness ebbed back away from the rushing of passion that came up to his limbs and over his face as she drew him. And soon he was a perfect hard flame of passionate desire for her. Yet in the small core of the flame was an unyielding anguish of another thing. (179)

When their relationship does not deny heterosexuality by being passive and infantile, it denies it by being transcendent. Birkin denies his own physicality. He is always sick; "I think it is *criminal* to have so little connection with your own body that you don't even know when you're ill," Ursula remonstrates. (188) He prudishly calls sex "impurity" and longs for "the pure duality of polarization," where each one is "free from any contamination of the other." (193) "On the whole, he hated sex, it was such a limitation." (191) The implication is that sex is existentially repugnant to him ("the merging, the clutching, the mingling of love was madly abhorrent to him,"[191]), but physical revulsion is quite apparent.

Birkin tries to train Ursula to abandon physical sensuality, "the terrible assertion of her body, the unutterable anguish of dissolution." (184) His love is spiritual sex. When Birkin and Ursula make love they are not two humans meeting, but two disembodied metaphysical forces mingling.

> They threw off their clothes, and he gathered her to him, and found her, found the pure lambent reality of her for ever invisible flesh. Quenched, inhuman, his fingers upon her unrevealed nudity were the fingers of silence upon silence, the body of the mysterious night upon the body of the mysterious night, the night masculine and feminine, never to be seen with the eye, or known with the mind, only known as a palpable revelation of living otherness.
> She had her desire of him, she touched, she received the maximum of unspeakable communication in touch, dark, subtle, positively silent, a magnificent gift and give again, a perfect acceptance and yielding, a mystery, the reality of that which can never be known, vital, sensual reality that can never be transmuted into mind content, but remains outside, living body of darkness and silence and subtlety, the mystic body of reality. She had her desire fulfilled. He had his desire fulfilled. For she was to him what he was to her, the immemorial magnificence of mystic, palpable, real, otherness. (312)

Such mystical sexuality is a contradiction in terms; sex divested of physicality is not sex.

On the other hand, Gerald and Gudrun are palpably physical, sexual lovers. Gerald is promiscuous, a "Sultan," Gudrun calls him, (385) "a whole saturnalia in himself." (384) Their passion is the antithesis of Birkin's mystic marriage. Gerald and Gudrun are associated with animals; the rabbit, horse, wolf, seagull and the "beast" are a few of their totem animals. Lawrence establishes the antitheses of Gerald and Gudrun to Birkin and Ursula, as the opposition of spirit and physis. In the wrestling match between Gerald and Birkin, for instance, Gerald is matter and Birkin the form that interpenetrates and realizes it.

> They seemed to drive their white flesh deeper and deeper against each other, as if they would break into a oneness. . . . [Birkin] seemed to penetrate into Gerald's more solid, more diffuse bulk, to interfuse his body through the body of the other as if to bring it subtly into subjection, always seizing with some rapid necromantic foreknowledge every motion of the other flesh, converting and counteracting it, playing upon the limbs and trunk of Gerald like some hard wind. It was as if Birkin's whole physical intelligence interpenetrated into Gerald's body, as if his fine, sublimated

energy entered into the flesh of the fuller man, like some potency, casting a fine net, a prison, through the muscles into the very depths of Gerald's being." (262)

But fundamentally the only difference between Birkin's marriage and Gerald's affair is that Birkin would transcend sex as he transcends flux, and Gerald plunges himself into sexuality as into a destructive element. And what is called in his case destructive sexuality, "the phosphorescent ecstasy of acute sensation," (375) is simply adult male sexuality.

Lawrence associates heterosexuality with destruction. Sex literally annihilates being in *Women in Love;* we are "always seeking to *lose* ourselves in some ultimate black sensation, mindless and infinite—burning only with destructive fires, ranging on with the hope of being burnt out utterly." (376) Such self-annihilation could plausibly be a reference to the temporary suspension of ordinary self-consciousness which occurs in sex. But heterosexuality in the novel always entails permanent self disintegration. Sex is the "Flux of Corruption" (375) because it is an "ecstasy of reduction," a "reducing ourselves part from part—reacting in intimacy only for destruction." (376) Thus genital sexuality is "sundering" and "frictional" in that it makes for division, "reducing the two great elements of male and female" in active battle instead of uniting them in perfect passive self-creation, in "the immemorial magnificence of mystic, palpable, real otherness." (312) In other words, sex according to Lawrence in *Women in Love* is corrupt because it is a separation from primal unity.

The fall into knowledge—that is, into self-consciousness and separateness—is a fall from oneness into sexual polarity. It is a descent from eternity into flux and strife, and this descent and this separation are what Birkin would avoid with his transcendental supersexual ideal. His equilibrium denies the motion inherent in sexual polarity. Thus, with Ursula, he feels

> ...it was such peace and heavenly freedom, just to fold her and kiss her gently, and not to have any thoughts or any desires or any will, just to be still with her, to be perfectly still and together, in a peace that was not sleep, but content in bliss. To be content in bliss, without desire or insistence anywhere, this was heaven: to be together in happy stillness. (244)

But when Ursula tries to introduce sex, Birkin quashes it as divisive:

> For a long time she nestled to him, and he kissed her softly, her hair, her face, her ears, gently, softly, like dew falling. But this warm breath on her ears disturbed her again, kindled the old de-

71

structive fires. She cleaved to him, and he could feel his blood changing like quicksilver.
"But we'll be still, shall we?" he said.

"Stellar equilibrium" imitates the pre-sexual relationship of the mother and child, which is, in terms of the sense of one's being, perhaps the stablest human relationship possible.

By extension, Gerald is the physical man, and Birkin the asexual. The beauty and solidity of Gerald's body is reiterated in the novel, while Birkin's form is minimized. Birkin displays male sexuality only once, when dancing in the Reunionsaal. "Even Birkin was behaving manfully," Lawrence notes. (400) Such sexuality is conceived of as predatory: "there were odd little fires playing in his eyes, he seemed to have turned into something wicked and flickering, mocking, suggestive, quite impossible. Ursula was frightened of him, and fascinated. Clear, before her eyes, as in a vision, she could see the sardonic licentious mockery of his eyes, he moved towards her with subtle, animal, indifferent approach." (402) Later she finds "his licentiousness was repulsively attractive," (403) and wonders "why not be bestial, and go the whole round of experience? She exulted in it. She was bestial." However the next morning Birkin and Ursula, who acted but faint imitations of the genuinely sensual Gudrun and Gerald, return to their usual ephemeral state.

Women in Love purports to show how one kind of relationship purifies the self into perfected "singleness of being," and how another kind disintegrates the self. The latter, destructive relationship is called "sensation-seeking," a "frictional," and "reductive process," "the passion for putting asunder." (376) Of this Gerald and Gudrun are guilty, by association. The rhetoric of the novel favors "spiritual" sexuality by associating it with the life process, and condemns Gerald and Gudrun's kind of sexuality by associating it with death. Birkin and Ursula pledge their troth surrounded by "fresh, luminous" nature; (304) but the "demonic marriage" (234) of Gerald and Gudrun is plighted in the "underworld," suggesting "abhorrent mysteries" (234) which are never directly named. It is "sinister, obscene," sworn in blood, and blessed by the devil incarnate, the rabbit Bismarck.

Both Gerald and Gudrun are associated with death, but it is a rhetorical association intended to persuade us that genital sexuality is deadly. Gerald and Gudrun, says Birkin to Ursula, have been "born in the process of destructive creation," they are "part of the inverse process, the blood of destructive creation." (164)

"If we are *fleurs du mal,* we are not roses of happiness," Birkin says to her.

> "But I think I am," said Ursula. "I think I am a rose of happiness."
> "Ready-made?" he asked ironically.
> "No—real," she said, hurt.
> "If we are the end, we are not the beginning," he said.
> "Yes we are," she said. "The beginning comes out of the end."
> "After it, not out of it. After us, not out of us."
> "You are a devil, you know, really," she said. "You want to destroy our hope. You *want* us to be deathly."
> "No," he said, "I only want us to *know* what we are."
> "Ha!" she cried in anger. "You only want us to know death."
> "You're quite right," said the soft voice of Gerald, out of the dusk behind. (165)

Gerald is, according to Birkin, self-destructive. "A man who is murderable is a man who in a profound if hidden lust desires to be murdered." (27) He is Cain because he once—in an act not without sexual symbolism—shotgunned his brother. He is Hermes the thief, who robs the earth of its coal and the workers of their humanity. Gerald carries with him a taint, an undefined guilt. "There's one thing about our family, you know," he says, "Once anything goes wrong, it can never be put right again—not with us. I've noticed it all my life—you can't put a thing right, once it has gone wrong." (176) He, like a Nibelung, carries an ancestral curse.

However the association of sex and death in *Women in Love* is not purely existential, it is also moral—specifically, puritanical. Lawrence links the two: the state of one's being depends on one's sexuality, or the lack of it.[9] The demonic cosmos of the novel reflects the sexual schizophrenia of the mind-body split. The upper half of the universe is the realm of spirituality; the nether regions represent a lumping together of everything in man that is considered obscene, either sexual or excretory. It contains symbols of the subconscious urges, the "lower" consciousness, all the powerful things that are repressed, and fearsome because repressed.

Thus *Women in Love* associates the sexual "sensation-seekers," the *"fleurs du mal,"* with the primitive and the demonic. Sex is linked with primitivism in the case of the London bohemians. Halliday's servant Hasan is "half a savage," (166) and Halliday himself owns primitive carvings, including the African goddess in labor. (67) Gudrun's carvings are pseudo-primitive, "full of primitive passion," and "like a flash of instinct." (32) Gerald has an interest in "primitive man, books of anthropology," (235) as well as having "explored the Amazon." (57) He discourses on savages to Minette (59) who is identified with the carved African goddess. To cement the analogy between their primitivism and sexuality, Lawrence names one bohemian Libidnikov.

The mythical embellishment of the novel also associates the sexual with the demonic. Gerald is Hermes, the god who travels between the upper and lower regions. He is Hades, lord in the underworld of Beldover and Whatmore, as Gudrun is Proserpine.[10] He is a Nibelung, a being from an ancient race whose element is water, whose wealth is a curse; and Gudrun is Brunhild, likewise of mysterious origin. Nottingham and London are regions of Hell, subterranean or submarine. Even the present phase of the cosmic process—the Flux of Corruption—is associated with Aphrodite, the dark, sensual side of human nature. Birkin says:

> "We always consider the silver river of life, rolling on and quickening all the world to a brightness . . . flowing into a bright eternal sea. . . . But the other is our real reality— . . . the black river of corruption. And our flowers are of this—our sea-born Aphrodite, all our white phosphorescent flowers of sensuous perfection, all our reality nowadays." (164)

The demonic plays an important part in all of Lawrence's fiction. Nature and foreign places provide counterparts to society, and are sources of powers inimical to social order. From *The White Peacock* on, the demon lover takes his rebel stance outside civilization. He symbolizes the deeper human drives and brings an influx of erotic power to a vitiated, repressed society.[11] He "saves" a woman and together they escape the social order— such is the plot of most of Lawrence's novels. As Widmer points out, this most intense form of Eros is necessarily outside and antithetical to the social order.[12] Lawrence also uses the demonic to show that society is antihuman in that its morality is the enemy of vitality. Demonism is a passionate, positive stance, essentially an assertion of the unconscious.

The contradiction in *Women in Love* is that society itself is demonic. It is hell, and as such the inverse of what society should be. It also embodies man's sexual urges; and therefore those who rebel against it deny sex. Birkin incongruously takes the part of the demon lover. He is the outsider who traffics with primordial powers. Hermione calls him a "dreadful satanist," (36) and he rescues Ursula from stultifying bourgeois life. However Birkin as a character lacks the dark, suggestive power of Ciccio or

Don Ramon or Don Cipriano, of Mellors, Count Dionys or even so crude a demon lover as Annable, precisely because he is utterly without erotic power. The world he wants to escape to is neither dark nor potent: "In my world it is sunny and spacious," he tells Ursula. (354) "The world beyond this just a bit" that he seeks is blissfully free of sex and sex's conflict.

On the other hand, Gerald and Gudrun are charged with erotic power. The "mystery" they share is dark, potent "underworld knowledge." (234) Although Birkin and Ursula also experience the "mysterious night" in their sex, their darkness is not dangerous but benign, a "good immediate darkness" (310) that brings surety and contentment. Sex between Gerald and Gudrun is dangerous: "through her passion was a transcendent fear of the thing he was . . . ah, how dangerous! . . . such an unutterable enemy." (324) And for him, "her fingers had him under her power. The fathomless, fathomless desire they could evoke in him was deeper than death, where he had no choice." The struggle in passion is deadly. Gerald's constant desire is "like a doom upon him." (390) Because their sex is based on fear it becomes a power struggle. Gudrun's "pity for him was as cold as stone, its deepest motive was hate of him, and fear of his power over her, which she must always counterfoil." (434) Ironically their attempts to control passion become more deadly than the passion itself.

Gerald embodies both the demon world and civilization, both passion and control. The two couples leave England, where it is impossible to be free:

> "Don't you love to be in this place?" cried Gudrun. "Isn't the snow wonderful! Do you notice how it exalts everything? . . . . One does feel *übermenschlich*—more than human."
>
> "One does," cried Ursula. "But isn't that partly the being out of England?"
>
> "Oh, of course," cried Gudrun. "One could never feel like this in England, for the simple reason that the damper is *never* lifted off one, there. It is quite impossible really to let go in England, of that I am assured." (385)

But Gerald isn't so enthusiastic:

> "It's quite true," said Gerald, "it never is *quite* the same in England. But perhaps we don't want it to be—perhaps it's like bringing the light a little too near the powder magazine, to let go altogether, in England. One is afraid of what might happen, if *everybody else* let go."
>
> "My God!" cried Gudrun. "But wouldn't it be wonderful if all England did suddenly go off like a display of fireworks."

"It couldn't," said Ursula. "They are all too damp, the powder is damp in them."
"I'm not so sure of that," said Gerald.

There is a strong sense, with Gerald, that he contains forces that must be kept under his control.

He has an over-strong sense of responsibility: "he has been so insistent, so guarded all his life," (170) He is afraid of "letting go," and when he does, the result is disaster. Out in the boat with Gudrun he momentarily forgets his responsibility for the water, and lapses out "for the first time in his life, into the things about him. For he always kept such a keen attentiveness, concentrated and unyielding in himself. Now he had to let go, imperceptibly he was melting into oneness with the whole." (170) Immediately, as if by cause and effect, his sister drowns.

Gerald's letting go in the presence of Gudrun signifies not only a loosening of sexual inhibitions, but a lapsing out of his sense of himself, which she provokes. This same lapsing occurs when he goes to Gudrun's house. His greatest disaster is of course his final lapsing out into death, which is also connected to his passion—by this time, a murderous lust—for Gudrun. There is thus a conjunction of sexual and existential guilt in the novel, and both are associated with death.[13] Death because failure to be whole is, of course, the death of the self. But more than that, death because sexuality invites punishment.

Women in Love is puritanical tragedy, where to assert one's male sexuality is the hubris that attracts divine retribution. Gerald's flaw is that he is proud of his physical attractiveness and his sexual prowess. The symbolic epitome of his male pride is his mastery of the Arab mare at the railroad crossing. He asserts himself against the horse:

> A sharpened look came on Gerald's face. He bit himself down on the mare like a keen edge biting home, and *forced* her round. She roared as she breathed, her nostrils frenzied. It was a repulsive sight. But he held her on unrelaxed, with an almost mechanical relentlessness keen as a sword pressing into her. Both man and horse were sweating with violence. Yet he seemed calm as a ray of cold sunshine. (104)

The sexual symbolism is thinly veiled. Gudrun recalls the incident almost entirely in sexual terms:

> Gudrun was as if numbed in her mind by the sense of indomitable soft weight of the man, bearing down into the living body of the horse: the strong, indomitable thighs of the blond man clenching the palpitating body of the mare into pure control; a sort of soft

white magnetic domination from the loins and thighs and calves, enclosing and encompassing the mare heavily into unutterable subordination, soft-blooded subordination, terrible. (106)

"I should think you're proud," Gudrun calls to him. (105) She is sexually excited by his pride, but ultimately excited by it to destroy him.

Gudrun is the agent of Gerald's destruction, and the ritual of his death provides an insight into the puritan morality of the novel. His death is a mock crucifixion. As Christ (Crich) he forms a demonic pietá with Gudrun, who all along has been forced unwilling into the role of his mother. At his death, she and Loerke celebrate an unholy communion in the snow with *schnapps* and *keks*, the blood and body of Gerald. The mother of Christ dominates the scene: not only is Gudrun a demonic Mary, but Gerald when he is out skiing seeks the Marienhütte as his goal. (451) Later he dies going "to the summit of the slopes, where was the Marienhütte." (465) After his death, Birkin thinks Gerald might have saved himself, found the pass and "where the Marienhütte hid among the naked rocks." (469) "Gerald might have found this rope. He might have hauled himself up to the crest. He might have heard the dogs in the Marienhütte, and found shelter." But it is a misleading goal, for woman does not mean salvation for Gerald, she means death.

Mother and death are joined rhetorically when Loerke says to Gerald: "Maria! You come like a ghost." (462) Struggling up the final ascent of his Calvary Gerald sees something standing out in the snow.

> It was a half-buried crucifix, a little Christ under a little sloping hood at the top of a pole. He sheered away. Somebody was going to murder him. He had a great dread of being murdered. But it was a dread which stood outside him like his own ghost.
> Yet why be afraid? It was bound to happen. To be murdered! He looked round in terror at the snow, the rocking, pale, shadowy slopes of the upper world. He was bound to be murdered, he could see it. This was the moment when the death was uplifted, and there was no escape.
> Lord Jesus, was it then bound to be—Lord Jesus! (465)

Gerald perishes in a hollow basin of snow, out of which rises "a track that brought one to the top of the mountains." (466) That is, he dies in the womb of the gigantic female body of the mountains.

The most insidious female symbol in the death scene is the moon. In Lawrence the moon is always a barometer of a woman's condition. Ursula, for instance, is at the height of her power over Birkin in "Moony" when the moon is full, and at the end of "Excurse," when she is subdued by Birkin, there is no moon at all. When Gerald leaves Gudrun's house, he has been made whole, but she withheld herself from him (which is the beginning of destruction in the affair), hence there's only "a piece of a moon in a vague sky." (342) A sinister moon presides over Gerald's death scene: "to add to his difficulty, a small bright moon shone brilliantly just ahead, on the right, a painful brilliant thing that was always there, unremitting, from which there was no escape." (464) This probing moon is an all-seeing eye that suggests an insistent conscience.

In fact in *Women in Love* Lawrence inverts Freud's contention that the superego is paternalistic in overtone and origin; instead, conscience is feminine. Gerald trains Gudrun to punish him, courting his own death at the hands of his conscience. When she strikes him she says, "It's you who make me like this, you know." (162) Lawrence's inversion shows the difference between the oedipal conscience in a patriarchal culture such as Freud's, and oedipal guilt feelings in a truly mother-dominated culture such as Lawrence's. Repression and punishment are not associated with the stern father but with the stern mother. (By extension, God is not a heavenly father, but God the mother.)

In this situation the only permissible sexuality is feminine. Hence *The Rainbow* brims with life because the first principle is the divine feminine, and that is an acceptable form of sexuality. *Women in Love* is primarily about heterosexuality, and is consequently full of retributive death. Gerald's death is a punishment for being masculine—by castration of his being, so to speak. He is unmanned, reduced to the state of unformed, infantile nothingness and lapsing out. Birkin avoids the same fate by avoiding male sexuality; what passes between him and Ursula insofar as it is sexual at all is only feminine, that is, maternal.

Women in Love concludes with Birkin mourning for his dead masculinity in the person of the frozen Gerald. Crich is now "like a dead stallion . . . a dead mass of maleness, repugnant." (471) The description stresses his corpse's masculinity: "it was the frozen carcase of a dead male." (468) Birkin's desire is thwarted for the *blutbrüderschaft* that would symbolize self-integration. Ursula is not enough because the relationship with her does not generate the male wholeness that is needed as much as certainty of being. In his next novels Lawrence deals with the theme of integrating sex and spirit, and maintaining ontological certainty, by means of an alter ego. Homosexuality is his metaphor.

4

SOLIPSISM:
AARON'S ROD AND *KANGAROO*

Coming to *Aaron's Rod* and *Kangaroo,* one is struck by the crudeness of their execution. In *The Rainbow* and *Women in Love* Lawrence constructs psychological allegory out of patterns of images more subtle than descriptive language. But *Aaron's Rod* and *Kangaroo* confront the reader with bald, discursive psychological probing, with joyless and ultimately pointless satire, with pseudo-politics, and with mystical discourse devoid of the poetry that usually redeems such writing in Lawrence. The books are semi-autobiographical pastiches that jumble essay, novel, diary and travelogue.

According to Richard Aldington, both *Kangaroo* and *Aaron's Rod* were written quickly, and sent to the printer in first draft.[1] The books seem to corroborate Aldington in their formlessness. They are organized mainly on the principle of free association, evident in the verbal wanderings of the heroes of *Aaron's Rod,* and the meanderings of Somers in *Kangaroo,* who seems to have read the essays of D. H. Lawrence. These debates of Lawrence with himself are tacked onto—but not integrated into—plots that are both minimal and indifferent. The discrepancy between action and preachment violates whatever possibilities for organic coherence exist in *Aaron's Rod* or *Kangaroo.* Consequently, in spite of their superficial "freshness" and "vividness,"[2] these novels as novels display a radical lack of life.

This is partly because *Aaron's Rod* and *Kangaroo* reflect Lawrence's obsessiveness. He defended the "continual, slightly modified" repetition of *Women in Love* as true to the action of the mind in emotional crisis. In *The Plumed Serpent* obsessive repetition takes the form of chants, where a mind paralyzed by emotion transforms it into a rigid, and effectively liturgical, structure—but a structure nonetheless. However in *Aaron's Rod* and *Kangaroo*

79

obsessiveness finds no outlet in forms; there is repetition but nothing coheres, develops, or resolves. "This gramophone of a novel," as Lawrence calls *Aaron's Rod,* is uncomfortably close to the realm of writing as psychotherapy. "One sheds one's sicknesses in books," Lawrence says, "repeats and presents again one's emotions to be master of them."[3] But the denial of form is also symptomatic in a larger sense; when Lawrence ignores form, he in effect ignores his audience. Whatever of the reader's loyalty survives the string of wooden debates usually succumbs to an unsympathetic morality: fascism, misogyny, and nonspecific rancor. In *Aaron's Rod* and *Kangaroo* Lawrence is thumbing his nose at his audience, and his disregard for the reader is consistent with the general tenor of rejection and withdrawal. "I want the world to hate me," Aaron thinks, "because I can't bear the thought that it might love me. For of all things love is the most deadly to me." (256)

If anything could be said to unify either of these amorphous works, it is their consistent pattern of withdrawal and repudiation. Lawrence tries to establish a new value system and a new ego psychology, because the world-view of the previous novels is no longer tenable. In *Sons and Lovers, The Rainbow* and *Women in Love,* one's reality is predicated on relationship, for one exists through others; these novels deal with union and the difficulty of balance in relationship. They assume that some kind of relatedness is a necessity. But *Kangaroo* and Aaron's Rod do not make this assumption; in fact they attempt to refute it, and deny the need for relationship entirely.

In *Aaron's Rod* the hero develops through progressive rejections:

> He was breaking loose from one connection after another: and what for? Why break every tie? Snap, snap, snap went the bonds and ligatures which bound him to the life that had formed him, the people he had loved or liked. He found all his affections snapping off, all the ties which united him with his own people coming asunder. And why? ... What was there instead?
> There was nothingness. There was just himself, and blank nothingness .... He could not persuade himself that he was seeking for love, for any kind of unison and communion. He knew well enough that the thought of any loving, any sort of real coming together between himself and anybody or anything, was just objectionable to him. No—he was not moving *towards* anything: he was moving violently away from everything. And that was what he wanted. Only that. Only let him *not* run into any form of embrace with anything or anybody—this was what he asked. Let no new connections be made between himself and anything on earth. Let all the old connections break. This was his craving. (174-75)

First Aaron escapes his wife Lottie (so called because if Aaron, like Lot's wife, should look back on home he would be petrified). She is a serpent who half-hypnotizes him: "Why have you come back to me?" she asks him. "Her arms gave him a sharp, compulsory little clutch round the waist. 'Tell me!' she murmured, with her appeal liquid in her throat."

> But him, it half overcame, and at the same time, horrified. He had a certain horror of her. The strange liquid sound of her appeal seemed to him like the swaying of a serpent which mesmerizes the fated, fluttering, helpless bird. She clasped her arms round him, she drew him to her, she half roused his passion. At the same time she coldly horrified and repelled him. He had not the faintest feeling, at the moment, of his own wrong. But she wanted to win his own self-betrayal, out of him. He could see himself as the fascinated victim, falling to this cajoling, artful woman, the wife of his bosom. (122)

Yet Aaron manages to disengage himself, only to be seduced by Josephine Ford. This precipitates the 'flu that nearly kills him.

After recovering from Josephine, Aaron goes to Italy, where he becomes involved in an affair with the Marchesa del Torre. She gives Aaron back "the male godliness, the male godhead" (250) he thinks he has lost, but she jeopardizes him as did her predecessors. Aaron's desire for her puts him in "a sort of trance or frenzy," and "whirled away by the evening's experience and the woman," he has his pocket picked. (225) Aaron feels that he has been violated, and that because of the woman: "Yes—and if I hadn't rushed along so full of feeling," he thinks, "if I hadn't exposed myself: if I hadn't got all worked up with the Marchesa, and then rushed all kindled through the streets without reserve: it never would have happened. I gave myself away, and there was someone ready to snatch what I gave. . . . I should always be on my guard: always, always, with God and the devil both, I should be on my guard." (226) Aaron takes the experience as a lesson on the necessity of absolute mistrust, especially of sexual "temptation."

Aaron's Rod reflects a deep general mistrust of reality, which is expressed as misogyny. For whatever biological reasons, and there are indications that tuberculosis was beginning to take its toll with Lawrence by 1922, fear of infection pervades the novel. There is a strong puritanical streak in him that requires that male sexuality be punished, sometimes by sickness. Birkin is sickened several times by Hermione, and laid up by Ursula as "Magna Mater"; laid up, as he says, "for my sins, I suppose." (193) In "Introduction to These Paintings" Lawrence links fear of disease and sex, explaining that in the Renaissance arose a horror of syphilis, which caused a suppression of sexual life; as a result the mental life replaced the intuitional. "The terror-horror element which had entered the imagination with regard to the sexual and procreative act was at least partly responsible for Puritanism." (*Phoenix*, 555) But the women in Lawrence's novels are also symbols; they are objectifications of reality, the Other, the Not-me that creates and defines the self through its contact with it. The nature of women in the novels is the nature of reality itself. In *The Rainbow*, where reality is seen as endless growth and plentitude, woman is a fount of life. In *Women in Love* reality is ambiguous, and so is woman: the cosmos can be a source of vital replenishment (Ursula), or it can mean destruction (Gudrun). Ultimately the "reality" woman reflects is the state of the self projected onto the universe. In *The Rainbow* reality is plentitude because the self is sensed as growing. In *Women in Love* reality is ambiguous because the self's equilibrium between being and not-being is precarious. In *Aaron's Rod* the balance has swung far to the side of invasion and death; the women are plague-bearing monsters because the self is diseased. The underlying assumption of the novel is that reality is a source of infection, hence women, who represent that reality, are carriers of disease.

All contact, especially sexual contact, is seen as contagion. In her sexual aspect the Marchesa seems "like a demon," to Aaron, "wonderful and sinister." (241) She affects him with a "touch of horror." Her appeal, like Crystabel's, is that of a snake. Aaron notes her

> strange, naked, remote-seeming voice! And then the beautiful firm limbs thrust out in that dress, and nakedly dusky as with gold-dust. Her beautiful woman's legs, slightly glistening, duskily. His one abiding instinct was to touch them, to kiss them. He had never known a woman exercise such power over him. It was a bare, occult force, something he could not cope with. (42)

Never has the female body been made to seem more ominous in Lawrence.

> "[Aaron] was aware of [the Marchesa's] beautiful arms, and her bosom; her low-crowned, thick hair, parted at the centre: the sapphires at her throat, the heavy rings on her fingers: and the paint on her lips, the fard. Something deep, deep at the bottom of him hovered upon her, cleaved to her. Yet he was as if sightless, in a stupor. Who was she, what was she? He had lost all his grasp.... The woman was silent mostly, and seemed remote. And Aaron felt his life ebb towards her. He felt the marvelous rich beauty of her arms and breast. And the thought of her gold-dusted smooth limbs beneath the table made him feel almost an idiot." (244)

82

Aaron is "terrified. He knew he was sinking towards her," (243) and when he sleeps with her she coils around him like a serpent, putting her arms "round him, that seemed such frail and childish arms now, yet withal so deadly in power. . . . And yet, even as he kissed her, he found her deadly. He wanted to be gone. He wanted to get out of her arms and her clinging and her tangle of hair and her curiosity and her strange and hateful power." (254) Afterwards Aaron feels "curiously blazed, as if some flame or electric power had gone through him and withered his vital tissue." (255) To him the Marchesa is Cleopatra, the incarnation of the sexual vampire, and he is not her Antony—that is, not her victim.

Aaron ends the affair to save himself, because the Marchesa "would drink the one drop of his innermost heart's blood and he would be carrion. As Cleopatra killed her lovers in the morning." Three times Aaron is threatened by women, and twice Rawdon Lilly, as disinterested in sex as he is in society, restores him. This time Lilly provides an undefined ideal beyond heterosexual love. (Aaron "had perhaps a faint sense of Lilly ahead of him; an impulse in that direction: or else merely an illusion." [174]) At the end of the novel Aaron learns his lesson at last, when his flute is destroyed in an explosion. In effect his symbolic penis is blown off, signifying the end of his attempts at heterosexual relationship.

Lawrence's misogyny focuses on the sex act. Almost always in Lawrence sex is never simply sex; it is an existential act, a crucial communion with reality—the Other than oneself—that creates or destroys the self. "Sex is the actual crisis of love. For in sex the two blood-systems in the male and female concentrate and come into contact, the merest film intervening. Yet if the intervening film breaks down, it is death." (SCAL, 66) Such a conception does not permit a clean distinction between psychic and somatic mingling. Whether the self is created or nullified in sex is expressed in somatic terms, in somatic images of "birth" of the self, "death" of the self, or vampirizing of vitality.

In Aaron's Rod both self and body are diseased by sex. "It is love which gnaws inside us like a cancer," one character remarks, and by way of illustration, Aaron's seduction by Josephine not only poisons his insides quite literally, it taints his integral being. "I felt, the minute I was loving her," Aaron says, "I'd done myself. And I had. Everything came back on me. . . . I felt it—I felt it go, inside me, the minute I gave in to her. It's perhaps killed me." And again, "It's my own fault, for giving in to her. If I'd kept myself back, my liver wouldn't have broken inside me, and I shouldn't have been sick." (84) The collapse of Aaron's liver is equally the collapse of his ego. "My soul's gone rotten," he tells Lilly.[4]

Previously in the novels the body is a symbol for the inner consciousness that is Lawrence's main concern. The body reflects the state of the self. Thus coitus becomes a metaphor for a crisis of being; or a woman, to take another example,—especially in her role of mother—assaults man's integral being, and this is often symbolized by the physical harm she inflicts on him. Miriam and Mrs. Morel, for instance, "invade" Paul and sicken him. Hermione wants to possess Birkin, and tries to get at his mind, quite literally, with a paperweight. Gudrun succeeds in extinguishing Gerald's ego and thereby kills him. *Aaron's Rod*, however, does not create such an interplay between inner and outer states, for it is an external and emphatically physical book. In it ego and body are identified, for the most part, as literally the same. In comparison to Lawrence's use earlier of the mind-body split, *Aaron's Rod* shows an atavistic concept of the relation of mind and body, in which outward and inner states are not clearly separated. (This is not unlike the ancient Greek notion of sin as physical pollution to be literally washed away.) Thus according to the primitive logic of the book, woman infects man's body and thereby leaves his being "rotten" and "broken."

In a universe of disease such as this, the only option for survival is withdrawal, and the only heroism possible is self-sufficiency. Thus the object lesson of Aaron's disastrous encounters with women is solipsism, the self alone, and this is the burden of Rawdon Lilly's teaching. Lilly reenacts Aaron's repudiation of the physical on a spiritual plane. He is an ersatz Buddhist who preaches a kind of *ahimsa*, or detachment. Aaron's rejection is defensive: "he would hold himself for ever beyond [Lottie's] jurisdiction.... To be alone, to be oneself, not to be driven or violated into something which is not oneself, surely it is better than anything." (123) Lilly, on the other hand, attempts to be more positive, to vindicate withdrawal as a philosophical stance. "I think a man may come into possession of his own soul at last," Lilly says, "as the Buddhists teach—but without ceasing to love, or even to hate. One loves, one hates—but somewhere beyond it all, one understands, and possesses one's soul in patience and in peace—" (99). To Aaron Lilly seems an ideal of detachment; like the "happy lily, never to be saddled with an *idée fixe*, never to be in the grip of a monomania for happiness or love or fulfillment. It is not *laisser aller*. It is life-rootedness." (163)

As the novel progresses Lilly withdraws from a "humanity" which would engulf him, (much as women threaten to overwhelm Aaron). "Damn all masses and groups anyhow," Lilly says. "All I want is to get *myself* out of their horrible heap; to get out of the swarm. The swarm to me is nightmare and nullity— horrible helpless writhing in a dream.... It's only when the ghastly mob-sleep, the dream helplessness of the mass-psyche overcomes [man], that he becomes completely base and obscene." (114) Lilly assumes a divine indifference to things sublunary. His self-sufficiency and his centrality are stressed: "Aaron looked at Lilly, and saw the same odd, distant look on his face as on the face of some animal when it lies awake and alert, yet perfectly at one with its surroundings. It was something quite different from happiness: an alert enjoyment of rest, an intense and satisfying sense of centrality.... Not passivity, but alert enjoyment of being central, life-central in one's own little circumambient world." (283) At the conclusion of *Aaron's Rod* Lilly appears in a self-sufficient Nirvana, radiating divine peace.

Lilly's (or Lawrence's) brand of oriental philosophy shows the influence of the Brewsters, Buddhist friends of Lawrence.[5] However, Lilly's "Buddhism" is more decorative than correct. The central tenet of Buddhism is self-annihilation in Nirvana. Lilly propounds exactly the opposite: self-aggrandizement. He considers the self supreme, indestructible, irreducible. "You can't lose yourself," he tells Aaron, "neither in woman nor in humanity nor in God. You've always got yourself on your hands in the end." (285) "There's no goal outside you—and there's no God outside you. No God, whom you can get to and rest in. None." According to him the self is the ultimate reality. "You've got an innermost, integral unique self, and since it's the only thing you have got or ever will have, don't go trying to lose it," counsels Lilly. (286)

Lilly's final state of beatitude arises out of his recognition that "in so far as he is a single individual soul, he *is* alone—*ipso facto.*" And, he continues, "in so far as I am I, and only I am I, and I am only I, in so far, I am inevitably and eternally alone, and it is my last blessedness to know it, and to accept it, and to live with this as the core of my self knowledge." (237) In other words, *Aaron's Rod* attempts to invert the premise of the previous novels, that existence depends on relationship to an Other. Instead, it assumes—or attempts to assume—that existence procedes from isolation.

Now, the greatest good is simply to possess oneself in solitude. "The first law of life," Lawrence says in the essay on Poe, "is that each organism is isolate in itself, it must return to its own isolation." (67) "The moment its isolation breaks down, and there comes an actual mixing and confusion, death sets in." (SCAL, 66) *Aaron's Rod* is an account of a man learning to be alone, "taking one's way alone, happily alone," (163) and his "arrival at a state of simple, pure self-possession" without "degeneration into a sort of slime and merge." (162) To this end the love of woman— "slime and merge"—is rejected.

To Lawrence, Cooper's Natty Bumppo is a hero because he is almost sexless and centered in himself. "Rather than be dragged into a false heat of deliberate sensuality, he will remain alone. His soul is alone, for ever alone. So he will preserve his integrity, and remain alone in the flesh." (61) In another context, a savage woman in Melville has "soft warm flesh, like warm mud. Nearer the reptile, the Saurian age. *Noli me tangere.*" (136) And, "each soul *should* be alone. And in the end the desire for a 'perfect relationship' is just a vicious, unmanly craving. *'Tous nos malheurs viennent de ne pouvoir être seuls,'*" Lawrence quotes La Bruyère. (142)[6] Yet when Lawrence glorifies solipsism one feels he is making a virtue of necessity, for the self alone— "choosing to be alone, because by one's nature one is alone"— seems to be a weak attempt to justify withdrawal that is self-defense.

The function of Jim Bricknell in *Aaron's Rod* is to illustrate the utter failure to be self-sufficient. He is a "baby" with a "bellyache for love." (53) He wants to be made whole by love: "If only somebody loved me," he complains. "If only somebody loved me I should be all right. I'm going to pieces." (48) "I shall die," he says, "only love brings [life] back.... I feel myself restored in the middle—right here! I feel the energy back again." (74-75) But Lilly tells him, "it's nothing but love and self-sacrifice makes you feel you're losing your life." He means "self-sacrifice" literally, for Jim wants to lose himself in sexual love, as in the vague love-ideal of Christianity. Lilly condemns all forms of selflessness. "You want to go from passion to passion," he tells Aaron, "from ecstasy to ecstasy, from triumph to triumph, till you can whoosh away into glory, beyond yourself, all bonds loosened and happily ever after. Either that or Nirvana, the opposite side of the medal." (285) One must seek, according to Lilly, to confirm and articulate the self, not seek to obliterate it.

Yet Lilly-Lawrence's insistence on solipsism leaves him in a cul-de-sac. In previous novels the self requires women as the Other, to create and maintain it. Yet in *Aaron's Rod* contact with women is dangerous, and Lawrence would have the self stand alone. However there must be an Other. Consequently Lilly (or Lawrence) does not abandon all attempt at relationship, he simply substitutes man for woman as Other. Lilly makes Jim Bricknell and Aaron his disciples.

In *Aaron's Rod* the dynamic of a relationship between man and woman is "love"; between man and man it is "power." "There are only two great dynamic urges in *life*," Lilly says, "love and power." (284) Either "you want to love, or to be obeyed." "Love," because it involves depending on woman, destroys the self. According to Lilly the love urge which now binds society is worn out, and become a "bottomless pit" that swallows one's being up. The alternative Lilly chooses is "power," a mode of relationship where the self is not in danger of invasion.

The notion of "power" is central in Lilly's (and Lawrence's) so-called fascism. Lilly is a reformer with a horror of masses, as apparently is Lawrence: "as for myself," he writes in *Fantasia*, "I have a horror of riding *en bloc*." (96) The dislike arises out of a threat to the self. The many references to democracy in *Studies in Classic American Literature* show aversion to the "masses" and the "mush" of a self mingled in them. "It sounds as though [the self] had all leaked out of you, leaked into the universe." (165) "ONE IDENTITY! chants Democratic En Masse,... oblivious of the corpses under the wheels." (167) The nucleus of Lilly's (and Lawrence's) eminently unviable power politics is an emotional one-to-one relationship between men, based on obedience.[7]

Aaron's Rod and *Kangaroo* are often referred to as Lawrence's "political novels," but their politics are more symbolic than otherwise. The novels do not contain social programmes; they are not studies of society so much as they are poems in which "society" objectifies an inner state.[8] They are studies of primitive thinking, and that on the elemental level of self preservation. Man resolves to take some "further purpose, some passionate purposive activity" in society, in order to keep woman in line, and control her "love-craving" that "will run on to frenzy and disaster." "Woman's sensual individualism," says Lawrence in *Fantasia*, "draws man away from social purpose." (157,215) But in Lawrence the "social purpose" man seeks is rarely if ever evident as anything except meeting with groups of men, where the one-to-one relationship is the *raison d'être* of the gathering. This *blutbrüderschaft* is the crux of Lawrence's "social" and "political" thought of this period. "The mystery of manly love," Lawrence writes in the essay on Whitman, "the love of comrades.

Over and over he [Whitman, but it applies to Lawrence] says the same thing: the new world will be built on the love of comrades, the new great dynamic of life will be manly love. Out of this manly love will come the inspiration of the future." (SCAL, 168) Manly love is Lawrence's attempt to supplant women.

In essence the *blutbrüderschaft* is a means to create the sense of self. It is based on "power," and in *Aaron's Rod"* "power" is one man's ability to command the obedience of another because of his "greater soul." "Men must submit to the greater soul in man, for their guidance," Lilly instructs Aaron. (289) The leader is an aristocrat whose superiority arises out of his self-sufficiency: "Obey the man in whom you recognize the Holy Ghost," Lawrence writes, and by "Holy Ghost" he means completeness and integrity of being. "You've never got to deny the Holy Ghost which is inside you," Lilly says, "your own soul's self." (286) Thus "power" is a synonym for self-sufficiency, because power is wholeness:

> The urge of power does not seek for happiness any more than for any other state. It urges from within, darkly, for the displacing of the old leaves, the inception of the new. It is powerful and self-central, not seeking its centre outside, in some God or some beloved, but acting indomitably from within itself. (288)

Lilly embodies the power urge precisely because he is detached. A sort of Buddha, he is self-centered and independent: the "greater soul."

In previous Lawrence novels man derives his being from woman. She seems, at least to man, to possess a "life-centrality" and wholeness that he does not. Lilly and Aaron ruefully acknowledge her as "woman, the life-bearer, the life-source." (155) Her superiority stems not only from the fact that she can bear children,[9] but from her power to create (or destroy) man's being. *Aaron's Rod* presumes a Christian matriarchy where woman devours man as sacramental Christ-communion.

> Why of course, in our long-drawn-out Christian day, man is given and woman is recipient. Man is the gift, woman the receiver. This is the sacrament we live by; the holy communion we live for. That man gives himself to woman in an utter and sacred abandon, all, all, all himself given, and taken. Woman, eternal woman, she is the communicant. She receives the sacramental body and spirit of the man. (162)

Lawrence's "historical" matriarchy is a projection of the belief that women creates (or destroys) man's being. He depends on her "love" to create him. But by substituting power for love as a dynamic mode, Lawrence attempts to deny woman her centrality, and to reverse the paradigm. If men submit to the greater man for guidance, then "women must submit to the positive power soul in man for their being." (289) It is not her "subservience" that Lilly foresees. "No slavery," he says, but "a deep unfathomable submission ... woman will submit, livingly, not subjectedly." (289) That is, she will depend on man for her sense of her self, not, as now is the case, he depends on her. Her "submission" is not "slavery" because ego-dependence is outside the realm of volition: it is the utter dependence of necessity.

Thus the bid for "power" in *Aaron's Rod* is man's attempt to usurp woman's wholeness and her influence over his being, by putting an end to "love," which is his need for her to create him, and substituting "power," which is his own wholeness and independence that imitates hers. Since it would deny woman as Other, *Aaron's Rod* must find new metaphors for self. The self is no longer created and recreated in coitus, as it was in *The Rainbow*. Nor does the self arise out of the balance between man and woman, as in *Women in Love*. Nor is it created and confirmed by "social purpose," since one function of the myth of the matriarchy in Lawrence is to feminize society and make it inimical to man. In *Aaron's Rod* one's being is shored up against the onslaught of woman-love by self-aggrandizement, which takes the form of male-glorification, for the self is now seen as male.

The self is objectified in the body of man. In previous novels the female body provided the crucial images of the self as something gestated and born; in *Aaron's Rod* male supremacy is self-supremacy, for the male body represents the self that stands alone. It is ironic (but perhaps predictable) that a novel so marred by disease should take for its center, both literal and figurative, the physically flawless young male body, Michelangelo's David. In this marble Aaron sees his ideal self.

"True myth concerns itself centrally with the onward adventure of the integral soul," Lawrence writes. (SCAL, 62) *Aaron's Rod* thus concerns itself with Aaron's journey to wholeness, which he finds in a male subculture in Florence, "a city of men." Before Aaron can find his new independent self he must lose his old, an event described in organic imagery reminiscent of *The Rainbow*.

> Having in some curious manner tumbled from the tree of modern knowledge, and cracked and rolled out from the shell of the preconceived idea of himself like some dark, night-lustrous chest-

> nut from the green ostensibility of the burr, [Aaron] lay as it were exposed but invisible on the floor, knowing, but making no conceptions.... Now that he was finally unmasked and exposed, the accepted idea of himself cracked and rolled aside like a broken chestnut burr, the mask split and shattered, he was at last quiet and free.

As it is used in the novel, without context, conviction or power, this organic imagery bears little relation to the development of Aaron's whole self. For the most part his self is expressed in images of physical maleness. Having shucked his artificial social identity, Aaron is nothing until he arrives in Florence. "Florence seemed to start a new man in him. It was a town of men." (208) "Here men had been at their intensest, most naked pitch, here, at the end of the old world and the beginning of the new. Since then, always rather puling and apologetic." In Florence maleness and self become one and the same.

The center of the book is the center of the city, the Piazza della Signoria, where stands Michelangelo's David. Aaron finds "one of the world's living centres, here, in the Piazza della Signoria. The sense of having arrived—of having reached a perfect centre of the human world; this he had." In Aaron's epiphany there are two things evident; one is that his new self arises out of maleness. The Piazza is "packed with men: but all, all men." That Aaron feels "a new self, a new life-urge rising inside himself," is Lawrence's attempt to substitute male generative power (erection) for female (birth) in creation of the self. But this masculine imagery is overshadowed by images of centrality; the Piazza gives Aaron precisely that sense of self-containment and self-centrality that he earlier attributed to woman with her "life-centrality." The essence of woman is her self-sufficiency, from which her power to create springs, and it is this essence that the male in *Aaron's Rod* would take from her for his own. David, the "genius of Florence," is "the white, self-conscious, physical adolescent." (207) Standing foward against the dark undifferentiated background he symbolizes the self alone, "manly virtue, which stands alone and accepts limits." (SCAL, 80) In the image of David, Aaron is recreated.

Male aggrandizement develops logically into homosexuality, but the homosexuality in *Aaron's Rod* (like the fascism in the novel) is much more a symbol of self than it is an erotic gesture. Lawrence's homosexuality is an attempt to define and reinforce one's being. The "David and Jonathan" relationship, as he calls it, gets at least cursory mention in every novel, beginning with

"The Poem of Friendship" in *The White Peacock*. Siegmund has a double, Hampson, in *The Trespassers*. Paul Morel establishes an alliance with his antithesis, Baxter Dawes. Tom Brangwen mentions a school chum who was one of the most important relations in his life. Birkin is Abel to Gerald's Cain, David to his Jonathan. This "homoeroticism" as Lawrence describes it, is narcissistic, and for that reason an act of self-definition.[10]

> I believe [a certain poet] would have loved a man, more than a woman: even physically: like the ancients did. I believe it is because most women don't leave scope to the man's imagination—but I don't know. I should like to know why every man that approached greatness tends to homosexuality, whether he admits it or not: so that he loves the *body* of a man better than the body of a woman— ... I believe a man projects his own image on another man, like a mirror. But from a woman he wants himself reborn, reconstructed. (CL, 250)

The relationship between a David and a Jonathan defines the self also because it is inclusive. Invariably one male is sensual, one spiritual; one "masculine," one "feminine"; the alter ego is a complement who provides what the self lacks. The relationship is an attempt to integrate the two halves of a single personality, an act which would make one whole. Thus Aaron's being is confirmed by Rawdon Lilly, his alter ego. The two men are complements: Lilly is analytical, verbal, asexual; Aaron is physical, emotional. The two are "like brothers," and Lilly quips, "Save for my job—which is to write lies—Aaron and I are two identical little men in one and the same little boat." (105) (By extension, if Aaron is Lawrence escaping from his working-class past, Lilly is Lawrence the successful litterateur.) Lilly wants Aaron "livingly to yield to a more heroic soul," meaning his own, and Aaron can either "die" or "yield." That is, he can, without Lilly, be only nonexistent; or he can, with Lilly, be whole through "life-submission" to him.

The difficulty with Lawrence's homosexual metaphor is that it comes full circle. Beginning as an attempt to exist without women, it nevertheless ends as an imitation of them. This is readily apparent in the nature of Aaron and Lilly's ménage in Florence, where Lilly is "as efficient and unobtrusive as any woman" darning her husband's socks, and Aaron is the surly spouse. (93) Lilly chastises Aaron:

> "You talk to me like a woman, Aaron."
> "How do you talk to *me*, do you think?"
> "How do I?"
> "Are the potatoes done?"

The parody reaches grotesque proportions with a mock delivery. Aaron languishes in childbed: "there was no getting anything definite out of the sick man—his soul seemed stuck, as if it would not move." (90) Lilly rubs him with oil, "as mothers do their babies whose bowels don't work." He is the midwife to Aaron's bowel-movement "baby," and the couvade signifies the birth of Aaron's new soul. "The spark had come back into the sick eyes, and the faint trace of a smile, faintly luminous, into the face. Aaron was regaining himself." (91) Later on, after Aaron has lost his flute and found a new identity that does not depend on women, he is again in childbed. "But here you are," Lilly chides him, "in bed like a woman who's had a baby. You're all right, are you?" (280) Both times Aaron, with help from Lilly, has given birth to his new self.

These imitations of motherhood in the alter-ego relationship indicate that in spite of the attempt to exclude women and substitute man alone, the terms of being in Lawrence are still in large part feminine. That is, the self is born of woman—or, barring that, born of man who is imitating woman. In this respect *Aaron's Rod* presents a concept of self which is essentially that of the rite of passage. The novel is a fantasy in which men undo the power of women: Aaron loses his woman-defined self through a mock death at Lilly's "men's house," and he is reborn through men into an exclusively male society. Yet, also like a rite of passage, the novel represents no true emancipation. Its attempt to discredit the birth power of women only pays such power greater homage.

In *Kangaroo*, however, Lawrence does succeed in divesting men of the need for women, and in achieving for men a true solipsism. The rite of passage becomes the central theme of the novel. Ben Cooley, or "Kangaroo," is an Australian revolutionary leader who wants to put an English writer, Richard Lovat Somers, in an undefined quasi-messianic place in his religious-political movement. Kangaroo is a composite figure, a hermaphrodite who incorporates what is most appealing, and at the same time most threatening, in both mother and father. He calls himself "her-me," and to the point.

Kangaroo's politics are a brand of benevolent paternalism based on the personal appeal of the father. "Man again needs a father," he says, "a quiet, gentle father who uses his authority in the name of living life, and who is absolutely stern against anti-life. I offer no creed. I offer myself." (111) Kangaroo would be a "Jehovah-like" leader, (108) "a patriarch, or a pope representing as near as possible the wise, subtle spirit of life." (110) Yet phys-

ically Kangaroo resembles a woman, with his maternal body
which seems "beautiful, to Somers—one might love it, intensely,
every one of its contours, its roundnesses and downward-
drooping heaviness." (112) Kangaroo displays the faceless immo-
bility, the massive prone hips and belly of an earth mother. "He
lay there rolled in his chair, with his face almost buried in soft
leather, and his big hips sticking out. . . . He swung round in his
chair, swinging his heavy hips over and lying sideways." (121)
He is like a mother to Somers in that his presence is "so warm.
You felt you were cuddled cosily, like a child, on his breast, in
the soft glow of his heart and that your feet were nestling on his
ample, beautiful 'tummy.' " (117) Several times Somers checks
his desire to touch Kangaroo, especially to lay his hand on the
other man's stomach. (136) In effect Kangaroo is the oedipal
mother, who combines the worst traits of both parents and ultimately tries to destroy her son.[11]

As always in Lawrence, the mother's weapon is "love." Kangaroo's new politics are based on love for mate and fellow man.
But Kangaroo's "love" for Somers is warmth that masks willfulness. He has "only to turn on all the levers and forces of his
clever, almost fiendishly subtle will, and he could triumph. And
he knew it." (108) As woman's love is destructive in *Aaron's Rod*,
so Kangaroo's principle of universal Love is a form of aggression.
Of humanity, " 'I *love* them,' he shouted, in a voice suddenly
become loud and passionate. 'I love them. I *love* you, you woman
born of man, I do, and I defy you to prevent me.' " (120) Kangaroo will overwhelm with "love" anyone who opposes him, and
engulf their being. "You're too much like Abraham's bosom,"
Harriet Somers tells him. "One would feel nowhere." (117)

Kangaroo as the apostle of Love in the abstract has as a pre-
decessor Jim Bricknell, in *Aaron's Rod*.

> "Don't you think love and sacrifice are the finest things in life?"
> said Jim. . . . I think [Love] is, Love and only love," said Jim. "I
> think the greatest joy is sacrificing one's self to love."
> "To *someone* you love, you mean," said Tanny.
> "No, I don't. I don't mean someone at all. I mean love—love—
> love.
> "But you can't sacrifice yourself to an abstract principle," said
> Tanny.
> "That's just what you can do. And that's the beauty of it. Who
> represents the principle doesn't matter. Christ is the principle of
> love," said Jim.
> "But no!" said Tanny."It *must* be more individual. How can you
> sacrifice yourself to an abstraction?"
> "Ha, I think Love and your Christ detestable," said Lilly. "A
> sheer ignominy." (72-73)

Kangaroo's love is oppressive because it is Love in the abstract, which denies individuality. "Don't love me," Somers complains to him. "Don't want to save mankind. You're so awfully *general*, and your love is so awfully general: as if one were a cherry in the syrup. Don't love me. Don't want me to love you. Let's be hard, separate men." (213) Kangaroo, like the mother in Lawrence, has the power to annihilate her son by denying his existence. ("Either you are with me," Kangaroo tells Somers, "and I *feel* you are with me: or you cease to exist for me." [213]) But Somers wants to escape "the white octopus of love," (344) and be his own man.

Instead of submitting to Kangaroo, Somers rejects him. At a political meeting the leader is shot in the belly (significantly), and he pines and dies because Somers will not say he loves him. His dying words are "you've killed me. You've killed me, Lovat." (343) Despite a superficially realistic presentation, *Kangaroo* has a strong undercurrent of mythic pattern and primitive fantasy. Essentially the novel is a rite of passage like Aaron's Rod, but it is a rite that fails. Somers, like Australia, should be reborn through Kangaroo; but Somers will not cooperate, as Australia will not, and the "child" is not forthcoming. The "mother" dies in childbirth, and Kangaroo's death represents the existential power of women to create man, symbolically and finally smashed.[12]

Kangaroo would keep Somers a child; the leader calls him "like a child. I know that is part of the charm of your nature, that you are naive like a child. But sometimes you are childish rather than childlike. A perverse child." (210) "But man, you are *perverse*," Kangaroo bellows; "what's the matter with you?" (211) "You are a dear boy, in spite of yourself," he tells Somers. "Oh yes, you are. There's some demon inside you makes you perverse, and won't let you be the dear, beautiful thing you are. But I'm going to exorcise that demon." (135) Somers gives "a short laugh, the very voice of the demon speaking." It is Somers' "devilish" perverseness, objectified as his "demon," that enables him to break free of Kangaroo.

Somers' demon is both his separate self in resistance and his manhood; they are the same. " 'You see,' said Somers, trying hard to be fair, 'what you call my demon is what I identify myself with. It's my best me, and I stick with it. I think love, all this love of ours, is a devilish thing now: a slow poison.' " (136) Somers' demon is related to his dark god, who "enters us from below, not from above."

94

> Kangaroo sat bunched up like some creature watching round-eyed out of a darker corner.
>
> "How do you mean, enters us from below?" he barked.
>
> "Not through the spirit. Enters us from the lower self, the dark self, the phallic self, if you like."
>
> "Enters us from the phallic self?" snapped Kangaroo sharply.
>
> "Sacredly. The god you can never see or visualize, who stands dark on the threshold of the phallic me."
>
> "The phallic you, my dear young friend, what is that but love?"
>
> Richard shook his head in silence.
>
> "No," he said, in a slow, remote voice. "I know your love, Kangaroo. Working everything from the spirit, from the head. You work the lower self as an instrument of the spirit. Now it is time for the spirit to leave us again; it is time for the Son of Man to depart, and leave us dark, in front of the unspoken God: who is just beyond the dark threshold of the lower self, my lower self. There is a great God on the threshold of my lower self, whom I fear while he is my glory. And the spirit goes out like a spent candle." (134)

Somers' dark god is his primitive self: his libido (for want of a better word). Thus he, returning rebellious from his quarrel with Kangaroo—and therefore reaffirmed as a man—considers seducing a neighbor. "Somers looked at her quickly, a smile round his eyes, and a curious, smiling devil inside them, cold as ice." (139) He is in "a devil of a temper...a wicked, fiendish mood that made him *look* quite handsome...And at this moment she was fascinated, and when she said, in her slightly contralto voice: 'You're not in a temper with *me*, though, are you Mr. Somers?' She was so comely, like a maiden just ready for love, and like a comely, desirous virgin offering herself to the wayfarer, in the name of the god of bright desire." Somers feels "weaponlike desire. He knew it. The god Bacchus. Iacchos! Iacchos! Bacchanals with weapon hands." (142)

For Lawrence the part of the self given over to primitive drives and impulses is seen as a male. Conversely, the civilized self, the superego is feminine. Thus to Kangaroo, since he is essentially the repressive mother, Somers' demon seems dangerous and animalistic. "I can see there is a beast in the way," he replies to Somers' discourse on the "great gods." "There is a beast in your eyes, Lovat, and if I can't conquer him then—woe-betide you, my dear. But I love you, you see." (136) The contest between Kangaroo and Somers' demon is again the struggle between male sexuality and feminine repression that occurs in most of Lawrence's novels. At least one character in *The White Peacock*, in *Sons and Lovers*, and in *Women in Love* succumbs to a woman who attacks his sexuality.

Somers rejects the man-to-man relationship that was the crucial existential relationship in *Aaron's Rod*. He will not participate in the absurd and brutal games of the diggers and refuses Jack Calcott's sticky offer of "mate" love.

> All his life he had cherished a beloved ideal of friendship— David and Jonathan. And now, when true and good friends offered, he found he simply could not commit himself, even to simple friendship. The whole trend of this affection, this mingling, this intimacy, this truly beautiful love, he found his soul just set against it.... He didn't want a friend... Not mates and equality and mingling. Not blood-brotherhood. None of that.
> What else? He didn't know.... Perhaps the thing that the dark races know. (104-105)

"What a holy horror man-and-man love would be," Somers thinks, "mates or comrades." (201) When Calcott embraces Somers, it is "a tense moment for Richard Lovat. He looked at the dark sea, and thought of his own everlasting gods, and felt the other man's body next to his." (89) He opts for his own "everlasting gods," and the "sweetness of everlasting aloneness." (335) In effect Somers can reject Calcott, as he can reject Kangaroo, because Lawrence internalizes the male alter ego of *Aaron's Rod* as Somers' demon. Through his dark gods Somers achieves existential self-sufficiency and perfect solipsism.

Somers is torn between different kinds of relationship—to Kangaroo, to Calcott and to his wife Harriet—and attempts to reject them all. When Somers rejects Kangaroo's philosophy of love, Lawrence in effect rejects his own earlier attitudes on love relationships. Kangaroo says,

> "All that man ever has created or ever will create, while he remains man, has been created in the inspiration and by the force of love. And not only man—all the living creatures are swayed to creation, to new creation, to the creation of song and beauty and lovely gesture, by love... I believe the sun's attraction for the earth is a form of love... Love is mutual. Each attracts the other. But in natural love each tries at the same time to withhold the other, to keep the other true to its own beloved nature. To any true lover, it would be the greatest disaster if the beloved broke down from her own nature and self and began to identify herself with him, with his nature and self.... The earth and the sun, on their plane, have discovered a perfect equilibrium. But man has not yet begun... Man has loved the beloved for the sake of love, so far, but rarely, rarely has he *consciously* known that he could only love her for her own separate, strange self: forever strange and a joyful mystery to him." (133)

Somers (or Lawrence) denies this. He repudiates the infinite generation of *The Rainbow* and the stellar equilibrium of *Women in Love*. He wants his dark gods to make him independent of his wife, who appraises the situation critically.

> He had nothing but her, absolutely. And that was why, presumably, he wanted to establish this ascendency over her, assume this arrogance. And so that he could refute her, deny her, and imagine himself a unique male. He *wanted* to be male and unique, like a freak of a phoenix. (177)

His dark god would permit him to stand alone by providing an existential Other. The God is seen, as was woman previously, as a generative power because it creates the self. "The purest lesson our era has taught is that man, at his highest, is an individual, single isolate, alone, in direct soul-communication with the unknown God, which prompts within him." (307-308)

Somers-Lawrence now insists that the source of being is male:

> he, this self-same Richard . . . must open the door of his soul and let in a dark Lord and Master for himself, the dark god he had sensed outside the door. Let him once truly submit to the dark majesty, break open his doors to this fearful god who is master, and enters us from below, the lower doors; let himself once admit a Master, the unspeakable god: and the rest would happen. (178)

Thus man's self-sufficiency and the dominance that follows from it stem from the fact that there is "in him also the mystery and lordship—of Hermes, if you like—but the mystery and lordship of the forward-seeking male." (176)

Yet Hermes, who was Gerald Crich's dark god as he is now Somers', has in *Kangaroo* more overtones of hermaphrodism than of male sexuality. The allegorical bark of Somers' marriage is rechristened "Hermes," ostensibly to signify Richard's mystic "lordship." But the name contains "*her* and *me*," as Lovat points out; and his attempt at masterdom is likewise hermaphroditic.

Somers submits to the dark god in him who is "Lord and Master for himself" as passively as a woman receiving a lover. Admittedly a "she-man," Somers plays the woman to his own male self. He is "forced to recognise the devil in his own belly. . . . nothing conjured away that bellyful of black devilishness with which he was *enciente*. He really felt like a woman who is with child by a corrosive fiend. In his lower man, just girning [sic] and demoniacal." (165) He notes "the long gestation of the soul within a man, and the final parturition, the birth of a new way of knowledge, the new God-influx. . . . only the dark god in [Harriet] answering the dark god in me has got my soul heavy and fecund with a new sort of infant. But even now I can't bring it forth." (272)

As in *Aaron's Rod,* man imitates the birth power of woman to bring forth his new self. Thus the death of Kangaroo enables Somers to give birth to himself, and he feels "such a pain in his stomach, as if something were torn there. . . . the torn feeling at the pit of his stomach was so strong, he sat down and shoved his fists in his abdomen."

> So he lay down, and at length fell into a sort of semi-conscious-ness, still pressing his fists into his abdomen, and feeling as he imagined a woman might feel after her first child, as if something had been ripped out of him.

And again, as in *Aaron's Rod,* this imitation is an attempt to in-corporate both genders and so be self-sufficient. But in Kangaroo the alter ego of the previous novel becomes one's demon or dark gods, and the birth metaphor is all but abandoned.

In *Kangaroo* the character closest approximating Somers' alter ego, or demon, is William James Trewhella, or "Jaz." With him Somers feels "a strange, different bond of sympathy" that is "hardly sympathy at all, but an ancient sort of root knowledge." (129) This affinity is Somers' recognition of Jaz as part of himself, for Jaz is the id incarnate. "I like him," Somers says. "He lives by himself and keeps himself dark—which is his nature." (60) Jaz is inimical to civilization. He, like his counterpart John Thomas, is identified with the ancient race of Cornwall, "the place of the pre-Christian human sacrifice."

> Human sacrifice! [Somers] could feel his dark, blood-consciousness tingle with it again, the desire of it, the mystery of it. Old pre-sences, old awful presences round the black moor-edge, in the thick dusk, as the sky of light was pushed pulsing upwards, away. Then an owl would fly and hoot, and Richard lay with his soul departed back, back into the blood-sacrificial pre-world, and the sun-mystery, and the moon-power, and the mistletoe on the tree, away from his own white world, his own white, conscious day. (243)

Jaz has the primitive "Celtic" consciousness that is "nearer the magic of the animal world." (210) He, like the dark gods, is iden-tified with sensual maleness.

Yet in *Kangaroo* this sensual maleness is not so much physical as it is transcendental—or rather, descendental. Somers describes the god of the old religions as "phallic," the God from whom the dark sensual passion for love emanates, not only the spiritual love of Christ. [Somers] wanted men once more to refer the sensual passion of love sacredly to the great dark God, the ithyphallic, of the first dark religions. And how could that be done, when each dry little ego was just mechanically set against any such dark flow, such ancient submission [to] the first, dark ithyphallic God whom men had once known so tremendous. (205)

However the god's phallicism is not expressed in male sexual activity. Somers, for instance, rejects the chance to seduce Victoria Calcott because "flashes of desire for a visual object would no longer carry him into action. He had no use for them." (143) He chooses to worship the drive in himself, rather than its object.[13] In doing so he transforms sexuality beyond the need for physical manifestation or connection. His phallicism is a turning within, "a downslope into Orcus, and a vast sacred phallic darkness, where one was enveloped into the greater god as into an Egyptian darkness. He would meet there or nowhere. To visual travesty he would lend himself no more." In effect Somers' descent into the "vast phallic sacred darkness" is a descent into his own unconscious. His "phallic" self is a region of his being that is ultimately antecedent to gender.

The unconscious is objectified as Australia—itself "down under"—an atavistic continent "void of speech." (352) The bush resists civilization as though it were consciousness: "was the land awake? Would the people waken this ancient land, or would the land put them to sleep, drift them back into the torpid semi-consciousness of the world of twilight." (180) It is "the previous world. . . . that had waited, it seemed, since the coal age. . . . What was the good of trying to be an alert conscious man here? You couldn't. Drift, drift into a sort of obscurity, backwards into a nameless past, hoary as the country is hoary. Strange old feelings wake in the soul: old, non-human feelings." (179) Australia is a state of vegetative awareness in which one "drifts back, becomes darkly half vegetable, devoid of pre-occupations. Even the never-slumbering urge of sex sinks down into something darker, more monotonous, incapable of caring: like sex in trees. The dark world before conscious responsibility was born." (180)

Australia is much like Jaz Trewhella, in that remoteness and treachery are their main characteristics. Somers feels that the "aboriginal daimon" of Australia (his unconscious) has entered his body so that sleep is "almost a pain, and too full of dreams." (143) He dreams that Australia overwhelms him.

But the dream had been just this. He was standing in the living-room at Coo-ee, bending forward doing some little thing by the couch, perhaps folding the newspaper, making the room tidy at the last moment before going to bed, when suddenly a violent darkness came over him, he felt his arms pinned, and he heard a man's voice speaking mockingly behind him, with a laugh. It was as if he saw the man's face too—a stranger, a round, strong sort of Australian. And he realized with horror: 'Now they have put a sack over my head, and fastened my arms, and I am in the dark, and they are going to steal my little brown handbag from the bedroom, which contains all the money we have' (144)

Likewise Jaz is a "traitor."

"You seem very thick with Trewhella," said Kangaroo [to Somers] at last.

"Not thick," said Richard. "Celts—Cornish—Irish—they always interest me. What do you imagine is at the bottom of Jaz?"

"Treachery."

"Oh, not only," laughed Somers.

"Then why do you ask me if you know better?"

"Because I don't really get to the bottom of him."

"There is no bottom to get to—he's the instinctive traitor, as they all are."

"Oh, surely not only that."

"I see nothing else. They would like the white civilization to be trampled underfoot piecemeal. And at the same time they live on us like parasites." Kangaroo glowered fiercely.

"There's something more," replied Richard. "They don't believe in our gods, in our ideals. They remember older gods, older ideals, different gods." (209)

The "older gods"—like the unconscious—cannot be trusted by the civilized self.

When the gods "come through the gate" of consciousness "they are personified," Lawrence writes, as Thor, Bacchus, Venus, and others. "But outside the gate it is one dark God, the unknown. And the Unknown is a terribly jealous God, and vengeful." (291) He is Moloch, Astafte, Ashtaroth, and Baal, a "hell-god." The unconscious is the "God of vengeance" because it is repressed. "The god is the mysterious life-suggestion, tapping for admission. And the wondrous Victorian Age managed to fasten the door so tight, and light up the compound so brilliantly with electric light, that really there *was* no outside, it was all in." (290) The revenge of the god who is denied is central in *Kangaroo;* Lawrence elaborates in his demonology the traditional psychoanalytic hypothesis of repression into the unconscious. For

100

this reason the book is dominated by images of eruption and revolution.

Somers' unconscious erupts in dreams, and in the memories of
the chapter "The Nightmare," where his wartime experiences return to him.

> He realized that all the time, since the year 1918, ... deep in his
> unconsciousness had lain this accumulation of black fury and fear,
> like frenzied lava quiescent in his soul. And now it had burst up:
> the fear, then the acute remembrance. So he faced it out, trembling
> with shock and bitterness, every detail. ... why had it all come
> back on him? It had seemed so past, so gone. Why should it sud-
> denly erupt like white-hot lava, to set in hot black rock round the
> wound of his soul? (265)

As a writer, Somers descends often into his unconscious. He sits
"alone with his own soul, alone with his eyes on the darkness
which is the dark god of life. Alone like a pythoness on her
tripod, like the oracle alone above the fissure into the unknown."
(287) He finds "strange, cruel, pregnant words: the new term of
consciousness." "But usually, nowadays, when he tapped his unconscious, he found himself in a seethe of steady fury, general
rage." (164) The chapter " 'Revenge!' Timotheus Cries," as its
title suggests, is likewise about an explosion of subconscious
rage.

The revolution impending in Australia corresponds to the
threat of revolt by the unconscious and the instincts. Kangaroo
(the super-ego) says that "the greatest danger to the world today
is anarchy, not bolshevism. It is anarchy and unrule that are coming on us—and that is what I, as an order-loving Jew and one of
the half-chosen people, do not want." (211) Lovat wants "chaos."
The other man calls him "like a wayward child!" (211) "You are
such a fool, Lovat, that you can't see that once you break the last
restraints on humanity today, it is the end. It is the end. Once
burst the flood-gates, and you'll never get the water back under
control. Never."

In *Kangaroo* the cosmos itself reflects revolt. A newspaper arti-
cle transcribed into the chapter "Volcanic Evidence" announces
that the earth threatens to erupt. "EARTHQUAKES/Is Australia
Safe?/Sleeping Volcanoes." (167) Somers reads this "almost thrill-
ing bit" of journalism "with satisfaction. If mother earth herself
is so unstable, and upsets the apple-cart without caring a straw,
why, what can a man say to himself if he *does* happen to have a
devil in his belly!" (170) Lawrence juxtaposes this seismological
upheaval to Somers' contention that "the day of the absolute is

101

over, and we're in for the strange gods once more." (149) Hope for an apocalypse is never far from the surface in *Kangaroo*.

The closest the novel approaches cataclysm is the tropical storm that culminates the Somers' stay in Australia. It blasts the land for three days; "darkness raging in waters around [,] it was like the end of the world." (357) The ocean destroys the beach: "Richard tried to walk under the cliffs, but the whole shore was ruined, changed: a whole mass of new rocks, a chaos of heaped boulders, a gurgle of rushing, clayey water, and heaps of collapsed earth." (360) The "malevolence of this ocean" (361) frightened Somers, and what was previously his own symbol for himself—his element, if you like—becomes "a cold, dark, inhospitable sea." (367)

The ocean is a central symbol in *Kangaroo,* one which reflects Lawrence's evolving concept of self. To Somers it first signifies his freedom from the entanglements of life on land. When he is faced with Jack Calcott's stifling affection, he wants to "be cold, cold and alone like a single fish, with no feeling in his heart at all except a certain icy exultance." (124) The sea comes to stand for his solipsism, the "icily self-sufficient vigor of a fish." When faced with Kangaroo's "love," Somers wants "to get out of this lit-up cloy of humanity, and the exhaust of love, and the fretfulness of desire. Why not swing away into cold separation? ... Why not break the bond and be single, take a fierce swoop and a swing back, as when a gannet plunges like a white metallic arrow into the sea." (137) Somers wants the "vertebral consciousness" of fishes because it is "pre-mental" consciousness, which he sees as perfect solipsism. "The fish is absolutely stone-wall limited in its consciousness, to itself. It knows no other." (305) Somers spends much of his time alone by the sea, where he once watches dolphins flash out "from the foamy horror of the land." (336) Kangaroo is his "last embrace with humanity. Now, all he wanted was to cut himself clear. To be clear of humanity altogether, to be alone." (271) He wants "to turn to the old dark gods, who had waited so long in the outer dark." These gods of his unconscious are objectified in the sea, "the sea of his own inward soul, his own unconscious faith, over which his will had no exercise." (154) Thus much of *Kangaroo* takes place by the edge of the sea; the shore signifies the boundary between conscious and unconscious states, the transition between which always holds great fascination for Lawrence.

When Somers communes with the sea he communes with his own unconscious—his Other—and thereby creates and sustains himself. Thus the image of the unconscious as an inexhaustible sea of life replaces the image of birth from woman in Lawrence's psychology of the self. Somers' individuality is given him by the sea. This is the significance of the seashells that he brings the dying Kangaroo; they are his integral self alone, which Kangaroo does not understand or respect. Somers presents the shells to Kangaroo as if they were his self.

> And very slowly[Kangaroo] began to look at the shells, one by one. There were black ones like buds of coal, and black ones with a white spiral thread, and funny knobbly black and white ones, and tiny purple ones ... and then those that Richard had put in, worn shells like sea ivory, marvellous substance, with all the structure showing: spirals like fairy staircases, and long, pure phallic pieces that were the centres of big shell. ... Richard liked these especially.
>
> Kangaroo looked at them briefly, one by one, as if they were bits of uninteresting printed paper.
>
> "Here, take them away," he said, pushing the box aside. And his face had a faint spot of pink on the cheek.
>
> "They may amuse you some time when you are alone," said Richard apologetically.
>
> "They make me know I have never been born," said Kangaroo, huskily. (329-330)

The presence of the God is expressed in images of flowing: "the sensitive influx of the dark," and the "new God-influx." (272) Into Somers' being surges "a new flood of the God-darkness, the living unutterable" that is "ever-present living darkness inexhaustible and unknowable."

Lawrence insures man's self-sufficiency by making the unconscious a supra-individual power that becomes a fountain-head of life. Thus Somers survives Kangaroo as well as Calcott, because his manhood becomes more than mortal and more than his own. It is deified as the dark God, a source of infinite power. "The only thing is the God who is the source of all passion," he says. "Once go down before the God-passion and human passions take the right rhythm." (202) The great God stabilizes, and giving centrality gives life: "because," Somers continues, "without the polarized God-passion to hold [men] stable at the centre, break down they would. With no deep God who is the source of all passion and life to hold them separate and yet sustained in accord, the loving comrades would smash one another, and smash all love, all feeling as well." (202)

The "unknowable darkness" in the universe of *Kangaroo* is called "all the God and the gods," both. (241) Essentially it is the dark god of Somers' unconscious in *Kangaroo* that gives rise to the notion of a great God that exists independent of individuals and has the power to generate life in them. In this respect Lawrence's religion-cum-psychology is much like that of the transcendentalists of the last century, who gave the individual unconscious its apotheosis as the World Soul. The Oversoul (and the dark God) is thought to be infinite because unknowable. Like the unconscious represented by Somers' Australian sea, the World Soul is an oceanic cosmic unconsciousness. And "every *living* soul," says Lawrence, "is a well-head to this darkness of the living unutterable." (271) With Lawrence's God, as with the Oversoul, insofar as every individual reflects it in little in his unconscious, so he participates in it.

As a strategy for self-sufficiency, the apotheosis of the unconscious as the great God contains a paradox. Perfect solipsism embraces the whole cosmos. As the God is only an externalization of the unconscious, so the realms of the universe become in Lawrence only symbols for regions of inner being. *Kangaroo* and *Aaron's Rod* are confused and inconsistent in their distinction between internal and external, because they represent Lawrence in transition from an external existential system to an internal one. In other words, in the novels he works his way from one that depends on relationship to other people, to one that does not. At the conclusion of *Kangaroo* Somers sails from Australia on an ocean liner. The passengers throw streamers to their friends on land. "One by one the streamers broke and fluttered loose and fell bright and dead on the water . . . the ship inexorably drifted out. . . . the last streamers blowing away, like broken attachments, broken heartstrings." (366) The sailing signifies Lawrence-Somers embarking on the sea of his unconscious, turning within to make an interior journey. *The Plumed Serpent* follows him to Mexico, where Lawrence creates a self-enclosed, all-encompassing universe of one.

5

DEATH AND
THE PLUMED SERPENT

At the center of *The Plumed Serpent*, radiating through it like a dark sun, is the fact of death. From his first novel through *The Rainbow* Lawrence deals with coming into being; with how the self is created through relationship to other individuals, to society, and to nature. The middle novels consider how the self is maintained, first in relationship *(Women in Love)* and then in isolation *(Aaron's Rod, Kangaroo)*. Taking death as its subject, *The Plumed Serpent* completes the unity of the novels, which as a whole describe the history of the self from birth to childhood, adolescence to marriage, maturity to decay. There is, as one would expect, a correspondence between the novels and Lawrence's biography. The fear of physical sickness that so radically affects *Aaron's Rod* and *Kangaroo* disappears in *The Plumed Serpent*, and is replaced by an obsession with death; for when Lawrence wrote the Mexican novel he knew he was dying of tuberculosis. He hemorrhaged, apparently for the first time, in 1924.[1] In Mexico the following year he had a near-fatal illness. "Lawrence himself thought he would die," Frieda wrote. "There, after the great strain of his illness, something broke in me. 'He will never be quite well again, he is ill, he is doomed.' " (Nehls, II, 394)

The disease is reflected in *The Plumed Serpent*. In the "Fourth Hymn" of Quetzalcoatl, which is a hymn of death:

> Lo! I release the dragons! The great white one of the north,
> Him of the disappointed dead, he is lashing you and turning round.
> He is breathing cold corruption upon you, you shall bleed in your chests. (284)

THE ART OF SELF IN D. H. LAWRENCE

The book is one of several ghost stories Lawrence wrote about himself. Not the least of the characters is Joachim Leslie, the heroine's dead husband. Joachim is, like Lawrence himself, "a man fighting for something beyond ordinary life," (75) a crusader whose thankless efforts kill him, and who, dying, tells his wife: "I feel as if I'd brought you to the doors of life, and was leaving you there. . . . But perhaps when I'm dead I shall be able to do more for you than I have done while I was alive." In a sense *The Plumed Serpent* is the first of Lawrence's elegies for himself, as "The Man Who Died" is the last.

In *The Plumed Serpent* death is ubiquitous. The narrative begins with slaughter in a bull-ring, and concludes having recounted more than twenty deaths, most of them murders. Lawrence builds his plot out of assassination and bloody ritual, in which throats are slit and necks are broken; out of spiritual death; and out of metaphysical death: the disintegration of Mexico, and indeed, of the cosmos itself. "There is nothing but death ahead," Kate Leslie realizes, "unless I find something else." (79) Yet the alternative, it seems, is only another kind of dying, the death of her "civilized self." Civilization is disintegrating in a sort of reverse Bergsonian evolution. America is the "death continent," (83) where "the white man's Dead Sea consciousness," (68) comprised of "will' and "sensation" has as its counterpart in deterioration the "downdragging black fatality" of the Mexican psyche. Kate soon abandons her European companions and Mexico City, only to find that "this all-encroaching dragon of the horror of Mexico" (85) pulls her down with "a slow reptilian insistence." (77) Lawrence reiterates the "death-obsession of the Mexican land and people"; he dwells on the "dark-fingered quietness of death" in the natives, "and the mystic presence of death in their voices." (85) Mexico is a country whose cry is *"Viva la muerte!,"* (41) an "entombed" nation with a "dead god," Jesus. (148) It is a wasteland over which the protagonists labor, with their new religion, as if to revive a corpse.

Lawrence's tone is generally melancholy, and oftentimes downright morbid. In the "Fourth Hymn" of Quetzalcoatl the earth is a vision of hell:

> For I tell you, there are no dead dead, not even your dead.
> There are dead that sleep in the waves of the Morning Star with freshening limbs.
> There are dead that weep in bitter rains.
> There are dead that cluster in the frozen north, shuddering and chattering among the ice

And howling with hate.
There are dead that creep through the burning bowels of the earth,
Stirring the fires to acid of bitterness.
There are dead that sit under the trees, watching with ash-grey eyes
    for their victims.
There are dead that attack the sun like swarms of black flies to
    suck his life.
There are dead that stand upon you, when you go in to your woman,
And they dart to her womb, they fight for the chance to be born,
    they struggle at the gate you have opened,
They gnash when it closes, and hate the one that got in, to be
    born again,
Child of the living dead, the dead that live and are not refreshed.
I tell you, sorry upon you; you shall all die.
And being dead, you shall not be refreshed.
There are no dead dead. (283)

"Death" encompasses the act of conception, birth, and life, as well as the end of existence.

The Plumed Serpent performs for death what The Rainbow does for birth: taking it as a central metaphor, the novel extends its meaning, explores its ramifications, builds a system to hold it and a symbolic structure to show it. With The Plumed Serpent Lawrence returns to the mode of psychological allegory he developed in The Rainbow and Women in Love, a kind of allegory that communicates his perception of reality through dynamic pattern. The prototypical motion in The Rainbow is organic unfolding; nature, society and the individual germinate and grow endlessly. In The Plumed Serpent the dominant pattern is the act of dying; in all activity, even in "regeneration," what is emphasized is separation, the loss of cohesion and energy, the lessening of power. In The Rainbow even death is construed as a kind of birth, the beginning of a new thing. But death in The Plumed Serpent is not a gentle passing away that leads to greater life; it is not that loosening of harsh mental consciousness that accompanies the birth of the living self. The attitude toward death in the Mexican novel is fundamentally negative. Nor in The Plumed Serpent do we find characters like Paul Morel and Gerald Crich, who have a Whitman-like longing for death as an ultimate consummation. The Plumed Serpent records a struggle for survival, and if it dwells on death, does so only in order to defeat it.

Lawrence's non-fiction prose written after 1921 registers this shift in the significance of death, in its overriding use of terms such as "energy," "vitality" and "life." Vitality is the theme of most of the essays in Reflections on the Death of a Porcupine (1925). Now concerned with how vitality is gained and kept, Lawrence's essays exclude almost every value other than life itself. "There is such a thing as life, or life energy," Lawrence writes in "Him with His Tail in His Mouth,"

> We know, because we've got it, or had it. It isn't a·constant. It comes and goes. But we *want* it.
> This I think is incontestable.
> More than anything else in the world, we want to have life, and life-energy, abundant in us.... Where it comes from, or what it is, we don't know, and never shall. It is the capital X of all our knowledge.
> But we want it, we must have it. It is the all in all.
> This we know, for good and all: that which is good, and moral, is that which brings us into a stronger, deeper flow of life and life-energy: evil is that which impairs the life-flow.
> But man's difficulty is, that he can't have life for the asking. 'He asked life of Thee, and Thou gavest it him: even length of days for ever and ever.' There's a pretty motto for the tomb! (*Phoenix II,* 428)

Vitality becomes, for Lawrence, not only the basis of morality but the basis of society. His utopia, both in the essays and in *The Plumed Serpent,* is based on the personal power of the "natural" aristocrat. An aristocrat is such, according to him, because he possesses superior vitality. "Being alive constitutes an aristocracy which there is no getting beyond. He who is most alive, intrinsically, is King." (*Phoenix II,* 483) Vitality is as well the sole aesthetic criterion. A novel, says Lawrence, must be "quick" and "interrelated in all its parts, vitally, organically." The hero must be likewise "quick," he must have a quick relatedness to all the other things in the novel." (*Phoenix II,* 422) Vitality is the greatest good, the end and aim of human existence. "More life!" Lawrence writes, "More *vivid* life! Not more safe cabbages, or meaningless masses of people. All creation contributes, and must contribute, to this: towards the achieving of a vaster, vivider cycle of life. That is the goal of living." (*Phoenix II,* 483) Now more than ever before Lawrence's world is utterly divided into the quick and the dead.

He attempts in the essays to define life and thus capture it; such efforts reveal above all that he fears to lose it. "We are losing vitality," he writes again and again, "losing it rapidly." *The Plumed Serpent* would deny death. The novel is repetitious because by repeating Lawrence would master the fact and the fear. The book is a literary monument to the repetition compulsion: in the religion of Quetzalcoatl "the Lords of Life are the Masters of Death." (414) The ambition of the novel—and this it has in common with all religions—is to conquer what ultimately cannot be overcome: the finiteness of human existence. There are, besides obsessive repetition, many other strategies against death in *The Plumed Serpent*. It is the purpose of this chapter to examine them.

Prominent among these strategies is the seasonal myth, taken mainly after Frazer's *Golden Bough*.[2] The skeleton of the plot in *The Plumed Serpent* is a sacred marriage that revives the wasteland. The heroine, Kate, pursues a quest out of civilization, represented by modern Mexico City, to the timeless realm of myth, the landscape of the Mexican interior. There she finds a "strange emptiness, everything empty of life!" (93) The life-giving power of water is emphasized by its very absence, by "the sense of life ebbing away, leaving dry ruin." (95) "The earth [is] utterly dry and stale." (91) Arid Mexico is the objective correlative of Kate's own inner wasteland; "she felt she could cry aloud, for the unknown gods to put the magic back into her life, and save her from the dry-rot of the world's sterility." (113) She penetrates to the heart of the wasteland to the equivalent of the sacred well of Frazer's myth, the lake at Sayula, with its water hyacinths and waters of regeneration. She becomes part of a revival of the old gods of Mexico, the religion of Quetzalcoatl, led by the *hacien-dado* Don Ramon and his lieutenant, Don Cipriano. Ramon battles with would-be assassins (the *agon*), and Kate saves him. The rainy season comes and she marries Cipriano, ascending to godhead as Malintzi in the Quetzalcoatl pantheon. The lake's and the season's highest fullness follows this sacred marriage, as does Kate's belief that she is finally, in these men, fulfilled and truly alive, and as does Mexico's acceptance of the new religion. But when the land becomes rich with the summer fullness, decay begins on the lake. "There was a smell of the piles of water-hyacinth decaying at the water's edges." (455) "Below [the mountain-slopes] was the lingering delicacy of green, already drying. The lake was full still, but subsided, and the water-hyacinth had drifted away." (482) The cycle—and the year—is complete.[3] Essentially the consolation of the cycle is that it denies linear (Christian) time and substitutes pagan, or cyclical. In a universe governed by the latter, nothing perishes, for the end leads only to the beginning.

Like his concept of time, Lawrence's concept of death—at least, as he presents it in *The Plumed Serpent*—is far from that of the orthodox Christian. The novel belongs in the tradition of religious mysticism that sees death not as an eternal transfiguration, but as the antithesis of life. Death is thus a state with structure and progression, and one that is in dialectical conflict with life.

This dualistic view is apparent in *The Rainbow,* and, to a greater degree, in *Women in Love,* as well as in *The Plumed Serpent.* In all three it provides the metaphysical axis on which the universe turns (as well as the structural axis on which the book turns). Lawrence's brand of gnosticism would incorporate death into life, and in so doing deny non-existence. This strategy would turn death inside out; it would follow life and death to the limits of human understanding, and find then that they are both the same: the serpent of eternity, Him With His Tail in His Mouth.

However it is apparent that in *The Plumed Serpent* no one strategy against death is enough, for Lawrence uses several, combining them into an unconventional—or, from another point of view, heretical—whole. A second strategy is to predicate that the universe contains a life-power from which men draw their vitality. The theme is not new in Lawrence; the life-force—the "Blood"—is virtually the main character in *The Rainbow.* The universe of *The Plumed Serpent* assumes that a similar power— "the life of the cosmos" (119)—dwells in the phenomenal world. This life power has affinities with the *anima mundi* of the transcendentalists, and Schopenhauer's "will."

The act of "communion" (119) with this power is central. It is exemplified in Ramon's trances and in Kate's experience of the "Great Breath." At the nadir of her life's sterility, Kate perceives that the cosmos is a corpse: "in the great seething light of the lake, with the terrible blue-ribbed mountains of Mexico beyond, she seemed swallowed by some grisly skeleton, in the cage of his death-anatomy." (116) Yet suddenly, as if the lungs of the countryside had inhaled, she is suffused with the "potency" of "the greater mystery, the higher power that hovered in the interstices of the hot air, rich and potent." (116) In the course of her conversion to the Quetzalcoatl religion the universe becomes alive to her. "She seemed to see the great sprouting of the fountain of non-human life. She seemed to see the great sprouting and urging of the cosmos, moving into weird life. And man only like green-fly clustering on the tender tips, an aberration there." (266-67) Kate is revived by this revelation of life. Lawrence's terminology is his own, but Kate's experience is the traditional one of religious-romantic nature mysticism, similar to Wordsworth's or Hopkins'

> Her weariness and her sense of devastation had been so complete, that the Other Breath in the air and the bluish dark power in the earth had become, almost suddenly, more real to her than so-called reality. Concrete, jarring, exasperating reality had melted

away and a soft world of potency stood in its place, the velvety dark breath in the inner air. Behind the fierce sun the dark eyes of a deeper sun were watching, and between the bluish ribs of the mountains a powerful heart was secretly beating, the heart of the earth. (119)

Communion like Kate's with the "greater life" is institutionalized in the religion of Quetzalcoatl; as with Kate, so with Mexico. The religion transforms the country by revealing that "the earth is alive and the sky is alive." (218) The god Quetzalcoatl is a celestial symbol of new life, but the crux of the religion lies in the teachings of Ramon, his earthly counterpart, who wants to "make a new connection between the people and god" (183) that will give men "the mystery of living." (394) He wants "living life"—heightened experience of the divine—to supplant mere dead mundane activity.

Lawrence reinforces the sense of life in the novel by using biological rhythms. The drums of Quetzalcoatl echo the heartbeat of the universe, and besides the cosmic heartbeat that thuds through the novel, there is universal inspiration and expiration in the swelling and waning sense of life, there is circulation and concentration of waters, "blood" and "lymph," which behave like the fluids of life. In addition to his use of the metaphor as a giant organism, Lawrence uses biological rhythms to structure the narrative. They shape *The Plumed Serpent* fully as much as the cycles of death and revival. The narrative proceeds by systole and diastole of greater and lesser tension; at times it moves, at times rests and reflects. There are pulsations in tone, from ornate mysticism to chatty travelogue. The focus expands and contracts regularly between individuals and a national view. Characters drift toward and away from each other in alternate periods of intellectual and blood awareness. Kate vascillates as predictably as a pulse between mysticism and skepticism, joy and despair.

Lawrence (and Ramon) stresses vitalism not for the sake of experience, but expediency. His object is to transfer life from the realm of the cosmic to man. "Seek life itself," Ramon says, "even pause at dawn and at sunset, and life will come back into us and prompt us through the transitions." (396) The "transition," implicitly, is death. "That which is life is vulnerable," Ramon continues, "only metal is invulnerable. Fight for the vulnerable unfolding of life. But for that, fight never to yield."[4] The contemplative Ramon shades off into his active alter ego, Cipriano, who urges his men to battle for "the second strength" that comes from "behind the sun," (397) the strength which will enable them to survive. Whether one follows the active or contemplative path, the goal of the religion of Quetzalcoatl is the same: to draw life-strength from the universe. This apparently was how Lawrence understood the animistic Amerindian religion that so impressed him in New Mexico. "The old Indians of the north still have the secret of animistic dancing. They dance to gain power: power over the *living* forces or potencies of the earth." (399)[5]

If one can draw life from the cosmos, why not from other living beings as well? From animism to cannibalism is a short jump, one that Lawrence sometimes makes. "Any man, creature, or race moving towards blossoming will have to draw immense supplies of vitality from men, or creatures below, passionate strength." (*Phoenix II*, 472) "The primary way, in our existence, to get vitality, is to absorb it from living creatures lower than ourselves. It is thus transformed into a newer and higher creation." (481) The heroine of "The Woman Who Rode Away" [1924] is sacrificed, quite literally, that the males of an indian tribe might win away her mana. In the ritual transfer of vitality the life is carved out of her:

> Only the eyes of the oldest man were not anxious. Black, and fixed, and as if sightless, they watched the sun, seeing beyond the sun. And in their black, empty concentration there was power, power intensely abstract and remote, but deep, deep in the heart of the earth, and the heart of the sun. In absolute motionlessness he watched till the red sun should send his ray through the column of ice. Then the old man would strike, and strike home, accomplish the sacrifice and achieve the power.
>   The mastery that man must hold, and that passes from race to race. (CSS, II, 581)

Kate's sacrifice is more subtle. She, like Ursula, Alvina, and others before her, relinquishes the individuality of her "very own will" (79) and her "civilized" self, that her men might survive. She, like her predecessors, becomes a goddess of sorts, an elemental being who supports but, devoid of will, cannot invade the male self. Kate's marriage to Cipriano is another instance of subjection by apotheosis.

Yet although Kate yields herself to Cipriano and Ramon numerous times for numerous reasons, none of them is sufficient to make the capitulation permanent. Sometimes she is overwhelmed because Cipriano is "Pan" and "the master of Fire," (351) who comes from "the world of shadows and dark prostration, with the phallic wind rushing through the dark," (348) and fuses her "into a molten unconsciousness, her will, her very self gone, leaving her lying in molten life." Elsewhere, she yields because she is "not real till she [is] reciprocal." (424) "Alone she was nothing. Only as the pure female corresponding to his pure male, did she signify." "Her halfness! Was there no star of the single soul?" (426) There is not, she learns; "the individual, like the perfect being, does not and cannot exist, in the vivid world. We are all fragments." Or again, Kate yields her self to the universal blood:

> . . . they demanded her acquiescence in the primeval assertion: *the blood is one blood. We are one blood*. It was the assertion that swept away all individualism, and left her immersed, drowned in the grand sea of the living blood, in immediate contact with all these men and these women. (457)

Yet Kate's ego, like a vampire, cannot be laid to rest. The last (and presumably equally temporary) death of her self comes about for the problematical reason that she does not want to grow "elderly and a bit grisly" in a European drawing-room. (482) "Without Cipriano to touch me and limit me and submerge my will, I shall become a horrible, elderly female."

In Kate's history, which consists largely of the repeated death of her self, Lawrence recapitulates most of his previous ego theories. "Stellar equilibrium," the metaphor of organic unfolding, the blood, and so on, appear in patchwork-quilt fashion. Their presentation is perfunctory, without verve or conviction. What is important in *The Plumed Serpent* is not the theories themselves, but the fact of the sacrifice, which is repeated over and over. By relinquishing her individuality to her men, Kate gives life to them, quite literally. By not doing so to her husband Joachim, she killed him. "If you could have given him your life," Kate is told, "he would not have even wanted to die." (451) She did not submit herself to "Joachim, the eager, clever, fierce sensitive genius, who could look into her soul and laugh into her soul; he had died under her eyes. . . . If she could have fanned his blood as Teresa fanned the blood of Ramon, he would never have died." (437-38) And if the religion of Quetzalcoatl fails, we can infer, it is because Kate once again does not sacrifice her self utterly to the masculine cause.

The fault, however, is not Kate's. The fallacy of Lawrence's strategy of animism, that would draw life from the cosmos, and of his "cannibalism," that would draw life from other human beings, (and of cannibalism in general) lies in their confusion of spirit and substance. Both his animism and "cannibalism" rely on a mode of primitive thinking that treats life as if it were matter;

113

as if it were palpable. But life and matter are not interchangeable; life inheres in matter and depends on it, but is not material, of course. Nor does it behave according to the laws that govern matter. If life were a substance that flowed, for instance, as Lawrence often describes it, it could (conceivably) be transferable, but it is not. Life can be created, but not transferred, and the irreducible fact of our existence is our limitation in the body. Our perceptions limit us in space as our life-span limits us in time. And since the boundaries of our bodies are the boundaries of our lives, we are left with our solipsism: the stone wall limits of our existence.

Faced with this irrefutable fact, his common human need to deny it made urgent by his sickness, Lawrence performs a sleight of hand in *The Plumed Serpent*. He transposes the meaning of "life," from a state of physical limitation to something more tractable and less "tragically" finite. To a psychologist of Lawrence's sophistication it is clear that one's self may ultimately be trapped in one's body, but one's sense of one's self is not. Therefore to deny the seemingly-inevitable fact of mortality Lawrence shifts his terms "life" and "death" from physical to existential. Existentially, "life" is the sense of one's self, and "death" is the loss of that sense of one's reality. (In this frame of reference Lawrence's animism and "cannibalism" as strategies to draw life from outside oneself are valid: for the ego "life"—the sense of one's existence—is drawn from cosmic or human alterity, for it resides in contact with an Other.) Lawrence substitutes the death of self for physical death, perhaps because the sense of non-existence—unlike actual death—has at least the possibility of being defeated.

Most of the death that pervades *The Plumed Serpent* is given the shape of psychic disintegration. The paradigm is the familiar one in Lawrence: engulfment or annihilation in nothingness, the antithetical destructions that threaten the weak ego. In this universe the white race perishes in isolated sterility, "widdershins, unwinding the sensations of disintegration and anti-life," (113) its relationships mere "mechanical connections," "where men die because they are cut off from "human contact." Therefore Kate begs, *"Let it not be all cut off for me!"*

At the other end of the spectrum is the fatal dissolution of the Mexicans. The "heavy black Mexican fatality" (22) is a "downsinking" into "the homogeneity of death." (83) Lawrence emphasizes that the Mexicans are "incomplete," "half-created," "uncreated." "Their eyes have no middle to them," Kate says.

"Those big handsome men, under their big hats, they aren't really there. They have no centre, no real *I*. Their middle is a raging black hole, like the middle of a maelstrom." (40) This incompleteness is deathly; a Mexican is a "half-being, with a will to disintegration and death." (116) Mexico is dying because its people are unintegrated—never having been integrated; "a people incomplete, and at the mercy of old, upstarting lusts,... never [having] been able to win a soul for themselves, never [having] been able to win themselves a nucleus, an individual integrity out of the chaos of passions and potencies and death." (147) In *The Plumed Serpent* dark and white races travel by opposite paths to the same fate: non-existence. Kate wonders about

> the dark faced natives, with their strange soft flame of life wheeling upon a dark void: were they centreless and widdershins too, as so many white men are now?
>
> The strange, soft flame of courage in the black Mexican eyes. But still it was not knit to a centre, that centre which is the soul of a man in a man.
>
> And all the efforts of white men to bring the soul of the dark men of Mexico into final clinched being has resulted in nothing but the collapse of the white man. Against the soft, dark flow of the Indian the white man at last collapses, with his God and his energy he collapses. In attempting to convert the dark man to the white man's way of life, the white man has fallen helplessly down the hole he wanted to fill up. Seeking to save another man's soul, the white man lost his own, and collapsed upon himself. (84)

Yet if death is psychic disintegration, life is the converse: the self made whole. The purpose of the religion of Quetzalcoatl is to bring life, i.e., to create psychic integrity. "The universe is a nest of dragons," Ramon says, "with a perfectly unfathomable life-mystery at the centre of it.... And man is a creature who wins his own creation inch by inch from the nest of the cosmic dragons. Or else he loses it little by little, and goes to pieces. Now we are losing it, in the ravishing and ravished disintegration. We must pull ourselves together, hard, both men and women, or we are all lost." And he repeats, "We must pull ourselves together, hard." (299) Ramon and Cipriano try to save the Mexicans by, in effect, pulling them together. Lawrence writes,

> If there is one thing men need to learn, but the Mexican Indians especially, it is to collect each man his own soul together deep inside him, and to abide by it. The Church, instead of helping men to this, pushes them more and more into a soft, emotional helplessness, with the unpleasant sensuous gratification of feeling themselves victims. (303)

In the novel Christianity is the death religion, partly because it worships a "dead god," but also because it encourages the self's

disintegration in observance which is "a sensual, almost vic-
timised self-abandon to the god of death.... It was not worship.
It was a sort of numbness and letting the soul sink uncontrolled."
(302) *The Plumed Serpent* is often called Lawrence's "religious"
novel, as distinct from his "political" ones, *Aaron's Rod* and
Kangaroo. But the "religion" of *The Plumed Serpent*, like the
"politics" of its predecessors, is primarily a metaphor for being.
According to the logic of the Mexican novel, if the imperfect self
is dying, then the perfect self will not, and it is the task of the
religion of Quetzalcoatl to make man immortal by making him
whole.

What constitutes this wholeness is revealed in the experiences
of the three main characters—Kate, Ramon and Cipriano—for
their lives are *exempla* of the progress to self-sufficiency. The nature of wholeness is also revealed in a more schematic fashion,
in the symbology of the religion of Quetzalcoatl. The religion can
be reduced, without violating its meaning (in fact, clarifying it),
to two symbols: the Morning Star, and the "greater sun" that is
"behind the sun." (129) These are also personified as Quetzalcoatl, "lord of both ways, star between day and the dark," (251)
and his "Father," the "master-sun, the dark one of the unutterable name." (135)

The "plumed serpent," as his name implies, reconciles opposites:

> I am Quetzalcoatl of the eagle and the snake.
> The earth and air.
> Of the Morning Star.
> I am Lord of the Two Ways. (374)

He is the symbol of equilibrium. "Without me," Quetzalcoatl
tells the Mexicans in a hymn, "you are nothing. Just as I, without
the sun that is back of the sun, am nothing." (134) Anterior to
Quetzalcoatl is a first principle "that made the sun and the world,
and will swallow it again like a draught of water." (134) It is the
"unknowable God-mystery," (371) called variously the "Father,"
the "Dark Eye," "God"; it is the image of a source, as a sun that
radiates life, and a "fountain that bubbles darkly at the heart of
the worlds." (248) Quetzalcoatl and the dark sun correspond to
the Christian (or Platonic) hierarchy, for the "Son" exists in the
realm of human experience, while the "Father," unknowable, is
beyond it.[6]

In *The Rainbow* and *Women in Love* the self turns primarily to
woman for its existence. In *Aaron's Rod* and *Kangaroo* it turns to
man. Having failed to establish a satisfactory relationship with
either, the self turns in *The Plumed Serpent* to the gods. How-

ever the images of divinity as Lawrence presents them in the
Mexican novel are actually images of human experience. These
gods are patterns, or paradigms of relationship. Since the purpose
of the Quetzalcoatl religion is to create the self and keep it
whole, it is only to be expected that its gods should, as they do,
embody the relationships to Other that accomplish the self. As
the religion has two gods, so the essential transfer of life, the
making whole, has two forms: it is an equilibrium between two
beings, and it is a flow of life energy from a great central source.

The notion of equilibrium is not new with *The Plumed Serpent*. The relation between Birkin and Ursula, for instance, is described as is Quetzalcoatl himself, as a balance between two
stars. Equilibrium presupposes a need to overcome an imbalance,
and indeed, for Lawrence, imbalance in relationship is generally
fatal. Ramon and Carlota, like Gerald and Gudrun before them,
exemplify this. "With a woman," Ramon says, "a man always
wants to let himself go. And it is precisely with a woman that he
should never let himself go. . . . but stick to his innermost belief,
and meet her just there." (298) His wife Carlota is a "ravisher."
"Absurd as it may sound," he tells Kate, "it is not I who would
ravish Carlota. It is she who would ravish me. Strange and absurd and a little shameful, it is true.—Letting oneself go, is either
ravishing or being ravished. Oh, if we could only abide by our
own souls, and meet in the abiding place." Kate, rather like Birkin, replies,

> But why don't you do as you say, stick by the innermost soul that
> is in you, and meet a woman there, meet her as you say, where
> your two souls coincide in their deepest desire? Not always that
> horrible imbalance that you call ravishing. (300)

Carlota "turns to her crucified Jesus," the victim god, and Ramon
to his "uncrucified and uncrucifiable Quetzalcoatl, who at
least cannot be ravished." (299) To relate in imitation of the
image of balance—Quetzalcoatl—is to keep the self whole. As
Ramon destroys Carlota, so Cipriano and Kate are intended to illustrate the converse: two identities in perfect balance. Their
marriage takes place "at twilight, between the night and the
day" "where man and woman, in presence of the unfading star,
meet to be perfect in one another." (361) "If there be no star,"
Ramon says, "no meeting ground, no true coming together of
man with the woman, into a wholeness, there is no marriage.
And if there is no marriage, there is nothing but an agitation."
(364) Marriages of "equilibrium" always seem to necessitate the
subjection of the woman in Lawrence. As with Ursula, so with

117

Kate. In the ceremony Cipriano kisses her "brow and breast"; she kisses his "heels and feet," (362) which indicates her subservience in the relationship. Eventually Kate achieves "perfect proneness." Consequently the Viedma marriage, like Birkin and Ursula's, is not a success. The "agitation" Ramon descries is the dialectic of existence—the self in eternal unstable conflict with Other, and its cessation in perfect equilibrium is as we saw in *Women in Love*, not only humanly impossible, but rationally inconceivable.

An alternative to equilibrium—or any kind of relationship—is solipsism, the self alone. But that too is unsatisfactory. There is an impulse to isolation in *The Plumed Serpent*, which arises out of revulsion from contact. Kate withdraws from the "contagion" of Mexico's "crawling evil" (19) much as Aaron and Lilly recoil from a universe that seems as if it could physically infect one's being. Kate is equally repelled by people: "I don't want them to touch me and I don't want to touch them." (274) Significantly, the first thing about Cipriano that impresses her is his "detachment." At the bull-fight where she first meets him, "even touching the crowd delicately with his gloved hand, and murmuring almost inaudibly the *Con permiso!* formula, he seemed to be keeping himself miles from contact." (19) Kate and Ramon indulge in a diatribe against relationship that recalls the conversations of Aaron and Lilly (one bitter voice, two speakers). She feels the "unconquerable dislike, almost *disgust* of people. More than hate, it was disgust." (276) As for Ramon, "with a certain pain and nausea, he realised the state she was in, and realised that his own state, as regards *personal* people, was the same. Mere *personal* contact, mere human contact, filled him, too, with disgust." "One must be able to disentangle oneself from persons, from people," he says. "People in some way *dominate* you." (275)

Yet an Other is indispensable, and dangerous as relationship might be, isolation is fatal:

> The fact remains when you cut a man off and isolate him in his own pure and wonderful individuality, you haven't got the man at all, you've only got the dreary fag-end of him...everything, even individuality itself, depends on relationship....
> It is in the living touch between us and other people, other lives, other phenomena that we move and have our being. Strip us of our human contacts and our contact with the living earth and the sun, and we are almost bladders of emptiness. Our individuality means nothing. (*Phoenix*, 193)

118

At first, like many characters in later Lawrence, Kate solves the problem by turning to an impersonal suprahuman Other, to living abstractions like the "greater mystery," (275) the "Great Breath," (116) or "greater sex." (143)[7] But as the novel proceeds, she is drawn into human relationships. In Kate, the impulse to isolation is countered by an equally strong need for connection; she vascillates between the men of Quetzalcoatl and solitude. Her life shows its sterility at the times when she has "made up her mind to be alone." (114) (Her room shows "the rather weary luxury and disorder, and the touch of barrenness, of a woman living her own life." [440]) Yet Kate early in the novel is, if "sterile," at least self-sufficient. As her history proceeds she learns the hard lesson of existential dependence, which is for Lawrence the lesson of life itself: she realises "for the first time, with finality and fatality, what was the illusion she labored under. She had thought that each individual had a complete self, a complete soul, an accomplished I. And now she realised as plainly as if she had been turned into a new being, that this was not so. Men and women had incomplete selves, made up of bits assembled together loosely and somewhat haphazard." (115) In other words, Kate discovers that she must relinquish her "barren" "true loneliness," (62) and in its place substitute need and relationship; only then will she "live," for contact, according to Lawrence, is life. "Man's life consists in a connection with all things in the universe." (*Phoenix II*, 478)

> But *living* and having *being* means the relatedness between me and all things. In so far as I am I, a being who is proud and in place, I have a connection with my circumambient universe and I know my place. When the white cock crows, I do not hear myself, or some anthropomorphic conceit, crowing. I hear the non-me, the voice of the Holy Ghost. . . . So it is with every natural thing. It has a vital relation with all other natural things. Only the machine is absolved from vital relation. (478)

And in a book about death, Lawrence presents a mysticism that is a pure and direct apprehension of life.

In *The Plumed Serpent* Lawrence uses events and characters as symbols in order to show how the conjunction of self and Other generates the sense of reality, or "life." It is as if he would penetrate to the nexus of relationship to isolate the essence of being. Life-giving contact is the essence of the Quetzalcoatl religion; as Ramon summarizes it in a sermon, "the touch, the look, the word that goes from one naked man to another is the mystery of living." (394) Kate touches the cosmos, literally, and knows she is alive:

> It was as if she could lift her hands and clutch the silent stormy potency that roved everywhere, waiting. "Come then!" she said, drawing a long slow breath and addressing the silent life-breath which hung unrevealed in the atmosphere, waiting. And as the boat ran on, and her fingers rustled in the warm water of the peace, and the power. (116-17)

The ceremonies of Quetzalcoatl ritualize contact, as with the "beautiful slow wheel of the dance," that Kate finds, "two great streams streaming in contact, in opposite directions." She is "identified in the slowly revolving ocean of nascent life, ... as the man whose fingers touched hers was gone in the ocean of life that is male.... The slow, vast, soft-touching revolution of the ocean above upon the ocean below, with no vestige of rustling or foam. Only the pure sliding conjunction." (143) Kate's marriage to Cipriano, bringing life to the cosmos, epitomizes the life-giving power of relatedness, which is symbolized also by the Morning Star. The mystery of relation is all. "If it is to be life," Lawrence writes in an essay, "then it is fifty per cent me, fifty per cent thee: and the third thing, the spark, which springs from out the balance, is timeless. Jesus, who saw it a bit vaguely, called it the Holy Ghost." (*Phoenix II*, 435) Lawrence calls it Quetzalcoatl, or equilibrium.

In the mystical perceptions that constitute a great part of the religion of Quetzalcoatl, equilibrium—that is, the God—represents the conjunction of self and Other that creates reality. In other (more traditional) words, it is the "wedding" of "subject" and "object," the *percipi esse* so beloved by Coleridge, Hopkins and other perceptual mystics. Thus at the wedding of Kate and Cipriano, Ramon says, "Where there is no star and no abiding place, nothing is, so nothing can be lost." (364) The religion of *The Plumed Serpent,* as Calvin Bedient notes, is that of the "aesthete" in the etymological sense, of "one who perceives."[8]

However Lawrence's interest in perceptual mysticism is prompted by more than a gratuitous religious-aesthetic impulse. It is significant that the experience of Quetzalcoatl denies time, that the God is eternal: "The Morning Star," Kate tells Cipriano, is "an abiding place between us, for ever." (362) And as it denies time, it denies death: "Your home at last is the Morning Star," Ramon says to his people. "Neither heaven nor earth shall swallow you up at the last, but you shall pass into the place beyond both, into the bright star." (219) Lawrence's image is of a perfect and therefore eternal balance. He uses equilibrium as a strategy against death with much the same logic that allows Donne to declare whatever dies was not mix'd equally. "I am undeparting," says Quetzalcoatl, "I sit tight/Between the wings of the endless flight." (196) Jesus, on the other hand, passes away because he is "lord of the one way." (250) The plumed serpent has no such fatal imbalance.

This consolation—if such it can be called—is perhaps no more than decorative; relying only on the logic of its images, it provides frail solace. However equilibrium is life-bringing in another and less purely poetical sense in the novel. Quetzalcoatl creates and preserves the self: "I will be with you," he tells the Mexicans, "so you depart not from yourselves." (196) He sings that, because of him, even physical death cannot destroy the integrity of the self. "And say to thy death: Be it so! I, and my soul, we come to thee, Evening Star. Flesh, go thou into the night. Spirit, farewell, 'tis thy day. Leave me now, I go in last nakedness now to the nakedest Star." (198) Flesh and spirit pass away, but individual being remains, through the intervention of Quetzalcoatl because he symbolizes the power of the perceptual experience to create the self.

"I do want to be alive," Lawrence writes in an essay. "And to be alive, I must have a goal in the *creative* universe. I want, in the Greek sense, an equilibrium between me and the universe.... And between us [him and a pet hen] there shall exist the third thing, the *connaissance*. That is the goal." (*Phoenix II*, 432) The moment of mystical perception is the "goal" not only because it gives a stronger sense of life than ordinary consciousness, which it certainly does, but also because it intensifies the sense of self. Perceptual mysticism as Lawrence describes it is a form of self-aggrandizement. It is antithetical to the mysticism that annihilates the self, as for instance, does Whitman's. (At least, Whitman's mysticism as Lawrence understood it: "Merging! And Death! Which is the final merge." And, "the transitions of the soul as it loses its integrity." [SCAL, 169, 170]) On the contrary, Lawrence's perceptual mysticism celebrates the self by intensifying the contrast between it and Other.

When Ramon communes with the cosmos, the experience creates his being. As he describes it,

> "There is no Before and After, there is only Now....
> "The great Snake coils and uncoils the plasm of his folds, and stars appear, and worlds fade out. It is no more than the changing and easing of the plasm.
> "*I always am,* says his sleep.
> "As a man in a deep sleep knows not, but is, so is the Snake of the coiled cosmos, wearing its plasm.

121

> "As a man coiled in a deep sleep has no tomorrow, no yesterday, nor to-day, but only *is*, so is the limpid, far-reaching Snake of the eternal Cosmos, Now, and forever Now.
>
> * * *
>
> "And only the sleep that is dreamless breathes *I AM!*
> "In the dreamless now, *I AM.*
> "Dreams arise as they must arise, and a man is a dream arisen.
> "But the dreamless plasm of the Snake is the plasm of a man, of his body, and his soul, and his spirit at one.
> "And in the perfect sleep of the Snake *I Am* is the plasm of a man, who is whole.
> "When the plasm of the body, and the plasm of the soul, and the plasm of the spirit are one, in the Snake *I Am.*[9] (193-94)

"I am weary of the thing men call life," Ramon says later. "I want to depart to where *I am* . . . to the Star where at last I have my wholeness, holiness." (279) It is the perception of alterity that creates the self. "What is the soul of a man," Lawrence asks, "except *that* in him which is himself alone, suspended in immediate relationship to the sum of things. Not isolated or cut off." (*Phoenix II*, 434) Lawrence's vision is that man's isolation—the "tragic" alienation of the human condition[10]—in fact gives man his "life," because it creates his sense of himself.

Ramon's contact is mainly with the cosmos. Kate and Cipriano, like Ramon, exemplify the life-giving power of relationship, but it is a different, lesser relationship. They have need primarily of each other. To Kate, Ramon has "the mystery, the nobility, the inaccessibility and the vulnerable compassion of a man in his separate fatherhood."

> She knew he was more beautiful to her than any blond white man, and that, in a remote, far-off way, the contact with him was more precious than any contact she had known. But then, though he cast over her a certain shadow, he would never encroach on her, he would never seek any close contact. It was the incompleteness in Cipriano that sought her out, and seemed to trespass on her. (206-207)

Furthermore, Kate and Cipriano are less than Ramon also in that their egos are not always utterly distinct from Otherness; they cannot "get beyond," in Lawrence's words, "the soft, quaking, deep communion of blood-oneness." (459) But Ramon, "admitting his blood-unison, . . . at the same time claimed a supremacy, even a godliness," for "he kept himself beyond. He was the living Quetzalcoatl." (459) Ramon's "godliness" lies in his great and unshakable sense of himself, and his passionate sense of the distance (or unlikeness) between himself and other things. He returns from his religious experiences with a stronger and more separate self, insulated against the mundane reality that would encroach on him. "He had to meet people [on] another plane, where the contact was different: intangible, remote, and without *intimacy*."

> His soul was concerned elsewhere. So that the quick of him need not be bound to anybody. The quick of a man must turn to God alone: in some way or other.
> With Cipriano he was most sure. Cipriano and he, even when they embraced each other with passion, when they met after an absence, embraced in the recognition of each other's eternal and abiding aloneness; like the Morning Star. (277)

"That which we get from the beyond," Lawrence continues, "we get it alone. The final me comes from the farthest off, from the Morning Star." Ramon is also Lawrence's attempt to get beyond relationship entirely, his most sustained and most intricate attempt to define a perfectly self-sufficient being.

Throughout Lawrence there exists (although often it is only implicit) an ideal of self-sufficiency. At times one senses a yearning for a state where the self is not bound by the necessity of relationship. Sometimes Lawrence symbolizes this ideal of perfect wholeness as childhood because it, like infantile consciousness, is anterior to the sense of (or need for) an Other. Also he symbolizes it as a state of grace.

By extension, the fact of existential necessity becomes the division of the sexes at adolescence, or a Fall into sexual need, or a crucifixion into partiality. In the "Tortoise Poems" Lawrence uses these images to describe solipsism and relationship.

> Why were we crucified into sex?
> Why were we not left rounded off, and finished in ourselves,
> As we began,
> And he [the tortoise] certainly began, so perfectly alone?
> ("Tortoise Shout" 11.9-12)

And in "Lui et Elle,"

> Alas, the spear is through the side of his isolation.
> His adolescence saw him crucified into sex,
> Doomed, in the long crucifixion of desire, to seek his
> consummation beyond himself.
> Divided into passionate duality,
> He, so finished and immune, now broken into desirous
> fragmentariness,
> Doomed to make an intolerable fool of himself
> In his effort toward completion again.
> (11.9-15)

123

The "Tortoise Poems" suggest why characters in *The Plumed Serpent* frequently become "virgin" or "innocent," often—paradoxically—through sex. Kate feels "a virgin again" (142) in the dance of Quetzalcoatl; Cipriano makes her "innocent" (430) because "that which he brought to marriage was something flamy, forever virginal." Sex with him makes her "again always a virgin girl." (431) "How else," she asks herself, "is one to begin again, save by refinding one's virginity. And when one finds one's virginity, one realises one is among the gods." Her "virginity"—like that of the tortoise—symbolizes the wholeness that she gets through conjunction with Cipriano.

The religious experience, too, makes one "pure." Ramon says, "When men meet at the quick of all things, they are neither naked nor clothed; in the transfiguration they are just complete, they are not seen in part. The final perfect strength has also the power of innocence." (278) And Ramon, through his trances, is "aloof, far-off and intangible in another day." (201) He seems to Kate to be "all for himself," to possess "a pure sensuality, with a powerful purity of its own."

> Ramon was handsome, almost horribly handsome, with his black head poised as it were without weight, above his darkened, smooth neck. A pure sensuality, with a powerful purity of its own, hostile to her sort of purity. With the blue sash round his waist, pressing a fold in the flesh, and the thin linen seeming to gleam with the life of his hips and thighs, he emanated a fascination almost like a narcotic asserting his pure, fine sensuality against her. The strange, soft, still sureness of him, as he sat secure within his own dark aura. And as if this dark aura of his militated against her presence, and against the presence of his wife. He emitted an effluence so powerful that it seemed to hamper her consciousness, to bind down her limbs.
>
> And he was utterly still and quiescent, without desire, soft and unroused, within his own *ambiente*. (202)

Cipriano at first also seems self-sufficient to Kate. ("They have got more than I," she thinks, "They have a richness that I haven't got.") (203) But Cipriano is not self-sufficient. He and Kate exist in the realm of sexual division, just as Ramon, since he turns to the gods for his wholeness, exists beyond it, in "the star of his manhood, ... proud and perfect." (219)

Ramon is opulently male, and his physical richness symbolizes his self-sufficiency in much the same way that women's bodies in earlier novels symbolized female plentitude of being. When Ramon confirms his self, in communion with the cosmos, it is symbolized as a confirmation of his maleness:

124

He was looking into the heart of the world; because the faces of men and the hearts of men are helpless quicksands. Only to the heart of the cosmos can man look for strength. And if he can keep his soul in touch with the heart of the world, then from the heart of the world new blood will beat in strength and stillness into him, fulfilling his manhood. (214)

To get this "manhood" is the purpose of the religion: "We've got to open the oyster of the cosmos," Ramon tells Cipriano, "and get our manhood out of it." (211) Lawrence, as in earlier novels, construes the self as male, and the male-aggrandizement of the religion of Quetzalcoatl—the phallic salutes, the male-orgasmic images of spurting fountains, the "spermy" waters of the sacred lake—is in essence self-aggrandizement. In his essays Lawrence uses "phallic" in an identitional rather than the more confined sexual sense:

It is the self which darkly inhabits our blood and bone, and for which the ithyphallus is but a symbol.... This self which lives darkly in my blood and bone is my *alter ego*.... And the sacred black stone at Mecca stands for this: the dark self that dwells in the blood of a man and of a woman. Phallic, if you like. But much more than phallic. (*Phoenix II*, 619)

Ramon is made perfect through mystical experience that is represented as a flow of energy from a central source. " 'The waters are coming,' he heard a servant say.... Then he threw aside his clothing, saying: I put off the world with my clothes."

And tense like the gush of a soundless fountain, he thrust up and reached down in the invisible dark, convulsed with passion. Till the black waves began to wash over his consciousness, over his mind, waves of darkness broke over his memory, over his being, like an incoming tide, till at last it was full tide, and he trembled, and fell to rest. Invisible in the darkness, he stood soft and relaxed, staring with wide eyes at the dark, and feeling the dark fecundity of the inner tide washing over his heart, over his belly, his mind dissolved away in the greater, dark mind, which is undisturbed by thoughts.

He covered his face with his hands, and stood still, in pure unconsciousness, neither hearing nor feeling nor knowing, like a dark sea-weed deep in the sea. With no Time and no World, in the deeps that are timeless and worldless. (212)

This oceanic consciousness is also described as a dark sun, "the fountain at the heart of the worlds," where Ramon's celestial counter-part, Quetzalcoatl, travels to be revived.

It would appear that Ramon's experience is actually a lapse rather than a confirmation of self. In this state, "mind dissolved away in the greater mind," self is coextensive with the universe. Whether one chooses to interpret it as the self made all or the self annihilated, depends in part on one's choice of metaphors. These may be incorporative (like Whitman's) or expulsive ("blowing out," *nirvana*). Thus Kate's "loss" of her "individual self" in "blood-unison" (456) results in essentially the same state as the "fulfillment fulfilling her soul" in the episode of the "Great Breath." (117) However Lawrence chooses to construe them differently. He considers the first a lapsing out of self, and sees the other as a mystic recognition of Otherness, a "communion of grace." The difference between the lapsing of "blood-unison" and the experience of the "dark sun" is essentially only one of means: the first is passive, the second, active; for both the end is the same. For Ramon to seek the oceanic consciousness is, according to Lawrence, an act of asserting the self against Other, and therefore creative. This "sun," in Lawrence's imagery, infuses existence into man and cosmos, and Lawrence insists that this creation is invariably a function of relationship. He cannot divest himself of the notions of self and Other, and that the "sun" is in essence an experience of Otherness, he leaves no doubt. "Life consists in a relation with all things," he writes in his essay "Aristocracy." Man's greatest and final relation is with the sun, the sun of suns: and with the night, which is moon and dark and stars. In the last great connections, he lifts his body speechless to the sun, and, the same body, but so different, to the moon and the stars, and the spaces between the stars." And, he continues, "in his ultimate and surpassing relations, man is given only to that which he can never describe or account for; the sun, as it is alive, and the living night." Ramon of course illustrates this connection:

> ... no man is man in all his splendour till he passes further than every relationship: further than mankind and womankind, in the last leap to the sun, to the night. The man who can touch both sun and night ... becomes a lord and a savior, in his own kind. With the sun he has his final and ultimate relationship, beyond man or woman, or anything human or created. And in this final relation he is most intensely alive, surpassing. (*Phoenix II*, 483)

There is, in other words, a relationship that is beyond relationship. Lawrence approaches antinomy in his existential imagery, because he is caught between assuming that relationship is necessary for existence, and positing a perfect being that is both the result of relationship and beyond it. Essentially he is trying to account for a jump out of the orbit of bipolar logic. His essays have little success, as he himself acknowledges. In "Reflections on the Death of a Porcupine" he reasons:

> 1. Any creature that attains to its own fulness of being, its own *living* self, becomes unique, a nonpareil. It has its place in the fourth dimension, the heaven of existence, and there it is perfect and beyond comparison.
> 2. At the same time, every creature exists in time and space. And in time and space it exists relatively to all other existences, and can never be absolved. Its existence impinges on all other existences, and is itself impinged on. . . .
> 3. The force which we call *vitality,* and which is the determining factor in the struggle for existence, is however, derived also from the fourth dimension. . . .
> 4. The primary way, in our existence, to get vitality, is to absorb it from living creatures lower than ourselves. . . . The best way is a pure relationship, which includes the *being* on each side, and which allows the transfer to take place in a living flow, enhancing the life in both beings.
> 5. No creature is fully itself till it is, like the dandelion, opened in the bloom of pure relationship to the sun, the entire living cosmos.

Unable to resolve the dilemma, Lawrence concludes ruefully:

> So still we find ourselves in the tangle of existence and being, a tangle which man has never been able to get out of, except by sacrificing one to the other. (*Phoenix II,* 469)

But in *The Plumed Serpent* the literary form frees him somewhat from the restrictions of discursive logic and enables him to capture—and indeed, account for—the contradictions in his notions of self.

Lawrence ellides self and Other in the novel by use of analogy. The narrative begins with a conventional fictional reality: Kate is set against other characters, and in the background is a society. Her train ride to Sayula is a transition to an inner reality, a universe of correspondences where cosmos, society and individual are identified. Thus Kate's aridity of spirit *is* Mexico's dryness, just as her revival *is* Mexico's; political strife in the country *is* the transition of the gods in the heavens just as the flow of life through the nation that follows *is* the new reign of Quetzalcoatl.

Analogy as Lawrence uses it obliterates normal spatial relations. "The hearts of living men are the very middle of the sky," (389) Ramon says. "Beyond me, at the middle, is the God." (80) The emptiness of the cosmos, "the waste space at the centre of life" (351) *is* the vacuity of the Mexicans, "the void in the middle of the peons." (40) The distinction between inside and outside becomes irrelevant: the drums of Quetzalcoatl sound "in the innermost far-off place of the human core," (138) and the old indians sing "to the inner mystery, singing not into space, but into the other dimension of man's existence, where he finds himself in the infinite room that lies inside the axis of our wheeling space." (137) There is a sort of telescoping focus in *The Plumed Serpent* that precludes any firm grasp of interior and exterior. Thus analogy disjoints the relation of subject to object, and instead of self and Other, we find a continuously-receding perspective, rather like a barber-shop mirror, of self-Other-self-Other. Furthermore this universe is self-reflexive in that self relates to a cosmic Other that is made in its own image.

In one sense, Lawrence's final image of the self is nothing less than the cosmos of *The Plumed Serpent* in its entirety. In *Women in Love* the cosmos is also patterned after the psyche, but in *The Plumed Serpent* the cosmos is not like a mind, it is a mind (or at least, an organism); it is not a backdrop in soft focus behind the characters, but part of a multiple focus, and one of the characters as much as Kate or Ramon. This, the last model of human personality that Lawrence devised, is his most complex. It is embodied in the emblem of Quetzalcoatl: the plumed serpent surrounded by the circle of the sun. It is expressed also in the image of a living cell, "the nucleus of life," (131) that the rituals of Quetzalcoatl and, eventually, much of the cosmos emulate. It is captured in "the peculiar gleaming farawayness, suspended between the realities, which ... was the central look in the native eyes. ... A look of extraordinary, arresting beauty, the silent, vulnerable centre of all life's quivering, like the nucleus gleaming in tranquil suspense, within a cell." (99) This is an image of perfect poise within centrality, of relationship suspended in a self-enclosed unit. It is an image of antinomy: a self that contains relationship and needs none.

Centrality is the key to the image. Ramon's effort is to keep himself centered in the maelstrom of existence. "I must keep myself together," he says, "keep myself within the middle place, where I am still." (301) The Other has always been antagonistic to the self in Lawrence. In *The Plumed Serpent* he objectifies this hostile reality as centripetal and centrifugal forces that tear at being or press in upon it. The book is a search for a center. Ramon is a center to Kate, as is Jamiltepec. ("A sort of Mecca to me," she says, "my inside yearns for it." [247]) Ramon and Cipriano make the lake "the centre of a new world," (358) and it is, in fact, like a huge cell in its palpitating, generative reality. Cipriano, in the trance where Ramon transforms him into a god, feels his "consciousness reeling in strange concentric waves, towards a centre where it suddenly plunges into the bottomless deeps, like sleep." (402-403) Cipriano is "swallowed up" (406) in his own center, as is Ramon in his trances. Twice Ramon asks him "Who lives," and is answered, "I." The third time, Ramon asks,

> "Is it perfect?"
> "It is perfect."
> "Who lives?"
> "Who—!"
> Cipriano no longer knew. (404)

His self disappears; he is in the "ultimate relationship" beyond "anything human or created," the relationship that is no longer relationship, where the terms "self" and "Other" no longer apply. Lawrence has in fact succeeded in freeing his character from the need for external environment, although not from the need for an Other.

In going "beyond" relationship, Cipriano, and more particularly, Ramon, turns to no more or less than his own unconscious. It is the Other that lies at the center of his own being (or, which is the same thing, at the center of the cosmos). He thus becomes both terms of the perceptual experience, both subject and object, perceiver and perceived. He achieves—at least in a theoretical sense—a perfect self-sufficiency, a self-contained relatedness that Lawrence symbolizes in the images of equilibrium enclosed in a circle.

That this ultimate relationship with the "sun" is actually with the unconscious, there can be little doubt. (The sun is also the image of the libido which is both interior and exterior, as it is described by Jung, whom Lawrence had read.)[11] In the experience of the cosmos, as of the unconscious, there is no conception of time, of subject and object, of cause and effect. The unconscious goes by contiguity and contraries, which is perhaps one meaning of Quetzalcoatl, symbol of relation, symbol of opposites. Since the unconscious is not hampered by the conceptual categories that limit the conscious mind, it gives the impression that it is infinite, as does the cosmos in *The Plumed Serpent*.

Lawrence expresses the sense of infinity in images of the cosmos as flux: "a sea of the glimmery, ethereal plasm of the world," (61) "the god-stuff [that] roars eternally, like the sea, with a sound too vast to be heard." The streaming of the cosmos is only a reflection of an interior ocean. Ramon sways like "dark seaweed" in the flux of his trances, and dives within himself, into the "ocean of the cosmos" after the "pearl" of his manhood. Once, he hears the noises of the external world sounding "on the outside of his ears, but inside them was the slow, vast, inaudible roar of the cosmos, like in a sea-shell." (199) Likewise Kate's descent into "blood-unison" leaves her "drowned in the sea of living blood," (457) and Cipriano in his trance plunges "into the bottomless deeps, like sleep."

These images of infinity become for Lawrence images of immortality. It is the last and most poignant strategy against death in *The Plumed Serpent*. Throughout the novel Lawrence juxtaposes two realities: the "concrete, jarring, exasperating reality" (119) of ordinary consciousness, and the interior cosmos: "a soft world of potency . . . the velvety dark flux from the earth, the delicate yet supreme life-breath in the inner air." Lawrence embodies the world of potency as the lake, "the great, lymphatic expanse of water, like a sea, trembling, trembling, trembling to a far distance, to the mountains of substantial nothingness." (105) In contrast to the living water is dry, dead land. "The lake stretched pale and unreal, far, far away into the invisible, with dimmed mountains rising on either side, bare and abstract." (350) This landscape is an image of a being, for the lake surrounded by the dead countryside is like the living unconscious within the arid confines of mental consciousness. It is Lawrence's familiar antithesis cast in new images. Like the unconscious, the lake seems infinite, stretching "pale and unreal into nowhere," (356) and the mountains seem finite, rising in "stiff resistance. . . . Distinct, frail distances far off in the dry air, dim-seeming, yet sharp and edged with menace." (105) It is as if to Lawrence finite limitation were fatal. "Life was vast, if fearsome," he writes, "and death was fathomless." (113) He would deny the finality of death, subsume both life and death in the endless flow of the unconscious, and by participating in the "sun," the infinity within him, never die.

Yet at the conclusion of *The Plumed Serpent*, we find that all strategy fails. Ramon cannot be divinely self-sufficient; he descends to the realm of human need in marrying Teresa. Even this relationship is not enough to prevent his disintegration. At the end of the book his efforts as a leader have left him "bled, bled, bled by the subtle, hidden malevolence of the Mexicans, and the ugly negation of the greedy, mechanical foreigners, birds of prey." (443) He is sick. "I am tired," he says, "these people make me feel I have a hole in the middle of me." (445) Kate is fearful because "he goes so remote, as if he might go away altogether into death." In the final moments of the novel, Ramon is like one of the dead. As his life was translated into terms of self-integrity, so his death is expressed primarily as psychic disintegration. "Do you feel awfully sure of yourself?" Kate asks him.

"Sure of myself?" he re-echoed. "No! Any day I may die and disappear from the face of the earth. I not only know it, I *feel* it. So why should I be sure of *myself?*

"And if you're not sure of yourself, what are you sure of?" she challenged.

He looked at her with dark eyes which she could not understand.

"I am sure—sure—" his voice tailed off into vagueness, his face seemed to go grey and peaked, as a dead man's, only his eyes watched her blackly, like a ghost's. Again she was confronted with this suffering ghost which was still in the flesh.

"You don't think you are wrong, do you?" she asked, in cold distress.

"No! I am not wrong. Only maybe I can't hold out," he said.

"And what then?" she said coldly.

"I shall go my way alone." There seemed to be nothing left of him but the black, ghostly eyes that gazed on her. He began to speak Spanish.

"It hurts my soul, as if I were dying," he said.

"But why?" she cried. "You are not ill?"

"I feel as if my soul were coming undone." (469)

"Unless one gets one's nobility from the gods," Ramon says, "and turns to the middle of the sky for one's power, one will be murdered at last." (479) Yet Ramon is dying. For a man near death, a prescription such as this is—and, in fact, as all of *The Plumed Serpent* is—must seem carrion comfort indeed.

Perhaps it is the urgency of death—the fact that his intuitions and systems are pitted against it—that makes *The Plumed Serpent* the *tour de force* of Lawrence's ego psychology. The novel contains restatements with variations of all his previous constructions of the psyche, and their development into final form. Furthermore, Lawrence creates in it his most complex model of personality, an attempt at a self-sustaining being. The faults of the Mexican novel, *qua* novel, stem mostly from the fact that it is a many-faceted perception of the self, by now ponderous and intractable in its complexity, that Lawrence attempts to wrest into fiction. The degree of abstraction in *The Plumed Serpent* is great, and the novel is burdened with schemes of ontology perhaps beyond the point fiction will bear.

All Lawrence's novels deal with the boundaries where the self stops and the rest begins. But none pushes past the limits of or-

dinary consciousness more variously and deliberately—one might
say, more clinically—than does *The Plumed Serpent*. In this
novel Lawrence sends the self on journeys of dissolution, much
as he entrusts his soul to the unknown in "Ship of Death," in
tentative reaching-out to the edge of awareness.

> We are dying, we are dying, so all we can do
> is now be willing to die, and to build the ship
> of death to carry the soul on the longest journey.
>
> A little ship, with oars and food
> and little dishes, and all accoutrements
> fitting and ready for the departed soul.
>
> Now launch the small ship, now as the body dies
> and life departs, launch out, the fragile soul
> in the fragile ship of courage, the ark of faith
> with its store of food and little cooking pans
> and change of clothes,
> upon the flood's black waste
> upon the waters of the end
> upon the sea of death, where still we sail
> darkly, for we cannot steer, and have no port.
>
> There is no port, there is nowhere to go
> only the deepening blackness darkening still
> blacker, upon the soundless, ungurgling flood
> darkness at one with darkness, up and down
> and sideways utterly dark, so there is no direction any more
> and the little ship is there; yet she is gone.
> She is not seen, for there is nothing to see her by.
> She is gone! gone! and yet
> somewhere she is there.
> Nowhere.

In this poem Lawrence explores to the brink of nonexistence.
In *The Plumed Serpent*, too, he travels toward the limits of self-
awareness, and returns as one might return from death, to record it.

6

THE LESSON IN
LADY CHATTERLEY'S LOVER

In *Lady Chatterley's Lover* the world has
passed into profound deadness. It is Law-
rence's vision of the modern dilemma, the self in isolation. Religion, "established upon the element of *union* in mankind," *(SLC,*
97) is defunct.

> For centuries the mass of people lived in [the rhythm of the cos-
> mos], under the Church. And it is down in the mass that the roots
> of religion are eternal. When the mass of a people loses the reli-
> gious rhythm, that people is dead, without hope. But Protestantism
> came and gave a great blow to the religious and ritualistic rhythm
> of the year, in human life. Nonconformity *almost* finished the
> deed. Now you have a poor, blind, disconnected people with noth-
> ing but politics and bank-holidays to satisfy the eternal human
> need of living in ritual adjustment to the cosmos in its revolutions,
> in eternal submission to the greater laws. *(SLC,* 105)

Society has lost its coherence; the classes have come apart into
awareness.

> The sense of isolation, followed by the sense of menace and fear,
> is bound to arise as the feeling of oneness and community with our
> fellow men declines, and the feeling of individualism and person-
> ality, which is existence in isolation, increases. *(SLC,* 109)

Reason, the modern addiction, has cut us off from the sense of our
own meaningfulness.

> The world of reason and science, the moon, a dead lump of earth,
> the sun, so much gas with spots: this is the dry and sterile little
> world the mind inhabits. The world of our little consciousness,
> which we know in our pettifogging *apartness.* This is how we
> know the world when we know it apart from ourselves, in the
> mean separateness of everything. *(SLC,* 107)

Perhaps the most striking thing about *Lady Chatterley's Lover* is its tone: elegiac, subdued. There is terrible resignation in the characters, and in Lawrence's voice. Mellors and Connie are two sparks of life in the universal gray, and even the woods where they meet are soon to be overwhelmed by the rising tide of industrial deadness. Nobody, not even Lawrence, seems to have faith in the "happy" ending, the comic wedding. Mellors "still has the warmth of a man," Lawrence writes in "A Propos of *Lady Chatterley's Lover*," "but he is being hunted down, destroyed. Even it is a question if the woman who turns to him will really stand by him and his vital meaning." (*SLC*, 109) The novel ends with Mellors declaration of optimism so faint it is all the more poignant:

> But a great deal of us is together, and we can but abide by it, and steer our courses to meet soon. John Thomas says goodnight to lady Jane, a little droopingly, but with a hopeful heart.

In this world meaning is lost. Mellors even in finding Connie seems to realize his profound lack of connection to his society and to anything greater than himself.

In large part the pessimism of *Lady Chatterley's Lover* is bearable only because the book, unlike any other novel by Lawrence, is romantic. When Lawrence wrote it he was sick almost to death with tuberculosis; presumably he was no longer able to have himself the sexual relationship he so glorifies in Connie and Mellors. He paints their intimacy in the bright, simple colors of nostalgia, excluding the bad but not the good. The essence of romanticism is this selective process. With Connie and Mellors all danger, and disillusion, all possibility of the self's disintegration in sex that exists earlier, are left out. The threat now lies in the world outside. Lawrence dwells lovingly on the man's body, on the woman's body, and on their perfect sex as though he were saying goodbye to them. But there is, at the same time, denying them, the current of his underlying fatalism, and the inevitable triumph of the encroaching deadness.

The deadness in *Lady Chatterley's Lover* is not only a function of Lawrence's fatalism; it is also a function of the book's form. The novel is an example of what happens when fiction ceases to be a process of discovery and becomes instead an act of summary and recapitulation. All of Lawrence's earlier themes appear: the antitheses of mind and body, conscious and unconscious, civilization and the demonic. Symbols and images from his previous novels float on the surface, connected not by any dialectical process within the book, but by the visionary cosmos he evolved earlier. Every metaphor is coherent, and every character intelligible within this system (which gives the full weight of meaning to Clifford's wheelchair or Connie's flowers). But it all has a certain ponderousness. Vital tension is absent. The book unfolds with a static, deliberate quality, like ritual.

The characters, too, lack vitality in comparison to those of the earlier novels. Lawrence has a fine touch with the realistic details of psychology—especially sexual psychology. And Connie and Mellors seem twice as alive in contrast to the deadness of their surroundings. But we perceive them as caricatures. Most Lawrence characters are caricatures, but we do not perceive them as such because they are informed with a developing idea of the self. Even the most exaggerated records a struggle to arrive at a new equilibrium with reality. The failure of vitality in *Lady Chatterley's Lover* only emphasizes that the sense of life in a novel (or character) depends on the exploration recorded in it. Any novel (or character) not conceived according to a new idea is without that particular subtle vibration of imaginative energy whose presence is so unmistakable in *Women in Love* and even *The Plumed Serpent.*

Much of Lawrence's nonfiction prose of the last years is also recapitulatory. He is didactic, not experimental. He has arrived at his final insight, which he only repeats in the hope of being understood. In *Lady Chatterley's Lover* Lawrence has found that a complex development of the idea of self is no longer necessary. All his previous convolutions of logic and symbolic structure are attempts at self-defense. The lesson in *Lady Chatterley's Lover* is that the best defense is to have no defense at all.

According to Lawrence, the modern age mistakenly uses reason as the means to create and maintain the self. In fact, modern psychology operates on the assumption that the self is strong in proportion to the dominance of reason over the unconscious. Similarly, modern philosophy (particularly phenomenology) posits that our sense of reality, including the reality of ourselves, arises from conscious reflection on what we know intuitively. But Lawrence believes that reason—the terrible wordiness of Clifford Chatterley, the intellectual interchanges of his friends—has grown out of proportion, and redefined a self that is grotesque. Worse, the more cut off and incomplete the self feels, the more reason struggles to control, like a consuming disease.

To be whole, according to Lawrence, we need to be in touch with our unconscious, and to be in touch with our unconscious we need—quite literally—sex.

> Perhaps [in *Lady Chatterley's Lover*] I shall have given some notion of my feeling about sex, for which I have been so monotonously abused. When a "serious" young man said to me the other day: "I can't believe in the regeneration of England by sex, you know," I could only say, "I'm sure you can't." He had no sex, anyhow: poor self-conscious, uneasy, narcissus-monk as he was. And he didn't know what it meant, to have any. To him, people had only minds, or no minds, mostly no minds, so they were only there to be gibed at, and he wandered around ineffectively seeking for gibes or for truth, tight shut in inside his own ego. (*SLC*, 91)

Sex is the antidote to being "tight shut in inside" the rational ego, because the sex act provides a direct inroad to the unconscious. The mind and the blood, as Lawrence says, are mutually exclusive. In sex the conscious mind is temporarily obliterated. He shows us this again and again with Connie Chatterley.

> She clung to [Mellors], with a hiss of wonder that was almost awe, terror. He held her close, but he said nothing. He would never say anything. She crept nearer to him, nearer, only to be near the sensual wonder of him. And out of his utter, incomprehensible stillness, she felt again the slow, momentous, surging rise of the phallus again, the other power. And her heart melted out with a kind of awe.
>
> And this time his being within her was all soft and iridescent, purely soft and iridescent, such as no consciousness could seize. Her whole self quivered unconscious and alive, like plasm. She could not know what it was. She could not remember what it had been. Only that it had been more lovely than anything ever could be. Only that. And afterwards she was utterly still, utterly unknowing, she was not aware for how long. And he was still with her, in an unfathomable silence along with her. And of this, they would never speak. (231)

Only in the unconscious can we know Otherness. The experience seems vital because people remain objects to us as long as they are known through the conscious mind. Only when we perceive them unconsciously, "sympathize," in Lawrence's word, do we assimilate them into ourselves (just as all learning takes place in sleep).

Through sex Connie is awakened not only to Otherness, but to the unconscious life in herself.

> She was gone in her own soft rapture, like a forest soughing with the dim, glad moan of spring, moving into bud. She could feel in the same world with her man, the nameless man, moving on beautiful feet, beautiful in the phallic mystery. And in herself, in all her veins, like a twilight.

"For hands she hath none, nor eyes, nor feet, nor golden Trea-
sure of hair..."
She was like a forest, like the dark interlacing of the oak-wood,
humming inaudibly with myriad unfolding buds. Meanwhile the
birds of desire were asleep in the vast interlaced intricacy of her
body. (188)

One's own unconscious seems vital because it is empirically perceived as such. It seems infinite, "the greater life," because in
that state we cannot perceive boundaries, time, cause and effect.
It is autonomous, operating constantly, with its own energies, independent of our will. It has the highly charged affect of all infantile or primitive states. It is animistic; emotions and drives are
projected outward and seen as "life." It peoples the cosmos with
the forces of light and dark, demons and angels, according to the
contraries which are its logic. Connie feels that she and Mellors
are like "the sons of God" and "the daughters of men," because
in the unconscious every being feels itself omnipotent. Unconscious experience has the quality of primal certitude, unmediated
by reason; it seems "right," divine, more potent than the "outer"
world where reason takes us, and which is perceived as hostile
(to our omnipotence), flat, "daylight," mechanical. In contrast to
the potent inner "living" world, the outer world seems mechanical because it is governed by cause and effect, and because the
people and things in it are objects, lacking the informing "life" of
unconscious projection. Every self has these two worlds in it.
The schizophrenic has been seduced by the inner world away
from the outer, "adult," reasoning one. The average modern man,
at least as Lawrence sees him, errs in the other extreme. But to
be whole we need both, and in proportion.

Lawrence is not advocating a steady diet of mindlessness; far
from it. "Life is only bearable when the mind and the body are
in harmony, and there is a natural balance between them, and
each has a natural respect for the other." (SLC, 87) The experience of the unconscious is an occasional act of renewal. It recon-
firms the self; afterwards we return to singleness. "So I love
chastity now," Mellors writes,

because it is the peace that comes of fucking. I love being chaste
now. I love it as the snowdrops love the snow.... And when the
real spring comes, when the drawing together comes, then we can
fuck the little flame brilliant and yellow, brilliant. But not now, not
yet! Now is the time to be chaste, it is so good to be chaste, like a
river of cool water in my soul. (374)

This rhythm of contact and withdrawal is one of the great
rhythms with which we are out of touch. "Ours is essentially a

tragic age" because reason has isolated us to death. But regeneration begins in singleness.

> The tragic consciousness has taught us, even, that one of the greater needs of man is knowledge and experience of death; every man needs to know death in his own body. But the greater consciousness of the pre-tragic and post-tragic epochs teaches us—though we have not reached the post-tragic epoch—that the greatest need of man is the renewal forever of the complete rhythm of life and death, the rhythm of the sun's year, the body's year of a lifetime, and the greater year of the stars, the soul's year of immortality. (*SLC*, 105)

The hardest lesson for us to learn is openness. "I believe," Lawrence writes, "there has never been an age of greater mistrust between persons than ours today: under a very superficial but quite genuine social trust." (*SLC*, 90) And, he concludes, "Don't trust *anybody* with your real emotions: if you've got any: that is the slogan of today. Trust them with your money, even, but *never* with your feelings. They are bound to trample on them."

Mellors has been battered by the world and withdraws into aloneness. But he finds this isolation is only another kind of death. Connie connects him up again:

> "And are you sorry?" she said.
> "In a way!" he replied, looking up at the sky. "I thought I'd done with it all. Now I've begun again."
> "Begun what?"
> "Life."
> "Life!" she re-echoed, with a queer thrill.
> "It's life," he said. "There's no keeping clear. And if you do keep clear you might almost as well die. So if I've got to be broken open again, I have." (165)

> He stood back and watched her going into the dark, against the pallor of the horizon. Almost with bitterness he watched her go. She had connected him up again, when he had wanted to be alone. She had cost him that bitter privacy of a man who at last wants only to be alone. (166)

Mellors has the misfortune of being born into the wrong age, when reason is supreme, (or, from another point of view, simply the misfortune of possessing "adult" rationality). Yet he makes the leap of faith, to tenderness, and vulnerability. "A man could no longer be private and withdrawn. The world allows no hermits. And now he had taken the woman, and brought on himself a new cycle of pain and doom. For he knew by experience what it meant." (166)

It was not the woman's fault, nor even love's fault, nor the fault of sex. The fault lay there, out there, in those evil electric lights and diabolical rattlings of engines. There, in the world of mechanical greedy, greedy mechanism and mechanized greed, sparkling with lights and gushing with hot metal and roaring with traffic, there lay the vast evil thing, ready to destroy whatever did not conform. Soon it would destroy the wood, and the bluebells would spring no more. All vulnerable things must perish under the rolling and running of iron.

He thought with infinite tenderness of the woman. Poor forlorn thing, she was nicer than she knew, and oh! so much too nice for the tough lot she was in contact with. Poor thing, she too had some of the vulnerability of the wild hyacinths, she wasn't all tough rubber-goods and platinum, like the modern girl. And they would do her in. As sure as life, they would do her in, as they do in all naturally tender life. Tender! Somewhere she was tender, tender with a tenderness of the growing hyacinths, something that has gone out of the celluloid women of today. But he would protect her with his heart for a little while. For a little while, before the insentient iron world and the Mammon of mechanized greed did them both in, her as well as him.

Mellors is heroic, in accepting vulnerability and tenderness. And he is tragic; he knows he will soon be lost.

The triumph of "the insentient iron world" is Lawrence's final vision. It is a rather hopeless conclusion to his life-long struggle for the self's autonomy. Connie and Mellors have discovered the experience with the greatest validity possible: wholeness through another human being. But it is not enough. In "The Man Who Died" (1929), Christ and the Priestess of Isis also discover their wholeness, but their contact leads to lasting regeneration, because they live in a "past" world (which may never have existed), where connection with something greater than the self—a social or religious idea in the broadest sense—is possible. But Connie and Mellors, like us, are up against the universal fragmentation of a scientific age.

To judge from the bleakness of *Lady Chatterley's Lover*, Lawrence's final insight is that his philosophy of existence can provide no salvation in our time. In this respect he was mistaken. His main concern—the sense of wholeness and meaningfulness—is now our main concern. Ideas similar to his about the development of the self have become part of our conscious experience, through popular and influential psychologies such as those of Erikson and Laing. His psychological systems are metaphorical, which makes them suspect (and/or unintelligible) to a society accustomed to "scientific" psychological explication. But though Lawrence appears mystical, he is fully empirical. The metaphors which constitute the core of his fiction illustrate exactly what modern ego psychology deals with, and what all of us would experience if we cared to listen to ourselves.

Lawrence's one greatest lesson is the necessity of wholeness, of integrating rational and non-rational experience. In the end he seems to have despaired of it, at least for the mass of mankind; *Lady Chatterley's Lover* is nothing if not a requiem for the irrational. But time has shown Lawrence's pessimism to be premature. Fifty years after the death of popular religion we commonly acknowledge the sterility of the unmitigated rational consciousness that is the only permissible consciousness in our daily lives; of civilization which considers the rational mind the only object worthy of "education," and which identifies our being with our rational selves. Much of recent psychology is an attempt to integrate, just as Lawrence did, rationality and the many areas of unconscious awareness into a meaningful self.

NOTES

Chapter 1. SONS AND LOVERS: The Struggle to Exist

1. The "Study of Thomas Hardy" (1914) and *Twilight in Italy* (1916) tell us a great deal about the ego psychology of *The Rainbow* (1915). "The Two Principles" (1919) and "The Crown" (1915, 1925) contain much of the substance of *Women in Love* (1921). *Studies in Classic American Literature* (1923) develop theories of the ego similar to those of *Aaron's Rod* (1922) and *Kangaroo* (1923), just as *Reflections on the Death of a Porcupine* (1925) and *Mornings in Mexico* (1927) clarify the ideas of self in *The Plumed Serpent* (1926).

2. "Every man comprises male and female in his being, the male struggling for predominance." (*Phoenix*, 488) On a cosmic level, Lawrence sees Being as a transcendent coitus:

> In the beginning, light touches darkness and darkness touches light. Then life has begun. The light enfolds and implicates and involves the dark, the dark receives and interpenetrates the light, they come nearer, they are more finely combined, till they burst into the crisis of oneness, the blossom, the utter being, the transcendent and timeless flame of the iris. (*Phoenix II*, 376)

Analogy gives Lawrence's narrative its tremendous evocative power. When Birkin and Ursula make love in "Excurse" they are as much cosmic principles as human beings:

> Quenched, inhuman, his fingers upon her unrevealed nudity were the fingers of silence upon silence, the body of mysterious night upon the body of mysterious night, the night masculine and feminine, never to be seen with the eyes, or known with the mind, only known as a palpable revelation of living otherness. (312)

3. Robert E. Gajdusek points this out in "A Reading of *The White Peacock*" (in *A D. H. Lawrence Miscellany*, ed. H. T. Moore [Carbondale: Southern Illinois University Press, 1959] p. 194).

4. Sigmund Freud, "The Most Prevalent Forms of Degradation in Erotic Life" (1912), in *The Collected Papers of Sigmund Freud*, ed. Joan Riviere in 5 volumes, (London: Hogarth Press, 1953) vol. 3, p. 502.

5. Reiff in his Introduction to *Psychoanalysis and the Unconscious* discusses the similarities between Lawrence and Freud. As a result of socio-economic changes at the end of the nineteenth century, the extended family lost its power, and the role of the mother was "grotesquely distorted into dominance, and the father's degraded into that of permanent *other*." (p. xi) Lawrence, unlike Freud, holds that the mother turns to her sons because the sexual relationship between the parents is out of joint, which was not unusual in the post-Victorian era. Also unlike Freud, Lawrence believes that it is the parent, not the child, who initiates the incest problem. (p. xvii)

6. In "The Theme of the Three Caskets" Freud hypothesizes that men deny the sexuality of the maternal image by fragmenting woman into a triple image, of mother, wife, destructress. These, he says, are the three forms assumed by the maternal image in a man's life: "the mother herself, the beloved one who is chosen after her pattern, and lastly the Mother Earth who receives him once more." *Complete Psychological Works of Sigmund Freud*, ed. James Strachey, London: Hogarth Press 1953-1966 in 23 volumes, Vol. 12, p. 301.

7. This displacement of unacceptable hostility to the mother is considered by Simone de Beauvoir to be the origin of the myth of the impossible mother-in-law. (*The Second Sex*, trans. H. M. Parshley, [N.Y.: Knopf, 1953] p. 161)

8. See "Apropos of *Lady Chatterley's Lover*" in *Phoenix II*, 487-518.

9. Erich Neumann, *The Origins and History of Consciousness* (New York: Pantheon, Bollingen Series, 1954), p. 17.

10. *Civilization and Its Discontents*, trans. James Strachey (New York: W. W. Norton & Co., 1963), p. 17.

11. Neumann, p. 17.

12. Strindberg describes it: "I forgot my sex in the arms of the mother who was no longer female but sexless." (in *Masculine/Feminine*, edited by Betty and Theodore Roszak [New York: Harper & Row, 1969] p. 12.)

13. Diana Trilling, "A Letter of Introduction to Lawrence" in *A D. H. Lawrence Miscellany*, p. 124.

14. Christian mysticism integrates the two states systematically, as part of the "ladder" to God. St. John of the Cross describes the dark night: "Inasmuch as not only is the understanding here purged of its light, and the will of its affections, but the memory is also purged of meditation and knowledge, it is well that it be likewise annihilated with respect to all these things, so that that which David says of himself in this purgation may be fulfilled, namely: 'I was annihilated and I knew not.' " (*The Dark Night of the Soul*, trans. E. Allison Peers [Garden City: Doubleday, 1962] p. 116.)

15. Graham Hough accuses Lawrence of this in *Dark Sun: A Study of D. H. Lawrence* (New York: Putnam, 1956) p. 51.

16. *The Divided Self: An Existential Study of Sanity and Madness* (Baltimore: Penguin, 1965) p. 45ff.

17. According to Laing, individuals with ontological insecurity often have a dread of being understood because "to be understood correctly is to be engulfed." (45) This suggests some relationship with Lawrence's life-long hatred of women who "understand" or who "know" a man, and why it is so often described as a destructive act. Other tendencies in the "schizoid individual" who is "subject to the dread of his own dissolution into non-being" are a "persistent scission between self and body," which is suggestive about early Lawrence; and the tendency to see human beings as machines, which is suggestive about later Lawrence. That Lawrence himself suffered from this syndrome is suggested by images he uses in his letters and elsewhere.

> I curse my age, and all the people in it. I hate my fellow man most thoroughly. I wish there could be an earthquake that would swallow everybody up except some two dozen people. Meanwhile we've got to watch it that we're not swallowed. (Nehls, I, 358)

> I find the Midlands full of the fear of death—truly. They're all queer and unnerved.... Last evening at dusk I sat by the rapid brook which runs by the highroad in the valley bed. When I got to the top—a very hard climb—I felt as if I had climbed out of a womb. (AH, 462)

J. M. Murry recounts that Lawrence once said "Jack is trying to kill me," and "one night," Murry says, "I heard him crying or moaning that I was 'an obscene bug that was sucking his life away.' " (in *Between Two Worlds: An Autobiography* [New York: Julian Messner, 1936] p. 417.) In Lawrence historical process, and such abstractions as "industrialism," "mechanicalism" and "democracy" reflect their existential origins. In *Kangaroo* he describes England's "war-panic" as loss of identity on a national scale. Because the "mob-spirit" ruled, according to him, "practically every man lost his head, and lost his own centrality, his own manly isolation in his own integrity, which alone keeps life real." (216) Lawrence's hatred of democracy, like John S. Mill's misgivings about it, stems from the fact that he believes that in democracy the individual is engulfed in the mass. This is the point of attacks on democracy in *Studies in Classic American Literature* and in *The Plumed Serpent* (p. 395, passim.).

18. Lawrence also condemns Walt Whitman (whose mind was very much like his own) because Whitman glorifies the experience of merging, and because Whitman finds everything female, "even himself," in that everything in Whitman's universe tends to absorb. "He found, as all men find, that you can't really merge in a woman, though you may go a long way. You can't manage the last little bit. So you have to give up and try elsewhere, if you *insist* on merging." And "Death is now his chant! Death! Merging! And Death! Which is the final merge. The great merge into the womb. Woman." (SCAL, 68-69)

19. That the mountain symbolizes woman—or more exactly, the womb—is also suggested by its crucifix and its Marienhütte. Gerald is a sacrificed Christ; Gudrun his mother Mary. Their relationship is a perverted *pietà*. The Marienhütte signifies that the "salvation" offered by woman to a man can also be his destruction.

20. Lawrence commonly reverses the threat of non-existence offered by a woman, and visits the crime on the perpetrator. In *Sons and Lovers* the spiritual vampirism of Miriam on Paul is reversed in Paul's affair with Clara. Paul practices vampirism on Clara in sex, in effect sucking her dry; at the opera he has a compulsion to kiss the vein in her arm (331) and at another meeting he sinks "his mouth on her throat, where he felt her heavy pulse under his lips. Everything was perfectly still. There was nothing in the afternoon but themselves." (311)

21. Likewise Ramon subjugates his second wife, Teresa, by figuratively enveloping her. She is his child-bride, and she says, "I shall not contradict him. How can I? My soul is inside him, and I am far from contradicting him.... That other way of women, where a woman keeps her own soul—ah, what is that but weariness!" (451)

THE ART OF SELF IN D. H. LAWRENCE

Chapter 2. THE RAINBOW: Coming of Age

1. At the opposite extreme is the impressionistic mode of characterization. Chekhov, for instance, creates his characters by building up details of surface, not presuming to give them an essence (or humor) which "explains" them. This acknowledges the improbability of the essentially literary assumption that we can know what a person really *is;* it imitates how we apprehend others in real life; and it maintains the radical elusiveness and unintelligibility of others.

2. This, Lawrence's revised theory of personality, resembles Freud's in that it assumes there is an unconscious (or blood consciousness) which in its relation to the conscious mind is like the iceberg, nine-tenths under water. Both men agree that this unconscious shapes our acts. The difference is that Freud mistrusts and fears the unconscious; whereas Lawrence, considering it the source of life and salvation, fears for it.

3. Walter Allen, in "D. H. Lawrence in Perspective," (in *Penguin New Writing* [Autumn, 1946] describes these "verbal mannerisms" as attempts to render the activity of the unconscious.)

4. Creative Evolution, in which *"élan vital"* is a key term, was published in 1907. Probably Lawrence had read the work by 1913, since from that time he used *"élan vital"* freely. (Rose Marie Burwell, "A Catalogue of D. H. Lawrence's Reading from Early Childhood," [*D. H. Lawrence Review*, vol. 3, no. 3, Fall, 1970 Fayetteville: Univ. Ark.]) Lawrence's debt to Bergson in *The Rainbow* appears to be considerable.

5. William York Tindall points this out in *D. H. Lawrence and Susan His Cow* (New York: Columbia University Press, 1939) p. 33.

6. The Rainbow provides ample illustration of Erik Erikson's hypothetical "inner bodily space." The book is dominated by the "abdominal consciousness" that he considers the distinguishing characteristic of femininity. (*Childhood and Society,* [2nd ed. New York: W. W. Norton, 1963,] p. 267.)

7. Other, minor resemblances between Lawrence's work and *Creative Evolution* suggest themselves. The rocket, like the phoenix which became Lawrence's trademark, arises out of the ashes of the past. The phoenix first appears in Lawrence in *The Rainbow* on a buttermold Will Brangwen carves for Anna. It is a symbol of their part in the generational process. In the novel rejection or casting away is often linked with images of ashes: Ursula in "the ash and grit of disillusion. . . . could only stiffen in rejection, rejection." (437) Both Lawrence and Bergson compare new life to spirit, and the past to matter that encumbers it. This is illustrated in the first battle encounter between Skrebensky and Ursula. He, who embodies outdated social forms (imperialism, militarism) hampers Ursula: "He held her very close, so that she could feel his body, the weight of him sinking, settling upon her, overcoming her life and her energy, making her inert along with him." (318)

8. The Rainbow, oddly enough for a modern novel, conforms to the last word on biblical exegesis, which is Dante's famous system of four levels of meaning. These he enumerated in the *Convivio* as: literal; allegorical (the truth hidden under a beautiful fiction); moral (tells us how to act); and anagogic (spiritual understanding beyond the senses).

9. Marvin Mudrick discusses the succession of life-styles in the three generations in "The Originality of the Rainbow," (*Spectrum III,* [Winter 1959] p. 3-28).

10. Two excellent discussions of this symbolism are H. T. Moore's "The Rainbow," (in *The Achievement of D. H. Lawrence,* eds. Hoffman and H. T. Moore [Norman, Okla. The University of Okla. Press, 1953] and Julian Moynihan's chapter on *The Rainbow* in *The Deed of Life: The Novels and Tales of D. H. Lawrence* (Princeton, New Jersey: The Princeton Univ. Press, 1963).

11. *Young Man Luther: A Study in Psychoanalysis and History* (New York: W. W. Norton, 1962), p. 41. Erikson postulates eight stages of growth, which can be briefly summarized as follows: 1. Early infancy, the crisis involving trust of the mother. 2. Infancy, where the prototypes of will and will-power develop, the crisis determining whether the individual will be dominated by autonomy or by shame and doubt; 3. The so-called phallic or oedipal stage, the crisis involving initiative vs. guilt; 4. The stage of systematic learning, tools, and rationale of action; 5. The identity crisis; 6. The crisis of intimacy; 7. Of generativity; 8. Of integrity. (p. 255ff.)

12. Erikson, p. 99.

13. Erikson, p. 101.

14. Erikson, p. 103.

15. Lawrence's punning is a bit more explicit than Dante, however. "And God the Father, the Inscrutable, the Unknowable, we know in the flesh, in Woman. She is the door for our in-going and our out-coming. In her we go back to the Father; but like the witnesses of the transfiguration, blind and unconscious." (Nehls, III, 1250)

16. The image of separating oneself from a matrix dominates Lawrence's ego psychology in "Study of Thomas Hardy." In this essay he discusses various ways to do this, such as action, knowing, and will.

> Now one craves that his life should be more individual, that I and you and my neighbor should each be distinct from the general mass. Then it would be a melody if I walked down the road; if I stood with my neighbor it would be pure harmony. (*Phoenix*, 432)
>
> Looking over the Hardy novels, it is interesting to see which of the heroes one could call a distinct individuality, more or less achieved, which an unaccomplished potential individuality, and which an impure, unindividualized life embedded in the matrix, either achieving its own lower degree of distinction, or not achieving it. (434)
>
> Yet in life, so often, one feels that a man who is, by nature, intrinsically an individual, is by practice and knowledge an impurity, almost a nonentity. To each individuality belongs, by nature, its own knowledge. Yet this is not so. Many a soul which we feel should have detached itself and become distinct, remains embedded, and struggles with knowledge that does not pertain to it. It reached a point of distinctness and a degree of personal knowledge, and then became confused, lost itself. (433)

17. Lawrence often objectifies outer self and inner self as social reality in contradistinction to erotic reality. Characters thus pass from one state to the other, questioning which is "real." Tom Brangwen's "own concrete life that was Cossethay," for example, fades before the erotic reality of life with Lydia. (27) The two states are also represented as physical realms. In *Women in Love* Ursula and Birkin relinquish society to become erotic outcasts. Through her affair with Birkin, Ursula's social self is abandoned. "She seemed to have passed into a kind of dream world, absolved from the conditions of actuality." (135) Later the dream becomes denser, and society more ephemeral. After their marriage the couple passes into the realm of erotic reality. The voyage to Europe, ending in Italy, symbolizes "this final transit out of life." (379) Lawrence only briefly suggests the nature of Italy in *The Rainbow* with an Italian *valet de chambre*, but in *The Lost Girl* he emphasizes that England is the social, Italy the erotic realm. The novel is predicated on the heroine's choice between them; Alvina vascillates between her role in English society and the vital reality of her love for an Italian. She doubts the relative reality of him and her English home. "In a minute Madame and Ciccio and all seemed to become unreal—the actual unrealities. . . . They *were* unreal, Madame and Ciccio and the rest. . . . Ciccio was just a fantasy." (162) Eventually she chooses Ciccio; her train trip to Italy, like Ursula's journey to Germany (and

Kate's to Lake Chapala in *The Plumed Serpent*) is a symbolic transit to permanent residence outside society in the realm of "actual unrealities."

18. Bruno Bettelheim, *Symbolic Wounds: Puberty Rites and the Envious Male* (New York: Collier, 1962) For a civilized counterpart, Melanie Klein posits a "femininity complex" in men ("Early Stages of the Oedipus Conflict" in *Contributions to Psychoanalysis 1921-1945* [London: Hogarth Press] pp. 206-207). Karen Horney discusses "womb envy" in *Feminine Psychology*, ed. Harold Kelman (New York: W. W. Norton, 1967).

19. *Male and Female: A Study of the Sexes in a Changing Society* (New York: Morrow, 1967) p. 98ff.

20. Rite of passage is a main theme in the story "Daughters of the Vicar." Birth symbols punctuate Alfred's transition from dependence on his mother. At first "polarized" to his mother, Alfred begins to be reborn when she takes to her bed, a tumor in her belly. He comes home from the mines and washes himself, emerging upside down and naked from the tub. (CSS, I, 170) His mother's death is his ego's birth trauma, when "he was afraid almost with obliteration. What was this new night ringing around him, and what was he?" (173) While she dies, "suffering seized him in its grip like two hands, in agony. He lay on the bed screwed up tight. It lasted so long, and exhausted him so much, that he fell asleep." At last he is delivered: "it seemed as if life in him had burst its bounds, and he was lost in a great, bewildering flood.... He himself was broken and spilled out amid it all. He could only breathe panting in silence." (176) His tears, disorientation and helplessness signify his newborn consciousness.

Chapter 3. CHAOS: WHO SURVIVES IN *WOMEN IN LOVE?*

1. Letter to Lady Cynthia Asquith (April 26, 1916) in *Selected Letters of D. H. Lawrence*, ed. Diana Trilling (New York: Farrar, Straus and Cudahy, 1958) p. 134.

2. Seymour Betsky considers that *Women in Love* deals with the "destruction of England by the industrial revolution" and the "disintegration of that collective tradition" shared by agricultural England. ("Rhythm and Theme: DHL's *Sons and Lovers*" in *The Achievement of D. H. Lawrence* p. 143.) Julian Moynihan sees *Women in Love* as reflecting the dissolution of European society as a result of the first World War. (*The Deed of Life* p. 72ff.)

3. "A Letter of Introduction to D. H. Lawrence" in *A D. H. Lawrence Miscellany*, pp. 114-130.

4. In his essay "The Two Principles," Lawrence contrasts two kinds of love:

> The coming-together of the sexes may be the soft, delicate union of pure creation, or it may be the tremendous conjunction of opposition, a vivid struggle.... From either of these consummations birth takes place. But in the first case it is the birth of a softly rising and budding soul, wherein the two principles commune in gentle union, so that the soul is harmonious and at one with itself. In the second case it is the birth of a disintegrative soul, wherein the two principles wrestle in their eternal opposition: a soul finite, momentaneous, active in the universe as a unit of sundering. The first kind of birth takes place in the youth of an era, in the mystery of accord; the second preponderates in the times of disintegration, the crumbling of an era. But at all times beings are born from the two ways, and life is made up of duality." (*Phoenix II*, 234)

Whether this union is cast in terms of "principles" or two human lovers, its issue is the same: a "soul," a being.

5. Wilhelm Reich, *Selected Writings: An Introduction to the Theory of Orgonomy* (New York: Farrar, Straus & Cudahy, 1960).

6. The Princess, in the short story of the same name, (1924) has a lethal virginal intactness described as inorganic hardness. She has a spirit "hard and flawless as a diamond," and "as a small child, something crystallized in her character, making her clear and finished, and as impervious as crystal." (CSS, II, 508, 476)

7. Another image of deathly finiteness that Lawrence uses often in *Women in Love* is the past. Hermione's Breadalby makes Birkin ponder "how sure, how formed, how final all the things of the past were—the lovely accomplished past—the house, so still and golden, the park slumbering its centuries of peace. And then, what a snare and a delusion, this beauty of static things—what a horrible dead prison Breadalby really was, what an intolerable confinement, the peace!" (91) The fatal allure of the "by-gone perfection" of the dead past is a strong theme in the "Breadalby" chapter. "Isn't it complete," Gudrun says of the house. "It is as final as an old aquatint." (75) (N. B. the pun on water.) This is the point of the games she and Loerke play in "Snowed Up":

> They praised the bygone things, they took a sentimental, childish delight in the achieved perfections of the past. Particularly they liked the late eighteenth century, the period of Goethe and of Shelley, and Mozart.
> They played with the past and with the great figures of the past, a sort of little game of chess, or marionettes, all to please themselves. (444)

Their games, too, signify lifelessness, this time in activity, instead of stasis.

8. "The Crown" essay describes the generation of reality through conflict: "Is not the unicorn necessary to the very existence of the lion, is not each opposite kept in stable equilibrium by the opposition of the other?" (*Phoenix II*, 366) "We say, 'I am the pure unicorn, it is for men to oppose and resist for ever that avid lion. If he ceased to exist, I should be supreme and unique and perfect, therefore

I will destroy him.' But the lion will not be destroyed. If he were, if he were swallowed into the belly of the unicorn, the unicorn would fly asunder in chaos." (367)

Simone de Beauvoir makes a similar observation, but in human terms. The difficulty, she writes, is that woman cannot fulfill man's "needs. Either she appears simply as a purely impersonal opposition, she is an obstacle and remains a stranger; or she submits passively to man's will and permits assimilation, so that he takes possession of her only through consuming her—that is, through destroying her. In both cases he remains alone." (*The Second Sex*, p. 129)

9. Lawrence redefines the mind-body split in existential terms in the essay "The Two Principles":

> Man is divided... into the upper and lower man: that is, the spiritual and sensual being... By spiritual we mean that state of being where the self excels into the universe, and knows all things by passing into all things. It is that blissful consciousness which glows upon the flowers and trees and sky, so that I am sky and flowers, I, who am myself. It is that movement towards a state of infinitude wherein I experience my living oneness with all things.... By sensual being, on the other hand, we mean that state in which the self is the magnificent centre wherein all life pivots, and lapses,... a magnificent central positivity,... a state portrayed in the great dark statues of the seated Lords of Egypt. The self is incontestable and unsurpassable. (*Phoenix II*, 235)

10. T. A. Smailes discusses some of this symbolism in "The Mythical Bases of *Women in Love*" (in *D. H. Lawrence Review* [vol. 1, no. 2, Summer, 1968] p. 129-36).

11. Kingsley Widmer, "Our Demonic Heritage" in *A D. H. Lawrence Miscellany* pp. 13-27.

12. Kingsley Widmer, *The Art of Perversity: D. H. Lawrence's Shorter Fiction* (Seattle: Univ. Washington Press, 1962) p. 120.

13. Karl Menninger illustrates what might be called the classical stereotyped explanation of the "inherent destructiveness" of male sexuality, in *Love Against Hate* (New York: Harcourt, Brace & World, 1942). Typically in such stereotyped thinking the sexes are polarized: to be feminine is to be passive and receptive; the essence of masculinity is to be active, "responsible" and "dangerous." (78) These are qualifications that Gerald fulfills. According to Menninger, Gerald as an industrialist is consummately masculine:

> Some of my colleagues distinguish another element in work, best described as an impulse toward mastery—controlling, reforming, organizing, directing, etc. They believe that such an impulse is an instinctual striving to use the powers of mind and body and is not motivated by hate. But to me this urge to master something, whether it be a mechanical puzzle or a complicated accounting problem or a recalcitrant horse, seems to be indistinguishable in its essence from the aggressive, destructive impulse, purposively and expediently directed. To the extent that something is mastered, some kind of resistance is broken down or overcome.... all of them are working *against* something in an effort to master a situation or a material and to produce something in the end. (135)

The difficulty with this sort of interpretation is that it assumes "aggressive" is "destructive." In Lawrence destruction has two main forms only, merging and annihilation, and they are utterly passive.

Chapter 4. SOLIPSISM: *AARON'S ROD* AND *KANGAROO*

1. Richard Aldington in the Introduction to *Kangaroo* (New York: Viking Press, 1960) p. viii.

2. Aldington, viii.

3. Quoted by Aldous Huxley in "D. H. Lawrence" in *A D. H. Lawrence Miscellany* p. 64.

In *Aaron's Rod* a returned soldier, Herbertson, is a victim of what Freud observed in some veterans and termed the "repetition compulsion." Herbertson comes to his friends "to talk war." "It was a driving instinct—to come and get it off his chest."

> And on and on he talked, over his wine and soda. He was not conceited—he was not showing off—far from it. It was the same thing here in this officer as it was with the privates, and the same with this Englishman as with a Frenchman or a German or an Italian. . . . every time it was the same thing, the same hot, blind anguished voice of a man who has seen too much, experienced too much, and doesn't know where to turn. None of the glamour of returned heroes, none of the romance of war: only a hot, blind, mesmerized voice, going on and on, mesmerized by a vision that the soul cannot bear. . . . The hot, seared burn of unbearable experience, which did not heat or cool, and whose irritation was not to be relieved. The experience gradually cooled on top: but only with a surface crust. The soul did not heal, did not recover. (108-109)

In a sense *Aaron's Rod* and *Kangaroo* are Lawrence's equivalents to Herbertson's war stories. As such they are purgation rather than communication, and private rather than public. "When a man writes a letter to himself," Lawrence remarks in *Aaron's Rod*, "it is a pity to post it to somebody else. Perhaps the same is true of a book." (256)

4. The theme of somatic disease and the disintegration of the psyche dominates most of the essays in *Studies in Classic American Literature* [1918-1923]. Cooper deals with "the collapse of the white psyche," (62) and Poe with "the disintegration processes of his own psyche," for "the human soul must suffer its own disintegration, consciously, if ever it is to survive." (65) "It is love that causes the neuroticism of the day. It is love that is the prime cause of tuberculosis" (68). Poe "died wanting more love, and love killed him. A ghastly disease, love." (81) In the essay on Hawthorne Lawrence writes that men are "stronger on LOVE than on anything: then there's nothing left for you to sin against except the Holy Ghost," one's self integrity. "And gradually, from within outwards, they rot. Some form of dementia. A thing disintegrating. A decomposing psyche. Dementia." (103)

5. See Earl and Achsah Brewster, *D. H. Lawrence, Reminiscences and Correspondence* (London: Secker, 1934).

6. Lawrence also writes, "Right to the end [Melville] could never accept the fact that *perfect* relationships cannot be. Each soul is alone, and the aloneness of each soul is a double barrier to perfect relationship between two beings." (SCAL, 142)

7. See Julian Moynihan, *The Deed of Life,* p. 98.

8. The significance of Lawrence's "social thinking" is a moot point. Raymond Williams writes that "the instinct of community was vital" in Lawrence's thinking. "Deeper and stronger, [DHL] argued, than even the sexual instinct." (in "The Social Thinking of D. H. Lawrence," in *A D. H. Lawrence Miscellany*, p. 301). Such literal interpretations, like Millett's in *Sexual Politics* (New York: Doubleday, 1969), ignore the high degree of poetic distortion in Lawrence's social pronouncements. Horace Gregory notes more acutely that Lawrence's sense of power could not be gratified in "leadership" because its source lay in the "definitely antisocial activity of translating his emotions into words. To be alone was

the first step toward a renewal at the source." (*D. H. Lawrence, Pilgrim of the Apocalypse: A Critical Study* [New York: Viking Press, 1933] p. 85)

9. Begrudging women their ability to bear children, *Aaron's Rod* ignores the commonplace that children are the reason for women's "biological enslavement" as well as their limited social role.

10. Erich Neumann corroborates Lawrence, that homosexual love between adolescents often has this narcissistic, mirror-image quality. In myth, he notes, one of the pair (often a pair of twins) is creative, one destructive. Neumann considers this manifestation of narcissistic "phallus-body love" the first stage of emancipation from the mother. (*Origins and History of Consciousness*, p. 96ff.)

11. The figure of Kangaroo is intelligible only as an oedipal mother. Graham Hough, for instance, finds Kangaroo an "unassimilated figure," but overlooks the fact that the book despite its realistic tone concerns a primitive fantasy of the parents (in *Dark Sun: A Study of D. H. Lawrence*, p. 97).

12. One hint that Lawrence is dealing with the theme of rejection of the mother is Somers' guilty dream about the woman he has repudiated. He insists on male activity from which his wife is excluded. Then he dreams of a woman "something like Harriet, something like his mother, and yet unlike her, a woman sullen and obstinate against him, repudiating him."

> Bitter the woman was grieved beyond words, grieved till her face was swollen and puffy and almost mad or imbecile, because she loved him so much, and now she must see him betray her love. That was how the dream woman put it: he had betrayed her great love, and she must go down desolate into an everlasting hell, denied, and denying him absolutely in return, a sullen, awful soul. [Somers laid his hand on her arm] "But I love you. Don't you *believe* in me? Don't you *believe* in me?" But the woman, she seemed almost old now—only shed a few bitter tears, bitter as vitriol, from her distorted face, and bitterly, hideously turned away . . . to the sullen dreary everlasting hell of repudiation. (p. 94)

13. "The most striking distinction between the erotic life of antiquity and our own no doubt lies in the fact that the ancients laid the stress upon the instinct itself, whereas we emphasize its object. The ancients glorified the instinct and were prepared on its account to honor even an inferior object; while we despise the instinctual activity in itself, and find excuses for it only in the merits of the object," (Sigmund Freud, "Three Essays on Sexuality" in *Complete Psychological Works of Sigmund Freud:* in 23 vols., vol. 7, p. 149.)

Chapter 5. DEATH AND *THE PLUMED SERPENT*

1. According to the Hon. Dorothy Brett, in Nehls, II, 356.

2. L. D. Clark in his study of Lawrence (*Dark Night of the Body* [Austin, Texas: University of Texas Press, 1964]) does an excellent job of tracing the mythic analogues of *The Plumed Serpent* in Frazer, in Aztec and Biblical myths, yoga, and so on.

3. Other details from the myth of the dying and reviving god are Malintzi's green and floral clothes; the *agon* between the new god Quetzalcoatl and the old god Jesus; the sacrificial victims: the seven dead after the attack on Jamiltepec, and the ritual sacrifice of "Huitzilpochtli's Night" where the victims are hooded, then strangled or have their throats cut.

4. In "Aristocracy" Lawrence writes,

> Man's life consists in a connection with all things in the universe. Whoever can establish, or initiate, a new connection between mankind and the circumambient universe is, in his own degree, a savior. Because mankind is always exhausting human possibilities, always degenerating into repetition, torpor, *ennui*, lifelessness. When *ennui* sets in, it is a sign that human vitality is waning, and the human connection with the universe is gone stale.... [Saviors] established a *new* connection between mankind and the universe, and the result was a vast release of energy. The *sun* was reborn to man, and so was the moon. (*Phoenix II*, 478)

5. Lawrence's essays about Indian religion make it clear that to him the goal of animism is to derive life:

> In the oldest religion, everything was alive, not supernaturally but naturally alive. There were only deeper and deeper streams of life, vibrations of life more and more vast. Rocks have more life than mountains. So rocks are alive, but a mountain has a deeper vaster life than a rock and it was much harder for a man to bring his spirit or his energy, into contact with the life of the mountain and to draw strength from the mountain, as from a great standing well of life, than it was to come into contact with the rock. And he had to put forth a great effort. For the whole life-effort of man was to get his life into direct contact with the elemental life of the cosmos, mountain-life, thunder-life, air-life, earth-life, sun-life. To come into immediate *felt* contact, and so derive energy, power, and a dark sort of joy. This effort into sheer naked contact, without an intermediary or mediator, is the root meaning of religion. (*Phoenix*, 146)

6. In one of the Hymns Quetzalcoatl says:

> I am the Son of the Morning Star, and child of the deeps.
> No man knows my Father, and I know Him not.
> My father is deep within the deeps, whence He sent me forth.
> He sends the eagle of silence down on wide wings
> To lean over my head and my neck and my breast
> And fill them strong with strength of wings.
> He sends the serpent of power up my feet and my loins
> So that strength wells up in me like water in hot springs
> But midmost shines as the Morning Star midmost shines
> Between night and day, my Soul-star in one,
> Which is my Father whom I know not.
> I tell you, the day should not turn into glory,
> And the night should not turn deep,
> Save for the morning and evening stars, upon which they turn. (373)

7. See Mark Schorer's "Lawrence and the Spirit of the Place" in *A D. H. Lawrence Miscellany*. Schorer discusses how in later Lawrence "the spirit of the place" replaces most characters.

8. *Architects of the Self: George Eliot, D. H. Lawrence and E. M. Forster* (Berkeley: University of California Press, 1972) p. 78.

9. This recalls the romantic transcendentalists, particularly Emerson. Coleridge's analysis of heightened perception, which he calls "imagination," is also very similar: "The primary imagination I hold to be the *living* power and prime agent of all human perception, and as a repetition in the finite mind of the eternal act of *creation* in the infinite *I AM*." [italics mine] (*Biographia Literaria* [New York: Dutton, 1962], p. 167.)

10. Wylie Sypher summarizes this position in *Loss of Self in Modern Literature and Art*. Bipolar logic, he says, predicates that the self is opposed to the world, which brings a "mistaken sense of individuality," and this heightened sense of the self causes "anxiety." (New York: Vintage Books, 1966) p. 128. Lawrence of course holds precisely the opposite view.

11. Mabel Luhan mentions in *Lorenzo in Taos* (New York: Knopf, 1932) that she sent Lawrence a volume of Jung in 1924.

Jung writes in *Psychology of the Unconscious,*

> The sun is adapted as is nothing else to represent the visible God of this world. That is to say, that driving strength of our own soul, which we call libido, and whose nature is to allow the useful and the injurious, the good and the bad to proceed. That this comparison is no mere play of words is taught us by the mystics. When by looking inwards (introversion) and going down into the depths of their own being they find "in their heat" the image of the Sun, they find their own love or libido, which with reason, I might say with physical reason, is called the Sun; for our source of energy and life is the Sun. Thus our life process, as an energic process, is entirely Sun. ([London: Kegan Paul, Trench and Trubner, 1916] p. 128.)

SELECTED BIBLIOGRAPHY

I.   WORKS BY LAWRENCE

NOVELS

Aaron's Rod. (1922) New York: Viking Press, 1961.

Kangaroo. (1923) New York: Viking Press, 1960.

Lady Chatterley's Lover. (1928) New York: Grove Press, 1959.

The Lost Girl. (1920) New York: Viking Press, 1968.

The Plumed Serpent. (1926) New York: Knopf, 1951.

The Rainbow. (1915) New York: Viking Press, 1961.

Sons and Lovers. (1913) *A Critical Edition,* Edited by Julian Moynahan, New York: Viking Press, 1968.

The Trespasser. (1912) London: Heinemann, 1955.

The White Peacock. (1911) Carbondale: Southern Illinois University Press, 1966.

ESSAYS

Apocalypse. (1931) New York: Viking Press, 1966.

Etruscan Places. (1932) New York: Viking Press, 1957.

Mornings in Mexico. New York: Knopf, 1928.

Psychoanalysis and the Unconscious (1921) and *Fantasia of the Unconscious.* (1922) Reprinted together. New York: Viking Press, 1960.

Sea and Sardinia. (1921) New York: Viking Press, 1963.

Studies in Classic American Literature. (1923) New York: Viking Press, 1961.

Twilight in Italy. (1916) New York: Viking Press, 1962.

Sex, Literature and Censorship. ed. H. T. Moore, New York: Viking Press, 1959.

POETRY, SHORT STORIES AND SELECTIONS

The Complete Poems of D. H. Lawrence. 2 vols. Edited by Vivian deSola Pinto and Warren Roberts. New York: Viking Press, 1964.

The Complete Short Stories of D. H. Lawrence. 3 vols. New York: Viking Press, 1964.

Four Short Novels of D. H. Lawrence. (1923) New York: Viking Press, 1965.

The Portable D. H. Lawrence. Edited by Diana Trilling. New York: Viking Press, 1969.

Phoenix: The Posthumous Papers of D. H. Lawrence. Edited by Edward D. McDonald. London: Heinemann, 1936.

Phoenix II: Uncollected, Unpublished and Other Prose Works by D. H. Lawrence. Edited by Warren Roberts and Harry T. Moore, New York: Viking Press, 1968.

St. Mawr (1925) and *The Man Who Died.* (1929) Reprinted together. New York: Viking Press, 1959.

II.   BIOGRAPHICAL MATERIAL

Chambers, Jessie [E. T.]. D. H. Lawrence: *A Personal Record.* Revised edition. New York: Barnes and Noble, 1965.

Lawrence, D. H. *The Collected Letters of D. H. Lawrence,* 2 vols., Edited by Harry T. Moore. New York: Viking Press, 1962.

_____. *Letters of D. H. Lawrence.* Edited by Aldous Huxley. New York: Viking Press, 1932.

_____. *Selected Letters of D. H. Lawrence.* Edited by Diana Trilling. New York: Farrar, Straus and Cudahy, 1959.

Lawrence, Frieda. *The Memoirs and Correspondence.* Edited by E. W. Tedlock, Jr. New York: Knopf, 1964.

_____. *Not I, But the Wind–.* New York: Viking Press, 1934.

Luhan, Mabel Dodge. *Lorenzo in Taos.* New York: Knopf, 1936.

Moore, Harry T. *The Intelligent Heart: The Story of D. H. Lawrence.* New York: Farrar, Straus and Young, 1954.

Murry, John Middleton. *Between Two Worlds, An Autobiography.* New York: Julian Messner, 1936.

Nehls, Edward. *D. H. Lawrence: A Composite Biography.* 3 vols. Madison: University of Wisconsin Press, 1958.

III.   SELECTED SECONDARY SOURCES

Bedient, Calvin. *Architects of the Self: George Eliot, D. H. Lawrence, and E. M. Forster.* Berkeley: University of California Press, 1972.

Clark, L. D. *Dark Night of The Body.* Austin: University of Texas Press, 1964.

Corke, Helen. *Lawrence and "Apocalypse."* London: Heinemann, 1933.

Eagleton, Terry. *Exiles and Emigres: Studies in Modern Literature.* London: Chatto and Windus, 1970.

Gregory, Horace. *D. H. Lawrence: Pilgrim of The Apocalypse, A Critical Study.* New York: Grove Press, 1957.

Hochman, Baruch. *"Another Ego": The Changing View of Self and Society in the Work of D. H. Lawrence.* Unpublished Ph.D. dissertation, Columbia University, 1964.

Hoffman, Frederick J., and Harry T. Moore, eds. *The Achievement of D. H. Lawrence.* Norman, Okla.: University of Oklahoma Press, 1953.

_____. *Freudianism and the Literary Mind.* 2nd ed. Baton Rouge: Louisiana State University Press, 1945.

Hough, Graham. *The Dark Sun: A Study of D. H. Lawrence.* New York: Putnam, 1956.

Kaplan, Harold. *The Passive Voice: An Approach to Modern Fiction.* Athens, Ohio: Ohio University Press, 1966.

Leavis, Frank R. *D. H. Lawrence, Novelist.* New York: Knopf, 1956.

Mailer, Norman. *The Prisoner of Sex.* New York: New American Library, 1971.

Millett, Kate. *Sexual Politics.* New York: Doubleday, 1969.

Moore, Harry T. *D. H. Lawrence, His Life and Works.* Revised edition. New York: Twayne, 1964.

_____. *A D. H. Lawrence Miscellany.* Carbondale: Southern Illinois University Press, 1959.

_____. ed. *D. H. Lawrence, A Critical Survey.* Toronto: Forum House, 1969.

Moynahan, Julian. *The Deed of Life: The Novels and Tales of D. H. Lawrence.* Princeton: Princeton University Press, 1963.

Nin, Anais. *D. H. Lawrence: An Unprofessional Study.* (1932) Chicago: The Swallow Press, 1964.

Sagar, Keith. *The Art of D. H. Lawrence.* Cambridge: Cambridge University Press, 1966.

Schorer, Mark. *D. H. Lawrence.* New York: Dell, 1968.

Spilka, Mark. ed. *D. H. Lawrence: A Collection of Critical Essays.* Englewood Cliffs, New Jersey: Prentice-Hall, 1963.

_____. *The Love Ethic of D. H. Lawrence.* Bloomington, Indiana: Indiana University Press, 1955.

Sypher, Wylie. *Loss of the Self in Modern Literature and Art.* New York: Random House, 1962.

Tindall, William York. *D. H. Lawrence and Susan His Cow.* New York: Columbia University Press, 1939.

Vivas, Eliseo. *D. H. Lawrence: The Failure and the Triumph of Art.* Evanston: Northwestern University Press, 1960.

BIBLIOGRAPHY

Widmer, Kingsley. *The Art of Perversity: D. H. Lawrence's Shorter Fictions*. Seattle: University of Washington Press, 1962.

IV.   WORKS CONSULTED IN PSYCHOLOGY AND PHILOSOPHY

Bergson, Henri. *Creative Evolution*. Translated by Arthur Mitchell. New York: Modern Library, 1944.

Bettelheim, Bruno. *Symbolic Wounds: Puberty Rites and the Envious Male*. Revised edition. New York: Collier Books, 1962.

Brown, Norman O. *Life Against Death*. Middletown, Conn: Wesleyan University Press, 1955.

deBeauvoir, Simone. *The Second Sex*. Translated by H. M. Parshley. New York: Knopf, 1961.

Erikson, Erik. *Childhood and Society*. 2nd ed. New York: W. W. Norton, 1963.

_____. *Identity and the Life Cycle: Selected Papers*. New York: International Universities Press, 1959.

_____. *Identity, Youth and Crisis*. New York: W. W. Norton, 1968.

_____. *Young Man Luther: A Study in Psychoanalysis and History*. New York: W. W. Norton, 1962.

Freud, Sigmund. *The Standard Edition of The Complete Psychological Works*. 23 vols. Edited by James Strachey. London: Hogarth Press, 1955-62.

Goodheart, Eugene. *The Cult of the Ego: The Self in Modern Literature*. Chicago: University of Chicago Press, 1968.

Jung, Carl G. *Psychology of the Unconscious: A Study of the Transformations and Symbolisms of the Libido*. London: Kegan Paul, Trench and Trubner, 1916.

Laing, R. D. *The Divided Self: An Existential Study of Sanity and Madness*. Baltimore: Penguin Books, 1965.

_____. *The Politics of Experience*. New York: Ballantine Books, 1967.

_____. *The Politics of the Family, and Other Essays*. New York: Pantheon, 1971.

_____, and A. Esterson. *Sanity, Madness and the Family*. Baltimore: Penguin Books, 1964.

Lederer, Wolfgang. *The Fear of Women*. New York: Harcourt, Brace and Javanovich, 1968.

Marcuse, Herbert. *Eros and Civilization*. New York: Vintage Books, 1962.

Neumann, Erich. *The Origins and History of Consciousness*. Bollingen Series XLII. New York: Pantheon 1954.

Schopenhauer, Arthur. *The Will to Live: Selected Writings of Arthur Schopenhauer*. Edited by Richard Taylor. Garden City: Anchor Books, 1962.

INDEX

Aaron's Rod, 2, 3, 12, 15, 19, 79-91, 105, 116, 141n., 149n., 150n.
adolescence, 2, 23, 105
  identity diffusion in, 39
adulthood, 2, 55, 105
Aldington, Richard, "Introduction to Kangaroo," 79
alienation, 34, 37-38, 47, 122, 133-136
allegory, 7, 31, 54-55, 79, 107
Allen, Walter, "D. H. Lawrence in Perspective," 143n.
allotropy
  in The Rainbow, 31-34, 49
  in Women in Love, 55-59, 62, 67
America, 106
Amerindians, 112, 114-115
analogy, 4, 33, 53, 127, 128
animality
  in The White Peacock, 5-6
  in Women in Love, 70f.
  in Kangaroo, 95-97
anima mundi, 110
animism, 112-114, 137
Annabel (in The Rainbow), 34, 37
Annabel (in The White Peacock) 5, 6, 75
Aphrodite, 48
apotheosis
  of unconscious, 104
  of women, 23-27, 36, 48, 112
"A Propos of Lady Chatterley's Lover," 134, 141n.
aristocracy, 108
"Aristocracy," 126, 151n.
Ashtaroth, 100
Asquith, Lady Cynthia, 147n.
Astarte, 100
Australia, 94, 99, 101, 102, 104

Baal, 100
Bacchus, 95, 100
Beardsall, Cyril (in The White Peacock) 8, 10
  Letty, 5
Bedient, Calvin, Architects of the Self, 120
Bergson, Henri, Creative Evolution, 30, 35, 106
Betsky, Seymour, "Rhythm and Theme, D. H. Lawrence's Sons and Lovers," 147n.
Bettelheim, Bruno, Symbolic Wounds, 146n.
Birkin, Rupert (in Women in Love), 21-23, 25, 52, 55-56, 59, 60-72, 74-78, 81, 117, 141n., 145n.
birth

  in The Rainbow, 31, 34-37, 43, 50, 55
  in Women in Love, 22-23
  in Aaron's Rod, 83, 90, 92
  in Kangaroo, 97-98
  in The Plumed Serpent, 105, 107
Blake, William, 53
blood, the, 10
  in The Rainbow, 30-38
  in The Plumed Serpent, 25-27, 110, 113
  in Lady Chatterley's Lover, 136
blood consciousness, 15, 29-30, 144n.
blutbrüderschaft, 64, 78, 87-88
Brangwen, Tom (in The Rainbow), 36, 38-42, 50, 145n.
  Lydia, 38-42
  Will, 7, 33-34, 37, 39-47, 50, 55, 144n.
  Anna, 7, 33, 34, 36, 39, 40-46, 144n.
  Uncle Tom, 34, 55
  Ursula (in The Rainbow) 36-37, 45-49
  (In Women in Love) 21-23, 55-56, 61-75, 81, 112, 117, 141n., 145n.
  Gudrun (in Women in Love) 12, 20-21, 56-68, 70-72, 75-78, 117
Brewster, Earl and Achsah, 85
Bricknell, Jim (in Aaron's Rod), 86-87, 93
Buddhism, 84-85, 88

Cain, 73
  and Abel, 91
Calcott, Jack (in Kangaroo) 96, 102
cannibalsim, 112-114
characterization, 1
  in The Rainbow, 28
  in Women in Love, 56-57
  in Lady Chatterley's Lover, 135
  Chekhov's, 144n.
Chatterley, Clifford (in Lady Chatterley's Lover) 20, 135
  Connie, 134-139
Chekhov, Anton, 144n.
childhood, 2, 20, 22, 105, 123
  in The Rainbow, 38-39, 43, 55
Christ, 7, 77, 88, 139, 143n.
Christian
  mysticism, 28, 44, 142n.
  idea of death, 109
  love, 13, 86
  time, 109
  religion in The Plumed Serpent, 115-116
Ciccio (in The Lost Girl), 12, 24, 74, 145n.

civilization, 7, 74-75, 145n.
  in *Aaron's Rod*, 99
  in *The Plumed Serpent*, 106, 112
  in *Lady Chatterley's Lover*,
    133-139
Clark, L. D., *Dark Night of the Body*,
  151n.
Cleopatra, 83
coitus
  as metaphor, 29-30
  in "The Crown," 36
  in *Women in Love*, 57, 59, 68, 70
  in *Aaron's Rod*, 83-84, 89
  in *Lady Chatterley's Lover*, 136
Coleridge, Samuel Taylor, 120, 152n.
consciousness
  male-female dualism, 4-5
  description of changing, 29f.
  evolution of modern, 37f.
  oceanic, 125-126
  cp. nonrational awareness, 134, 140
  cp. pre-mental, 102
  loss of in sex, 136-138
  ordinary, 131-132
Cooper, James Fennimore, 9, 86,
  149n.
Cornwall, 97
Crich, Mrs. (in *Women in Love*) 12,
  58
  Gerald, 19-22, 52, 57, 59-70, 72,
    76-78, 107, 117
"The Crown," 20, 43, 54, 141n.,
  147n.
Crystabel, Lady (in *The White Peacock*) 6

"Daughters of the Vicar," 32-33,
  146n.
"David" of Michelangelo, 89-90
David and Jonathan relationship, 90-
  91,96
Dawes, Baxter (in *Sons and Lovers*)
  91
  Clara, 9-10, 13-14, 16, 23-24, 29
death
  in *Sons and Lovers*, 14
  in *Women in Love*, 21, 52-59, 62-
    66, 72-76
  in *The Lost Girl*, 24
  in *Aaron's Rod*, 83, 86
  in *Kangaroo*, 94
  in *The Plumed Serpent*, 26, 105-
    111, 114-116, 119-121, 130-132
  in *Lady Chatterley's Lover*, 133-
    138
deBeauvoir, Simone, *The Second Sex*,
  40, 141n., 148n.

Demeter, 24
democracy, 87, 142n.
demonic, the
  in *Women in Love*, 73-77
  in *Aaron's Rod*, 82-83
  in *Kangaroo*, 94-101
  in *Lady Chatterley's Lover*, 134
disease
  in *Aaron's Rod*, 81-84, 89
  in *The Plumed Serpent*, 105, 114,
    118, 130
  and psychic disintegration, 149n.
"Divine Comedy, The" (Dante), 37,
  144n.
divinity
  of flesh, 7
  of blood, 30
  of male, 46, 81
Donne, John, 120
Durant, Alfred (in "Daughters of the
  Vicar"), 32-33, 146n.

ego
  normal development according to
    Freud, 17f.
  according to Lawrence, 18-19
  allegorical presentation of, 31
  identity diffusion of adolescence,
    39
  identified with body, 84
  ideal of perfect balance in stellar
    equilibrium, 21, 60-72, 97, 113
  in image of Quetzalcoatl, 120f.
  implosion, 18
  engulfment, 25
  contradictory impulses of weak
    ego, 18, 39-40, 44, 55-59, 64, 114
  Gerald's death exemplifies, 21
  see also self-sufficiency, ontolog-
    ical insecurity
ego psychology, 1-3, 17-18, 32, 37,
  38, 44, 80, 113, 131, 140
élan vital 30, 31, 35
Emerson, Ralph Waldo, 152n.
England, 56, 61, 75, 145n.
Erikson, Erik, 139
  Young Man Luther, 39-40
  and "inner space," 144n.
Eros, 5-6, 47, 74

fall, the, 35, 71, 123
Fantasia of the Unconscious, 10, 18,
  21, 32, 40, 87
fascism, 80, 87, 90
Florence, 89-90

Ford, Josephine (in *Aaron's Rod*) 81, 83
form and matter antithesis
  in *The White Peacock*, 5, 7
  in *The Rainbow*, 47, 49
  in "The Man Who Died," 49
  in *Women in Love*, 70
four ages of mankind, 35-36
Frazer, James, *The Golden Bough*, 23, 109
Freud, Sigmund, 13, 144n.
  Civilization and Its Discontents, 14
  "The Most Prevalent Forms of Degradation in Erotic Life," 9-10
  and ego development, 17
  patriarchal culture, 78
  "Theme of the Three Caskets," 141n.
  "Three Essays on Sexuality," 150n.
Futurists, 31

Gajdusek, Robert, "A Reading of *The White Peacock*," 141n.
Garnett, Edward, 8
gnosticism, 110
God
  in *The Rainbow*, 30
  self as, 45
  female, 78
  cp. Quetzalcoatl, 115-117, 120, 124, 127
gods,
  in *Women in Love*, 63
  in *Kangaroo*, 95, 97-104
  in *The Plumed Serpent*, 109-110, 122, 129, 132
Greek
  life, 45
  idea of sin, 84
Gregory, Horace, *Pilgrim of the Apocalypse*, 149n.

Hades, 73
Hardy, Thomas, 9
Hawthorne, Nathaniel, 9, 149n.
Herbertson, Capt. (in *Aaron's Rod*) 149n.
hermaphrodism, 92-93, 97-98
Hermes, 74, 97
"Him with His Tail in His Mouth," 108
Holy Ghost, 88, 120

homosexuality, 2, 150n.
  in *The White Peacock*, 8
  in *Aaron's Rod*, 78, 87-92
Hopkins, Gerard Manley, 110, 120
Horney, Karen, *Feminine Psychology*, 146n.
Hough, Graham, *Dark Sun*, 17
Houghton, Alvina (in *The Lost Girl*) 24-25, 112, 145n.
Huitzilpochtli (in *The Plumed Serpent*), 26
Huxley, Aldous, "D. H. Lawrence," 149n.

industrialism, 1, 37, 134, 139
instinct, 1, 5, 7-10
"Introduction to These Paintings," 81-82
Isis in "The Man Who Died", 139
Italy, 12, 24, 81, 89, 145n.

Jesus, 106, 117, 120
Jung, Carl, 129
  Psychology of the Unconscious, 152n.

Kangaroo (Ben Cooley in *Kangaroo*), 12, 92-96
Kangaroo, 2-3, 12, 15, 79-80, 92-105, 116, 141n., 142n., 149n., 150n.
Klein, Melanie, "Early Stages of the Oedipus Complex," 146n.

LaBruyère, Jean, 86
Lady Chatterley's Lover, 2, 20, 133-140
Laing, R. D., 139
  The Divided Self, 17-18
  and ontological insecurity, 39-40, 142n.
Lawrence, Frieda, 105
Leslie, Joachim (in *The Plumed Serpent*), 106, 113
  Kate, 12, 25-27, 106, 109-120, 122, 124, 127-128, 130, 146n.
Lievers, Miriam (in *Sons and Lovers*), 9-13, 16-17, 23
life force
  in *The Rainbow*, 30, 49
  in *The Plumed Serpent*, 110f.

Lilly, Rawdon (in *Aaron's Rod*) 19,
84-88, 91-92, 118
Lindley, Louisa (in "Daughters of the
Vicar"), 32-33
Loerke (in *Women in Love*) 56-57
Lost Girl, The, 2, 12, 15, 24-25,
145n.
love
Christian, 13
and identity, 14, 18
Birkin's idea of, 21
in *Aaron's Rod,* 80, 83-84, 86, 149n.
in *Kangaroo,* 93-96, 102
two definitions of, 64-65
"Love," 64
Luhan, Mabel Dodge, 152n.
"Lui et Elle," 123

male-female dualism
and consciousness, 4-5
in *Women in Love,* 71-72
Malintzi (in *The Plumed Serpent*)
24-25
"Man Who Died, The," 7, 106, 139
marriage, 2, 105
in *The Rainbow,* 47
in *Women in Love,* 22, 37, 59-65,
69
in *The Plumed Serpent,* 109, 117-
118, 120
Mary Madelaine (in "The Man Who
Died"), 7
masculinity
and identity, 13-14, 42, 45
in *Women in Love,* 78f.
in *Aaron's Rod,* 89-90
in *The Plumed Serpent,* 124f.
Menninger's definition, 148n.
matriarchy
in *The Lost Girl,* 12
in *The Rainbow,* 36-37, 42-45, 50
in *Aaron's Rod,* 88-89
Mead, Margaret, *Male and Female,*
50, 146n.
Mellors, Oliver (in *Lady Chatterley's
Lover*), 75, 134, 137-139
Melville, Herman, 86
Menninger, Karl, *Love Against Hate,*
148n.
Mexico, 26-27, 104-106, 109, 115, 118,
127
Mill, John Stuart, 142n.
Millett, Kate, *Sexual Politics,* 149n.
mind-body split, 1-2, 148n.
in *The White Peacock,* 7-10
and oedipus complex, 8-13

in *Sons and Lovers,* 27
in *Women in Love,* 73
in *Aaron's Rod,* 84
in *Lady Chatterley's Lover,* 134
misogyny
in *The White Peacock,* 6
in *Aaron's Rod,* 80f.
Moloch, 100
moon, 22-23, 77-78
Moore, Harry T., "The Rainbow,"
144n.
Morel
Gertrude (in *Sons and Lovers*),
10-12, 16-17, 23-24, 28
Paul, 9-19, 23-24, 28-29, 91, 107
William, 9, 13
Mornings in Mexico, 141n.
mother-incest, 10-14
Moynihan, Julian, *The Deed of Life,*
144n., 147n.
Mudrick, Marvin, "The Originality of
The Rainbow," 144n.
Murry, John M., 142n.
mysticism, 79
Christian cp. pagan, 44
and uroboric incest, 14-15
in *The Rainbow,* 28f.
in *Women in Love,* 69
in *The Plumed Serpent,* 109, 120-
125
Lawrence's seeming, 139
Christian, 142n.
myth
in *Sons and Lovers,* 13, 23-27
in *The Rainbow,* 27, 35-36
in *Women in Love,* 74
in *The Lost Girl,* 24
in *Aaron's Rod,* 89
in *The Plumed Serpent,* 25-27, 109,
151n.

Nethermere, 8
Neumann, Erich, *Origins and His-
tory of Consciousness,* 14, 150n.
New Mexico, 112
Nirvana, 85, 86, 126

oedipal mother, 45, 150n.
displacement of characteristics of,
16-17
split image, 10
in *The White Peacock,* 8-10
in *Sons and Lovers,* 10, 16-17

in *Women in Love*, 78
in *Kangaroo*, 93
in *The Plumed Serpent*, 25
oedipus complex
in *Sons and Lovers* cp. to Freud,
8-10, 27
in *Psychoanalysis and the Unconscious*, 19
Old Testament, 35
ontological insecurity, 17-21, 25, 27,
39-41, 47-48, 59f., 114

paganism, 36, 44
Pan, 112
Pancrazio (in *The Lost Girl*), 24
Pascal, Blaise, 19
patriarchy, 36
phallic principle, 46
phallic religion
in *Kangaroo*, 98-99
in *The Plumed Serpent*, 112, 125
Plotinus, 53
The Plumed Serpent, 2-3, 12, 15, 25-
26, 79, 105-132, 135, 141n., 142n.,
146n., 151n.
Poe, Edgar Allen, 85, 149n.
polarity
in *The Rainbow*, 31-33
in "Daughters of the Vicar," 32
in *Women in Love*, 71
in *Kangaroo*, 103
polarization
of egos, 7, 10, 21-22
of sex roles, 40-43
power, 87-89
primitivism
in *The White Peacock*, 7
in *The Rainbow*, 47, 51
in *Women in Love*, 73-75
in *Kangaroo*, 98-104
in *The Plumed Serpent*, 137
"Princess, The," 147n.
Proserpine, 74
protestantism, 13, 133
Psychoanalysis and the Unconscious,
10, 15, 18, 32, 40
psychopathology
Lawrence's own, 2, 80
ontological insecurity, 17f.
of mind-body split, 9f.
identity diffusion, 39f.
puritanism, 10, 44
Lawrence's, 30
in *Women in Love*, 73-77, 81f

Quetzalcoatl, 25, 26, 105-116, 119-
129, 151n.

The Rainbow, 2, 7, 20, 27, 28-51, 54-
55, 107, 116, 141n., 144n., 145n.
Ramon, Don (in *The Plumed Serpent*), 75, 109-111, 115-118, 121-
126, 128-131
Carlota, 12-13, 117
Teresa, 113
realism, 27, 31, 135
reason, 3, 29
in *Lady Chatterley's Lover*, 133,
135-138, 140
*Reflections on the Death of a Porcu-
pine*, 107, 127, 141n.
Reich, Wilhelm, *Introduction to the
Theory of Orgonomy*, 147n.
"character armor," 56
Reiff, Philip, "Introduction to *Psychoanalysis and the Unconscious*,"
141n.
religion
in *The Rainbow*, 30f.
in *The Plumed Serpent*, 25, 108f.
in *Lady Chatterley's Lover*, 133
revolution, 101, 127
rhythms
biological in *The Plumed Serpent*,
111
natural in *Lady Chatterley's Lover*,
138
rite of passage, 146n.
in *The Rainbow*, 50
in *Aaron's Rod*, 92
in *Kangaroo*, 92, 94
Rochard, Madame (in *The Lost Girl*)
12, 145n.
Roddice, Hermione (in *Women in
Love*), 13, 56, 74, 147n.

St. John, 28, 142n.
Saxon race, 7
Saxton, George (in *The White Peacock*), 5-7
Emily, 6
Meg, 7
Schopenhauer's "will," 110
Schorer, Mark, "Lawrence and the
Spirit of the Place," 151n.
self-sufficiency
in *Women in Love*, 66-67, 69
in *Aaron's Rod*, 85-90
in *Kangaroo*, 97f.
in *The Plumed Serpent*, 118-125
in *Lady Chatterley's Lover*, 137-
140

sensation
in *The Rainbow*, 48
in *Women in Love*, 55, 63, 71-73
in *The Plumed Serpent*, 106

Sex, Literature and Censorship,133-134, 136-138
sex roles
Victorian, in *The Rainbow*, 40-42
insistence on in *Women in Love*, 64f.
sexuality
modern, 1, 136-137
infantile, in *The White Peacock*, 8
mother as threat to, 10
infantile, in *Sons and Lovers*, 14
metaphor for identity, 14
and blood consciousness, 30f.
Lawrence misunderstood on subject of, 30
female, in *Women in Love*, 68-70
male, in *Women in Love*, 69-78
male, and sickness, 81-82
and repression, in *Kangaroo*, 95
male, in *Kangaroo*, 97
in *The Plumed Serpent*, 25
in *Lady Chatterley's Lover*, 136f.
"Ship of Death, The," 132
Siegmund (in *The Trespasser*), 6, 11-12, 91
Sisson, Aaron (in *Aaron's Rod*), 12, 19, 80-84, 91-92, 118
Lottie, 81, 90
Skrebensky, Anton (in *The Rainbow*), 7, 34, 45, 47-49, 55
Baron, 33
Smailes, T. A., "The Mythical Bases of *Women in Love*," 148n.
social purpose
in *The Rainbow*, 46-47
in *Aaron's Rod*, 87, 89
in *Kangaroo*, 96
social theory
in *Women in Love*, 53-54
in *Aaron's Rod*, 86-88
in *Lady Chatterley's Lover*, 136
Somers, Richard (in *Kangaroo*), 12, 92-94, 96-104
Sons and Lovers, 1, 8-10, 13-15, 23, 27-28, 55, 95, 143n.
spirituality, 9-10
of women, 5, 7, 12-13
in *Women in Love*, 70-73
stellar equilibrium, 21, 60-61, 65, 72
Strindberg, J. A., 142n.
Studies in Classic American Literature, 9-10, 83, 86, 87, 89, 90, 121, 141n., 142n., 143n., 149n.

"Study of Thomas Hardy," 4, 141n., 145n.
superego
in *Women in Love*, 78
in *Kangaroo*, 95, 101
Swedenborg, E., 53
Sypher, Wylie, *Loss of Self in Modern Literature and Art*, 152

Tempest, Leslie (in *The White Peacock*), 7
Thor, 100
time
Gudrun and, 63
in *The Plumed Serpent*, 109
Tindall, William York, *D. H. Lawrence and Susan His Cow*, 144n.
Torre, del, Marchesa (in *Aaron's Rod*) 81-82
"Tortoise Shout," 123
Trespasser, The, 6, 11, 15, 30, 91
Trewella, James (in *Kangaroo*), 98-100
Trilling, Diana, "A Letter of Introduction to Lawrence," 15, 54
tuberculosis, 81, 105, 134, 149n.
Twilight in Italy, 44-45, 48, 141n.
"Two Principles, The," 141n., 147n., 148n.

unconscious, 3
described by analogy, 31
in *Aaron's Rod*, 99-104
Victorian repression of, 100-101
in *The Plumed Serpent*, 129-130
in *Lady Chatterley's Lover*, 135-137
Freud's idea of cp. to Lawrence's, 144n.
underworld, 74-76, 94
uroboric incest, 14-19, 29
in *The Rainbow*, 43-47
in *Women in Love*, 68
in *The Plumed Serpent*, 25

Van Gogh, Vincent, 28
Venus, 100
Viedma, Don Cipriano (in *The Plumed Serpent*), 12, 25, 75, 109, 111-112, 116-118, 122, 124-125, 129-130

INDEX

visionary mode, 53-55, 134
visionary worldview, 53
  in *Women in Love*, 54
  in *Lady Chatterley's Lover*, 134
vitality, 107-108, 111, 135

War, First World, 53-54, 101
White Peacock, The, 1, 5, 7-8, 11, 19, 74, 91, 95
Whitman, Walt, 15, 28, 87-88, 107, 121, 126, 143n.
Widmer, Kingsley, *The Art of Perversity*, 74
will, 12, 137
  in *The Rainbow*, 43-44
  individuality and, 45
  female, 12, 63

  in *The Plumed Serpent*, 106
Williams, Raymond, "The Social Thinking of D. H. Lawrence," 149n.
"Woman Who Rode Away, The," 112
womb, 20-22
  "of creation," 36
  in *The Rainbow*, 43-50
  in *Women in Love*, 68, 77, 143n.
Women in Love, 2, 12, 19, 33-34, 37, 45, 50, 52-78, 79, 95, 105, 116, 128, 141n., 145n., 147n.
Wordsworth, William, 28, 110
world soul, 104

Yeats, William Butler, 53